The

ASK

The

ASK

How *to* Ask Anyone
for Any Amount
for Any Purpose

Laura Fredricks

Foreword by

Susan Earl Hosbach

Jon M. Wagner

Andrea McManus

JOSSEY-BASS
A Wiley Imprint
www.josseybass.com

Published by Jossey-Bass
A Wiley Imprint
989 Market Street, San Francisco, CA 94103-1741   www.josseybass.com

Jossey-Bass books and products are available through most bookstores. To contact Jossey-Bass directly call our Customer Care Department within the U.S. at 800-956-7739, outside the U.S. at 317-572-3986, or fax 317-572-4002.

Jossey-Bass also publishes its books in a variety of electronic formats. Some content that appears in print may not be available in electronic books.

Library of Congress Cataloging-in-Publication Data
Fredricks, Laura.
   The ask : how to ask anyone for any amount for any purpose / Laura Fredricks.
      p. cm.
   Includes bibliographical references.
   ISBN-13: 978-0-7879-7856-3 (cloth)
   ISBN-10: 0-7879-7856-6 (cloth)
   1. Fund raising. I. Title.

   HG177.F68 2006
   658.15'224--dc22

                        2005032333

Printed in the United States of America
FIRST EDITION
HB Printing   10 9 8 7 6 5 4 3 2 1

Contents

Foreword

SUSAN EARL HOSBACH, CFRE

*VICE PRESIDENT, RESOURCE DEVELOPMENT,
BOYS & GIRLS CLUBS OF MIDDLE TENNESSEE*

As the chief development officer for the Nashville-based Boys & Girls Clubs of Middle Tennessee, I know that personally soliciting donations is one of the hardest things our volunteers are asked to do. They know it's critical to the health and viability of the organization, but fear of rejection and the need to commit time to the process seem to dampen the enthusiasm.

Our organization has been in this community for over one hundred years, and as part of a national nonprofit, it is fairly well known. However, every gift is still precious and is needed to make a difference in the lives of our youth. Our organization is dependent on the private sector for philanthropic support and would not be able to continue helping kids in this community without the generosity of personal gifts. It is imperative that our staff and board meet regularly with donors and prospects to ask for support.

Knowing *how* to ask and understanding the donor and his or her intent are critical to this process. And it is a process. No matter how passionate one is about the mission or how much one believes in it, people still give to people, not causes. Personal solicitation is the key to maintaining and growing revenue for a nonprofit organization. No organization can afford to become dependent on grants or special events but should focus on the real source of giving—individuals. It takes research, preparation, training, listening, and a lot of encouragement to make the process work.

Laura Fredricks has written the perfect book, a thorough, one-stop tool for meeting fundraising goals for professional staff and volunteers alike. *The Ask* is a comprehensive guide that will help alleviate people's fears about personal solicitation. It provides training tips for the entire process, from research to how to ensure a "joyful yes." This book gives any fundraiser, whether volunteer or professional staff, the proficiency necessary to be confident in the solicitation process, no matter the size or the purpose of the request. It is a must-have reference guide for all development officers.

Jon M. Wagner, CFRE

Director of Development, Laguna Playhouse

I am a professional fundraiser for the Laguna Playhouse, a nonprofit, regional theater located in Laguna Beach, California. The playhouse was established in 1921, earning it the distinction of being the oldest continuously operating theater company on the West Coast. Like all nonprofit theaters, the playhouse cannot survive on ticket sales alone. Annual philanthropic contributions are required to balance the books. My job, and the job of my associates and many volunteers, is to ask for money.

How has the playhouse survived World Wars I and II, the Great Depression, and the virtual elimination of the California Arts Council and still managed to raise philanthropic support for more than eighty years? The simple answer is that thousands of people have been asked for their support by hundreds of other people who are possessed with a deep passion and belief in the mission of the Laguna Playhouse. Sounds easy enough, but those of us with fundraising experience know that for many people asking for money in a face-to-face meeting is intimidating.

Raising money is the key to the health and vitality of all charitable nonprofits. An organization may have a professional staff with responsibility for fundraising, but it requires the commitment and hard work of many volunteers in concert with the professional staff to be a truly successful organization. Indeed, the most important responsibility of nonprofit board members is to ask others for support.

It takes skill to be a successful fundraiser. Although some volunteers are blessed with natural ability, most need a little encouragement. All right—truth be told—a lot of encouragement. And direction. And a pat on the back. And a push now and then. And skills! Fortunately, those skills can be learned.

No matter how badly fundraising skills are needed, suggesting to our volunteers that they enroll in a fundraising course would probably strain our relationship with them. Our best volunteers are people with many responsibilities and multiple interests—family, career, and community. It takes all of our professionalism to get and keep their attention focused on our needs.

Laura Fredricks has written the perfect resource for the busy volunteer and professional. Unlike a textbook written for professionals, *The Ask* distills the critical skills needed for any fundraising campaign in a refreshing, easy-to-understand style. At the same time, *The Ask* does not take shortcuts. All the skills are here but without the heavy theory or history that makes some publications unreadable for those outside the fundraising profession.

This is a great resource for the professional as well. We have all experienced the occasional volunteer who is suspect of our methods. *The Ask* can serve as an important reference to share with volunteers to validate a fundraising strategy.

Considering a career in nonprofit fundraising? Learn the skills in *The Ask* before any others, and you cannot help but be successful.

ANDREA McMANUS, CFRE

PRINCIPAL, THE DEVELOPMENT GROUP,
CALGARY, ALBERTA, CANADA

During my sixteen years as a professional fundraiser I have often heard about the extra complexities of fundraising in Canada as compared to fundraising in the United States. Sometimes these differences are portrayed as advantages and sometimes as disadvantages.

Personally, I believe that these differences are reflections of our countries' unique national characteristics and histories and have little to do with the comparative dollars raised, volunteers committed, or overall successes. Sure, there are some differences—capital campaigns tend to feature much bigger numbers in the United States than they do up here north of the border, there are definitely more millionaires and billionaires down south just because of the greater population, and fundraising as a profession has generally evolved faster in the United States than it has in Canada.

But some of the oft-cited comparisons are just myths: for example, Canadians are more generous than Americans (not true), philanthropy is unique to the United States (also not true), and Canadian institutions don't generally require as much philanthropic support as U.S. institutions because of the level of government funding they receive (definitely not true). Canadian charities have as great a need as U.S. charities to make the right ask, in the right way, at the right time, and with the right volunteer with the right training and with the right support. Preparing our board members, executives, volunteers, and staff to make that ask may be the most important task we have as professional fundraisers.

The focus of my consulting firm, The Development Group, has always been on helping entire organizations to become philanthropically focused (rather than simply helping fund development offices with that focus) and to develop the capacity to turn that focus into increased donations. An organizational philanthropic focus calls for including everyone connected with the organization somewhere in the philanthropic process—and that can be scary for many people. I am convinced that fear of asking others for money belongs right up there with fear of heights, public speaking, or spiders. My own experience is that with rare exceptions, once nonprofessional fundraisers experience a prospect's interest in the organization or the joy of a yes, they are hooked—or at the very least feel more proud of their own commitment to helping their cause and are willing to make a second call.

So how do we properly prepare our people and our organizations for making the all important ask? One answer is certainly that most of us could and should do a better job more often! How we prepare our volunteers and how we prepare our organizations to raise the money and to receive and to steward the gifts is critically important to instilling the confidence we want our fundraising teams to have. I am always searching for good training resources—articles, books, videos—on how to make the ask. And they are scarce.

Laura Fredricks has written a book that will fill this void in your resource toolkit and will help you and your fundraising team to do your jobs better and achieve greater success. *The Ask* is a comprehensive and detailed resource that covers the whole process of leading up to, making, and stewarding the ask in a practical, thorough, and straightforward manner. It will help all fundraisers to prepare their organizations and their fundraising teams to confidently, willingly, and successfully ask for money. *The Ask* is a much-needed and welcome resource for all professional fundraisers, whether north or south of the forty-ninth parallel.

*I dedicate this book to everyone I have ever
asked or will ever ask for a gift.*

Preface

Some people would rather stand in the longest supermarket line than ask for money. Asking for money can bring on a flood of emotions, emotions that have their origins in how a person was raised; the economic climate when he or she was growing up; and the value and emphasis that was placed on earning, saving, spending, and giving back in those early years.

I wanted to write a book that was very different from the current books, seminars, and conferences that address asking for money. I cannot tell you how many people—people whose job is to raise substantial money as well as people whose primary job is not fundraising but who still need to know how to ask others for money—ask me for the steps, the "magic ask words," and the rules of persuasion for raising money. Well, I'm here to tell you there are no asking amulets that will guide you through the ask. Asking is loads of fun; it is all pure heart in loving what you do, loving whom you do it for, and finding your own voice and style. It takes practice, but before you know it you are in high gear to do several asks. Be careful, it can be addictive!

So what makes this book unique? I thought long and hard on what I could write that would put the world of asking into perspective, with a clear road map that anyone can follow. Yes, you can teach someone how to ask. This book is one-stop shopping for anyone who wants to learn how to ask, needs to train others to do the ask, or wants to perfect his or her own asking style. It will teach people *with or without fundraising experience* how to ask *individuals, in person,* for money for a local charity event or special project, for an enhanced annual gift, for a larger major gift, for a long-lasting legacy planned gift, or for a complex and challenging capital campaign gift. It covers facing the practical challenges of addressing your own views on money before making an ask; learning how you can ask for money, how you can work in concert with others to do an ask, and how and when you should or should not ask a friend for money; and knowing how many asks you can do within the time constraints of your job and your life. Perhaps the most practical, popular, and needed section addresses all the responses you will get to the ask. Dealing with these responses has caused askers to run, hide, duck for cover, freeze, change their professions, select a different volunteer position, or embrace the challenge in all its splendor. Have no fear; this book has myriad suggestions on how to listen, what to say, and how to follow up on each and every ask until you receive a solid and definitive answer. No one book to date has included all these aspects of the ask. Now you have that book.

This book is written in a conversational style. If you are engaged and entertained, you will learn more. Besides, who wants to read a dry book on the ask! I hope you will remember the stories and examples you are about to read and share them with your colleagues and friends. Above all, I hope that you smile as you read along and that when you finish the book you feel confident, perhaps a bit nervous but very willing to ask with confidence and conviction because you believe in yourself and your cause.

New York, New York   Laura Fredricks
November 2005

Acknowledgments

When I look over my career in fundraising, one person stands out, not just for me but for the profession of fundraising, Paulette V. Maehara, president and CEO of the Association of Fundraising Professionals (AFP). Role model, mentor, and friend, Paulette champions every day our role and prominent position as fundraisers, locally, nationally, and internationally in nonprofits, for-profits, and nongovernmental organizations. She constantly reminds us that our proud and enriching careers as fundraisers and business leaders can and will be the guiding force that will have the largest impact socially and economically in our communities, across the country, and in the world at large. There is no separation between my career and AFP. This organization of some 26,000 members internationally gave me the opportunity to learn, explore, and experiment and to teach life lessons in our wonderful world of fundraising. Thank you.

I have waited ten years to publish a book with Jossey-Bass. I need to thank Dorothy Hearst, whom I met at an AFP International Conference in 1994 when she spoke on "so you want to write a fundraising book?" I feel I have stalked her ever since, sending her proposals for books and videos. Then last year Jossey-Bass asked me to write this book! Persistence and patience pay off. It's the same in fundraising—*no* now does not mean *no* later. So here I am with the gift—this book.

A special thanks to Allison Brunner who guided me along this happy publishing trail and my editors—you really made me sound quite good in this book.

Also I need to thank the Pace University community, especially Team Philanthropy. You gave me the opportunity to come to an organization in high gear for transition and growth and to work with you to achieve new heights. All for one and one for all. We will accomplish great things—*watch us!*

Lastly, I need to thank my family and friends, who by this time are exhausted with hearing me talk about the book. It's here—and it's for you!

—*L. F.*

Introduction

The ask is the most essential element for any successful fundraiser to master. Without the right preparation and without a thorough knowledge of what an ask entails—before, during, and after the ask—fundraisers will find that their programs and capital campaigns will not meet funding goals. Every organization needs money for its special projects, its annual fund, its major gifts program, its planned giving program, and eventually, its capital campaign drive. *Asking people in person* is the only way a group can raise substantial funding year after year. If the professional fundraisers, top administrators, board members, volunteers, and others do not make the ask, the organization may not survive.

Many fundraisers, top administrators, board members, and volunteers fear or may be extremely hesitant to ask for money. This is true whether they are organizational veterans or novices and regardless of their age, fundraising position, and title. Many people raised in hard economic times feel they cannot ask others for money because these prospects are likely to be *savers* and unwilling to part with precious, hard-earned dollars. Others fear the simple fact that they may get a no answer; they fear that rejection. There are a myriad of other reasons why people find it so hard to ask for money even when they are so committed to an organization's mission. This book addresses those fears and psychological barriers so that people can feel empowered to ask for money.

People are not born fundraisers, just as they are not born with all the skills to be accountants, doctors, lawyers, or artists. To date I have not heard that anyone has "fundraising genes"! Asking someone for money is a skill and requires talent plus a serious commitment to a philanthropic cause. Definite tools and techniques need to be learned if one is to feel comfortable in asking for money and, most important, if one is to be *successful in getting money.* This book will provide you with this training. It will serve as a lasting reference guide for any fundraiser, top administrator, board member, volunteer, and anyone else who wants to learn fundraising to ask for any size gift. It is designed to address the clearly identified need of all professional and nonprofessional fundraisers, from any organization of any size, whether local, national, or international, to learn how to ask with confidence and conviction.

What is new about this book is that it presents the skills and techniques to *ask for any size gift for any purpose for any organization in one comprehensive volume.* Currently, there is no single book on the market that addresses the ask for *all* types of gifts, from special events and projects to annual to major to planned to capital campaign gifts. When a person takes a fundraising job or volunteers to do fundraising for a local charity such as a school, cultural organization, or hospital or to raise money for an international cause, he or she can now go to *one* place to learn how to ask for money—this book. Fundraisers, volunteers, and others who need to raise money but have never asked can now use this book as a reference to learn everything from start to finish about the ask. It is an extremely cost-effective way to learn the skill of asking.

Because this book addresses the moment you are preparing for and conducting the ask, it does assume that you know your prospects and target audience, that you have adequate research and knowledge about them, and that you have the leadership and volunteer base in place at your organization. It also assumes that you know what amounts constitute a high-end annual gift for your organization and a major gift for your organization and that you have a working knowledge of planned gifts and capital campaigns. However, this book does provide a checklist of what needs to be in place institutionally before you personally ask for the enhanced annual, major, planned, or capital campaign gift. After all, you don't want to be in the position of asking for money when your organization is not in a position to process, acknowledge, invest, and steward the gift. Additionally, because planned giving and capital campaigns are complex fundraising areas, I have provided simple charts outlining the most popular planned giving vehicles and donor benefits, and I have detailed the way in which capital campaign gifts are *stretch* gifts and distinct from other types of gifts.

WHO SHOULD READ THIS BOOK

This book is designed for the following sets of readers:

• *Fundraisers, for any size or type of local, national, or international organization, who have primary fundraising responsibilities.* Frontline fundraisers such as development directors and officers, annual giving directors and officers, major and planned giving directors and officers, and leadership gifts directors and officers can benefit greatly from this book because they are the people whose bottom line is to achieve yearly fundraising goals.

• *Top administrators whose sole responsibility is to make the organization fiscally sound, largely through solid and successful fundraising programs.* Top prospects and top asks always involve the top tier of a nonprofit's staff, such as the president, chief executive officer, vice president, provost, or chief medical officer. If these individuals feel awkward or postpone asking for large and often *transformational* gifts, the organization may not thrive. This book can help people in leadership positions become comfortable with and even enjoy asking for large sums of money.

• *Board members who are expected not only to make their own gifts but also to ask top prospects and their peers for gifts.* The art and skills of asking are often overlooked for board members. Many feel they have the knowledge and skills to ask; however, when it is actually time for the ask, they may postpone the meeting or be so unprepared for this important task that the ask is executed poorly and results in no gift. Board members can use this book to train for success in making the ask.

• *Donors and volunteers who are dedicated to and who give to the organization.* In many instances donors who have given at a certain level to the organization are approached to ask prospects, including peers and friends, for money to support it. These donors are usually accompanied during the ask by someone in a leadership position or a front-line fundraiser, but it is the donor who makes the ask. A donor's personal story, explaining why he or she made a gift to the organization, can be extremely moving and persuasive to these prospects. These donors may be role models as givers, but they can also really benefit from training, specifically training featuring role playing and best practices, on how to ask potential supporters for money.

• *People who work for or are otherwise involved with an organization in roles besides asking for money.* This group includes program officers, office managers, executive assistants, administrative assistants, and personnel from the human resource and finance and accounting units. Everyone who works for or is involved with the organization should have a vested interest in raising as much money for it as possible. These people need to be well versed in all facets of the ask presented in this book: the preparation, script, and rehearsal; the selection of the asker or asking team; the right timing for the right gift for the right purpose; the ask itself; the response to the objection or concern; and the follow through. In many cases their input on asking certain donors and other prospects for gifts is invaluable. Their interaction and personal relationship with select prospects and their long-standing institutional knowledge of the organization makes them a valuable asset to the personal ask; therefore it is critical that they have all the skills entailed in making the ask.

• *People who want to learn about fundraising.* There are countless people who, day after day, want to help an artist raise money for an upcoming show, help a block association sell raffle tickets, support a religious fund drive, expand local day-care services, or prevent a local theater from closing. They have heard about fundraising, but they have no experience with asking individuals for money. Fundraising is a new field, perhaps a side interest or new career opportunity, for them. They need a hands-on book such this one that will give them the knowledge and skills it takes to ask individuals for money.

THE ORGANIZATION OF THIS BOOK

Chapter One, "Hesitating to Ask for Money," will help you understand the psychology behind the fears and hesitations people have when asking for money. Money is an emotional firecracker because it defines our lives, how we live, and often whether we have been successful. These influential factors can often prevent people from asking for money. And because asking is a two-way street, this chapter explores the views on money of the person being asked as well as the views of the asker. Identifying these potential roadblocks up front is intended to give you a sense of confidence through the recognition that these issues affect many people. The secret is to move beyond these fears and to focus on the mission and the purpose, the reason why the money is needed for the organization.

Chapter Two, "Judging the Prospect's Readiness for the Ask," details in one simple formula how to judge the timing of the ask. In every class I have taught someone has always asked me, "When do you know the person is ready to be asked?" I use this formula as a litmus test: Interest + Education + Involvement + Assets + Inclination to Give = The Right Time to Ask. It has proven to be a wonderful and reliable guidepost.

Chapter Three, "Selecting the Right Person or Team to Do the Ask," will help you understand the importance of choosing the right person or team to make the ask. This entails considering many factors, such as the size and focus of the organization asking for the gift; the number of staff and volunteers who are skilled and knowledgeable in making the ask; the budget for expenses when travel is required; the time that can be devoted to the ask by frontline fundraisers, top management, board members, and volunteers; and the amount of the ask. These factors plus identifying the person who knows the prospect the best and the person or people who can function as the prospect's peers are all addressed.

Chapter Four, "Preparing for the Ask," details all the preparation that is needed before the ask can be made. Preparation for any ask takes time, commitment, a firm strategy, and organization. This chapter outlines setting the right tone; presenting a strong, positive image through body language and tone of voice; gathering and reviewing all prospect research on the person to be asked; reviewing all aspects of the gift proposal; and scripting the ask. Each ask needs its own script. The script includes the time frame for the ask, the warm-up, the transitional statements, the exact wording of the ask, the silent period that must take place after the ask is made, the prospect's anticipated response, the close and follow-up, and who speaks and who listens during the ask. Suggested transitional statements and other wording, including wording for the ask itself, are presented, as well as my *four questions for any asker.*

Chapter Five, "Asking for Special Event or Community Project Gifts and Increased Annual Gifts," addresses two levels of basic fundraising: (1) how nonfundraisers and volunteers can ask for money to support a special event such as a walk-a-thon, block association event, golf outing, or local artist's show, and (2) how to ask consistent givers to the annual fund for an increased gift. Many people whose full-time jobs are not fundraising want to help the community and worthy causes raise money. They volunteer to ask community members, business merchants, and friends, then they suddenly find they do not know how to go about it or what to say or not say to do the *presentation,* or *pitch.* This chapter lays out suggested scripts for making these important, mainstay asks. Additionally, it shows you how to ask people who have supported the annual fund at a good but modest level for an increased gift. The best way to bump a person up in his or her annual giving is to ask in person. This is the first step in turning this group of people into major donors.

Chapter Six, "Asking for Major Gifts," gives all the tips and techniques on how to ask anyone for a significant gift for any purpose. *The mainstay of any organization is asking for and getting major gifts.* Major gifts supply the money and backing the organization needs to stay in existence, to fulfill its mission, and to have the cash flow to take on new and exciting initiatives and programs. Askers need to feel comfortable, confident, and dedicated if the major ask is to be a success. This chapter addresses major gift levels for several types of organizations in order to respond to the needs of readers whose organization's major gift level is from $5,000 to $25,000, readers whose organization's major gift level is $250,000 to $2.5 million, and all those readers in between. It defines how major gifts are different from other types of gifts, states the basic elements that make up any solid major gift fundraising program, provides a checklist of the elements that need to be in place for any successful major gifts program, and illustrates the contrasts between major gift asks that might work and those that are highly effective.

Chapter Seven, "Asking for Planned Gifts," teaches you how to ask for the most popular forms of planned gifts: bequests, charitable gift annuities, and charitable remainder trusts. Planned gifts are unique in a fundraising program because they must meet more technical requirements than other gifts and they take longer to acquire, given that it often takes a prospect awhile to commit to this long-term gift. This chapter covers the importance of planned gifts to the institution and to the donors; the types of people who make planned gifts; the prospect pool for planned gifts; the prerequisites that should be in place before the institution embarks on a formal planned giving program; the coordination and integration with other fundraising programs, such as the annual and major gifts programs and capital campaigns, that must occur; and the need for internal and external marketing plans for planned gifts. Sample dialogues and illustrations of how any size group can ask for a bequest gift and build up to a charitable remainder trust are highlighted at the end of the chapter.

Chapter Eight, "Asking for Complex and Challenging Capital Campaign Gifts," shows you how and when to ask for a capital campaign gift while the organization's fundraising programs for such things as the annual fund and major and planned gifts are also ongoing. This chapter explores the importance and uniqueness of a capital campaign, including its distinct phases, its campaign gift levels, and the people who are campaign prospects. The chapter concludes by presenting a simple yet highly effective campaign marketing piece that can be used for a capital campaign ask and two specific examples of asking for capital campaign gifts.

Chapter Nine, "Addressing the Prospect's Response to the Ask," prepares you to respond to any response, lack of response, objection, or hesitation the person being asked may have after the special event or community project ask or the annual, major, planned, or capital campaign ask. It is filled with illustrations of the many types of responses the asker will receive once the ask is made. How the asker addresses each response is crucial to the success of the ask. This chapter shows you how to fluidly address each aspect of the prospect's concerns. It illustrates how you can keep the dialogue going so that you have the opportunity to meet again with the prospect and the ask remains "alive" and viable. This chapter gives tips on how not to be argumentative, how to be the best listener possible, and how to turn potential road blocks into building blocks. Suggestions on how to stay positive and how to read the prospect's body language, with appropriate responses to both body language and verbal responses, are also listed.

Chapter Ten, "Following Through with Each Ask," is the last chapter, and it brings the ask full circle to the point of a firm answer from the prospect. The ask that has no follow-through will most certainly result in no gift. This chapter lists the important steps that need to be taken after each ask. Each prospect being asked is different, which is why the organization needs a check-off list of what to do after each ask. The reality is that after one ask is made, many more asks will need to be made, and there are definite steps to take to ensure that the least amount of time lapses between an ask and its follow-through. The follow-through can take a few weeks, months, or years, depending on the size and purpose of the gift, and each organization must factor in the appropriate time for the necessary next steps. Of utmost importance is to follow through in a variety of ways with each and every ask until the gift is received or is *totally* out of the question.

This book has a natural flow and progression, so I highly recommend that you read it from start to finish. It is filled with tips, techniques, charts, checklists, examples, and great on-the-road stories about the ask. Also sprinkled throughout the book are boxes that present important *guiding principles.* There are ten of them, and they are crucial for any fundraiser or want-to-be fundraiser to know because they encapsulate the core values of asking for money. The last section of Chapter Ten recaps these ten guiding principles, with the goal of putting the ask into a manageable perspective and reinforcing the most important elements in any ask.

It is my hope that all this material will give you and your team the blueprint you need to do many asks for many purposes. The best part is that you will meet some wonderful, fascinating, and admirable people along the way. That alone should give you all the more reason to *ask,* early and often!

The

ASK

Hesitating to Ask for Money

*People do not ask for money because they have preconceived notions
about what the response to their request might be. They know many
good causes to support exist and one can't possibly donate to all of them.
They fear that by asking someone to donate that they are putting them
in an awkward position. They rationalize ahead of time that maybe
they will be told that they don't believe in the cause or they already donate to other charities and assume the answer will be no. This said, the
requests are never made.*

—Gene Hovanec, Vice President, Finance and Chief Financial Officer,
Vitesse Semiconductor Corporation, Camarillo, California

ASKING PEOPLE FOR MONEY SHOULD BE AN
enjoyable and rewarding experience, not something that people fear or put off until the last minute. This chapter will explore all
the reasons why people may have a fear about asking for money that
causes them to hesitate or not ask at all, to the detriment of their organization. Fear and hesitating to ask can be overcome when the
asker knows everything necessary about the prospect and the organization. Through cultivation the asker will learn much about the
prospect, and because cultivation is a two-way street, the asker should
share her or his own passion for and loyalty toward the organization.
This personal dialogue is an amazing process, and it usually reduces
the fear and hesitation about asking.

People give for a variety of reasons to a multitude of organizations. The key is to know the prospect inside and out, including her personal views and values about money and giving, and to know that the prospect shares the asker's admiration for the group that needs support; then asking will be an enjoyable and rewarding experience. The initial step in this process is to determine the prospect's views on money.

The topic of money is almost certain to open a floodgate, releasing emotionally charged memories for many of us. Just say the word *money,* and you have opened Pandora's box. Money can mean the following:

- It can define your stature in life.
- It can determine your success.
- It can be why you need to work and why you work where you do.
- It can determine when and if you can retire.
- It can set the parameters of what you can give to your loved ones now or in the future.
- It can make you reflect on whether you made the right choices in life.
- It can govern how much you can borrow.
- It can govern how much you will inherit.
- It can determine what and how much you can buy.
- It can govern what you do in your free time.
- It can determine where and how you live.
- It can be a factor in your selection of health care coverage.
- It can narrow or widen your vacation plans.
- It can play a positive or negative role in your relations with friends, colleagues, and business partners.
- It can influence other personal relationships.
- It can motivate you to be like others or to have similar things and similar lifestyles.
- It can govern how much you save.

- It can govern how much you can invest.
- It can be a positive motivational factor in your life.
- It can be a most stressful topic of conversation.

Discussing other people's money—how much they make, how they spend it, how much they have saved and invested—is not something we all grow up doing around the dining room table. It feels as if we are prying into an area that should be kept private. For instance, if someone you know has just landed a fantastic new job, is the first thing you say to him, "Terrific, how much are you making?" That's unlikely. Chances are that you congratulate the person but keep to yourself your speculation on what that job might pay. Yet if we are to ask people for money, we have to know their views about money and the lifestyle choices they make and why before we ask them for a gift. The asker has to be confident in doing the ask: know the prospect, know the organization inside and out so that the ask is made with conviction, and be proud to ask as many people as possible to support the mission of that organization because it is a worthy and deserving cause. A person making an ask does not get to this point overnight. It is important that we take a look at the fears people have in asking for money, understand the psychological barriers those fears can present to the ask, and learn some solutions so that we can comfortably and confidently "ask anyone for any amount" and enjoy the process.

What Fears May Prevent or Postpone the Ask?

The following list of fears is by no means exhaustive, but it does reflect the common issues that can get in the way of the ask:

- I don't know the person's views on money.
- I don't know how the person was raised and whether she experienced money as a positive or negative factor.
- Prospect research shows that the person has the assets to give, but why should he give his hard-earned, invested, or inherited money to our organization?
- I know she supports other causes; why would she support ours?

- There are numerous groups that do similar work, so why should he support us?
- What if she feels insulted that we asked for money?
- What if I ask him for too much or two little?
- How can I possibly ask a friend or relative for a gift?
- I just know she is going to ask me something I don't know. Shouldn't the organization president or CEO be doing this?
- Why can't I ask him for money in writing instead of meeting him in person?
- What if she says no and never speaks to me again?

Looking over this list, you will notice that some common themes pop up. The first theme is fear of not knowing the prospect well enough before making the ask. The second is understanding why people would part with their money. The third is learning what makes one's organization so special that people would elect to support it over other groups. The fourth is knowing one's organization inside and out, and the fifth is understanding the personal nature of the ask. The sixth, and perhaps most common, is simply the fear of rejection.

Identifying the most common fears, as we have just done, is the first hurdle. Now we need to explore what we can do about them. The following are concrete solutions and exercises you can use to "get beyond" the psychological barriers that can make any asker worry himself or herself out of making the ask.

KNOWING THE PROSPECT WELL BEFORE MAKING THE ASK

Essential to your success is knowing as much as you can about the prospect before making the ask. We will explore this theme much more in Chapter Two, but it is important to introduce the idea in the context of the asker's fears. Not knowing *how the prospect was raised and the role that money played in that person's upbringing* can make anyone hesitate to ask for money. People's views on money begin at home. How they were raised and the era in which they were raised can be the most important factors influencing their philanthropic giving. People who grew up during World Wars I and II or who lived through the stock market crash of 1929 often have "cautious spending habits" and hence a need to save (Nichols, p. 43, 2001). Even though they may give to charity, their priority is to save money so that everyone can be taken care of if something happens. People who are extremely religious are likely to tell you that they have always been taught to "give back" and "to help others in need." To them, giving is natural, it is expected, and they want to help others in any way they can. As long as they have the means to do so, they are more than willing to lend a hand to those less fortunate. If someone's parents, extended family members, mentors, colleagues, peers, or friends have supported a charity or several charities, there is a strong likelihood that this tradition will have been passed along, shared, and encouraged. Conversely, people who have lost major investments in technology stocks or lost a job are likely to tell you that they need lots of time to recoup losses before considering giving money to a worthy cause. Such reasons illustrate that understanding how and when a person was raised can give you a greater insight into his views on money.

You find out people's views on money and how they were raised during the cultivation stages. *Cultivation* is *everything you do up to the ask* (see Exhibit 1.1). It is the series of meetings, events, and conversations and the exchanges of correspondence you have with the people you will eventually ask for money. This is the time when you really get to know your prospects, and in turn they build a long and lasting trust with you and with the organization's leaders and volunteers. Cultivation is essential *before* any ask. While you are sharing information with your prospects about your organization and its leaders, finances, volunteers, and beneficiaries, you also have the golden opportunity to see, hear, and witness their lifestyle choices. You will know, for example, why they feel they are crusaders for controversial causes; why sent their daughter or son to a certain school; where and when they vacation; how important religion is to them and their family; why they chose to have or not to have a family; how they selected their career path; the importance to them of the cars, homes, second homes, and boats they have selected; how and why they volunteer; and last but not least, which charities they support. These things unfold naturally over time if you and others from your organization are diligent in building relationships with potential donors.

EXHIBIT 1.1. *Twenty Cultivation Techniques.*

1. Corresponding with and sending e-mails to prospects.

2. Calling prospects.

3. Meeting with prospects at their homes, offices, or a restaurant.

4. Having prospects meet the leaders of the nonprofit group, board or committee members, administrative officials, staff, and beneficiaries.

5. Giving prospects a tour of the group's facility.

6. Sending prospects personal messages attached to the direct mail they receive from your group.

7. Sending prospects holiday, birthday, congratulatory, sympathy, and anniversary cards.

8. Asking prospects for advice on a particular subject that is important to your group.

9. Having beneficiaries call, write, or visit prospects on a frequent basis.

10. Inviting prospects to the group's special events.

11. Asking prospects to host a reception, breakfast, lunch, or dinner gathering of select donors and prospects to promote the successes of the group or to inform donors and prospects about the progress of a project or program.

12. Asking prospects to volunteer for a special event committee, a standing committee, or advisory board.

13. Inquiring whether prospects have contacts, colleagues, or friends who would be interested in finding out more about your group.

14. Drawing on prospects' writing or communication talents and asking them to write an article for your group's newsletter or magazine.

15. Sending prospects newspaper and magazine articles on their interests, such as sports, theater, music, shopping, and literature.

16. Taking prospects out for their birthdays or to celebrate some other special event.

17. Joining prospects at a concert, race, game, hike, or walk when they extend an invitation to do so.

18. Featuring prospects in your group's internal publications.

19. Inviting prospects to give a speech, lecture, or workshop on their area of expertise to the group's beneficiaries, other prospects, administrators, or fundraising staff.

20. Having the leaders of the group periodically call, write personal notes, or e-mail prospects after they have met, just to keep the prospects informed about the group.

The Soft Approach

There are three approaches you can use to learn everything you need to know about the people you are going to ask for money. First is what I call the *soft approach.* In this approach you ask open-ended questions of prospects during your cultivation visits. Your goals are multifaceted. You want to know as much as you can about the prospects so that the ask will be seamless and effortless. Specifically, you want to know (1) a prospect's views on money; (2) how money affected the prospect in the past and how it affects her now; (3) the prospect's interest in your group over other groups; (4) the prospect's motivation to support your group in the past or interest in possibly supporting the group now; (5) the prospect's connection with any of your group's leaders, committee members, beneficiaries, or volunteers; and (6) the prospect's key areas of interest within your organization, such as a particular program or project or just the "good work your group does for so many deserving people."

Here is an example of how this works. Fundraiser Jon, who works for a summer youth camp, has met with a prospect, Jennifer, at her home and office several times to discuss how Jennifer can help the camp. Through these conversations, Jon has learned that Jennifer attended camp as a child, and she has reflected on how important camp was to her growth and self-esteem. She has not revealed any more details at this point in time. Jon takes Jennifer to the camp and introduces her to the camp director and the children at the camp. Afterward Jon asks Jennifer some light, open-ended questions that may not have been addressed in previous conversations. He might begin by saying:

"Jennifer, you seem to have a wonderful and engaging interest in our camp. The children really respond to you. Too bad you didn't have your sneakers with you; you could have joined them. Do you know any of the children here or anyone else associated with the camp?"

Or:

"Jennifer, many of our long-standing supporters attended camp. You mentioned before that you went to camp as a child. If you don't mind telling me, where did you go? Was this a good memory?"

This can be followed by a series of follow-up questions:

"How old were you when you went to camp?"

"Did you go for just one summer or a few times?"

"Is there anyone in particular you remember from your camp days—a camp director, other kids?"

"Was this an overnight or day camp?"

"Is this something you wanted to do or did your parents or someone else send you?"

"Jennifer, there are many summer camps you could be interested in. What makes our camp so special for you?"

Now, if you noticed, not one question contained the word *money* and not one question asked for "views on money." However, I guarantee that the answers to these questions will lead to Jennifer's views on money. She may respond that the summer camp is important because her parents couldn't afford to send her but private donations to the camp made it possible for her to attend. She may respond that her aunt and uncle sent her and now she in turn wants to help a child or several children attend. She may tell you that one year she attended a whole week and loved it, but the next year she couldn't because one of her parents became ill and she had to stay home and help the family. She may tell you that she feels the need to help inner-city youths learn the value of sharing and a sense of community so that they in turn will help others. She may state that she always wanted to do something for children because "it wasn't easy for her in the past," but now she is in a position to help others. The point is that soft, open-ended questions, combined with site visits and interaction with the organization's beneficiaries, will help you learn more about your prospects, which will put you at ease when you do the ask.

The Direct and Sincere Approach

Jon and Jennifer's dialogue went well and most assuredly will lead Jon down the path to discovering how Jennifer was raised, her current views on money, and her views on supporting the camp. But what if a prospect is not so agreeable to your questions, or what if you really struggle to find out how the person feels about money? The second approach to try is the *direct and sincere approach*. There is nothing wrong with simply asking someone some questions about money. But how you do this makes all the difference in the world. If you are sincere and can weave in some personal observations about the prospect that you have made during cultivation, you should have no problem. After all, the person knows you work or volunteer for a particular organization. The person knows it is your job to *raise money* so that your group can help thousands of worthy people or preserve acres of land or rescue countless abandoned animals. Consider, for example, the following dialogue, which begins with making a general, nonthreatening statement to the prospect:

"As you know it is so important to our group that we get to know our fabulous supporters and potential supporters like you. Money is not an easy subject to talk about, and in fact I always get a bit nervous and am hesitant to discuss the topic. I've learned so much over the past few years, working [or volunteering] for this group and sharing stories with our supporters. Some people really surprise me, and I am in awe of how they overcame such hard times, how they practically became self-made and yet still feel the need and desire to help others."

In my experience a statement like this gets a dialogue going in which prospects will share something about themselves, particularly about their background and their fondness for your group. But what if your prospect responds in one of the following ways:

"I know what you mean. I have a few people like that who work for me."

"I bet you have."

"That's terrific."

Well, you are getting close to what you need to learn in this discussion, but you are not quite there. You and the prospect are not discussing the prospect's views about money or personal accounts of the prospect's background. This is the fundraiser's opportunity to bring the conversation back to the more personal level. Here are examples of a variety of ways a fundraiser can focus the conversation to get prospects' views on money:

"Rachel, you've been so successful, an inspirational role model for our students. Thanks again for coming to speak to our student fraternal groups. I can't imagine there is any topic, even the topic of money, that would make you feel uncomfortable."

"Doug, you mentioned awhile ago that things are 'getting better now' for you, your mom, and your brother. We're so happy to hear this. If you don't mind my asking, is there anything we at the organization can do for you or your family?"

"Nancy, it is important to our group to know why you would consider investing your precious, hard-earned dollars with us. What motivates you to give? Out of the thousands of charities you could support, why us?"

"Christopher, whenever I watch you speak about our group you have such passion and conviction, can we bottle you? No, really, you are so confident, polished, and persuasive. Were you always like that? I can picture you as president of your high school class or the one who won all the civic prizes at graduation."

Notice again that you are not hitting the prospect over the head by asking, "How do you feel about money?" but you are taking a more direct approach by focusing on the prospect and weaving in points about what you have seen and heard during prior cultivation efforts.

I referred in the Introduction to the ten guiding principles that I believe are crucial to the ask. Here is the first one.

Guiding Principle 1

The more personal and sincere you are with the people you are cultivating, the quicker you will be able to make the ask.

This point is a guiding principle for a variety of reasons. During the conversations you need to have with prospects, it is very easy to get caught up in organization mechanics, such as the details of some new and wonderful program or project, the fundraising goals the group hit last year, the special event that broke all records, the new board members who will add miraculous strength to the board, or the newsletter or magazine the group just published. This results in what I call speaking *at* your prospects, not *with* them. Your conversations with your prospects, while remaining professional, should always be on a personal level; they should be warm and fuzzy without being phony. As a fundraiser you have to bring a whole lot of *you* to the table and be willing to share yourself with others. If you are speaking coldly and mechanically, I assure you it will take a whole lot longer to build trust, which will most certainly delay the time it will take to get to the ask. People who give to organizations need to feel that their investment is in good hands, with people they know, trust, and like at all levels of the organization. This calls for a personal touch, sincerity, and integrity at all levels, and it begins at the first meeting with your prospect and carries through at and after the ask.

The Share Yourself Approach

The third way to learn all you can about prospects' views on money and why prospects are interested in your organization is to talk about yourself and why you have a passion for this particular cause. This is in line with the first guiding principle, keeping it personal and sincere. By talking about yourself, I mean the following. Anyone who works or volunteers, or wants to work or volunteer, for a nonprofit organization must believe in the cause, the mission, the leadership, and the direction of the organization and must be proud of the hard work everyone is doing on behalf of the cause. I believe that this third way of *sharing yourself* is the easiest way to learn more about prospects, especially their views on money and how they were raised. The caveat I have with this approach is that you must be sure you are comfortable with this technique. Many very good and successful fundraisers and volunteers would rather give up their vacation time than use this approach. So I am not advocating that this is for everyone, but if it suits your personality—go for it!

This is how it works. During the cultivation period, when you are visiting with your prospect at home or work or have some private downtime before or after an event or meeting, simply *share* some personal history. For example:

"Sarah, you know, I don't think I ever told you that years ago my mother was a patient here. I still remember coming to this waiting room. Believe me it looks a lot better now. Back then we did not have flat screen TVs, a million magazines, or volunteers letting us know an estimated time when we could see the doctor or nurse. We've come a long way thanks to people like you who really care about this hospital. That's why I work here and support the patient program. How about you? What interests you the most about this hospital?"

"Jim, I don't often have the opportunity to tell people why I work for the community center. You see, I worked in many cities, and I was always a member of the local community center, and I could always count on the center for volunteer work opportunities and for the low-cost membership. I needed to stay in shape, and yes, what I really needed was an outlet to take a physical break from work and life. I was drawn to this community center because of its location and reasonable price but, more important, also for its community services. Our literary program, our food bank, and our sliding-scale membership are so good for our community. That's why I work here, that's why I make a yearly gift to our center. I see you here pretty regularly. What brings you here over other health clubs, and what draws you to considering a gift to this center?"

"Glenn, I always think it is important for people to know why I work for the cancer foundation. Many members of my family have suffered from cancer, and over my lifetime I have been committed to fighting this disease. We need a cure so that more families do not go through what my family and others have had to endure. Is that what draws you to our foundation?"

This is a very comfortable and casual way of getting closer to prospects so that the conversation can reveal values, what is important to both of you, and the choices you have made. It has the added bonus of *marketing* your organization, because you are telling your own unique story about why you work or volunteer for the organization.

Learning people's views on money, how they were raised, and why they are interested in your organization will most assuredly eliminate or at least lessen the fear and hesitation about making the ask. Additionally, the more you share of yourself with a prospect, the more comfortable you will be in making the ask, and your fears and hesitations should quickly dissipate. The best part is that you will be establishing long and lasting friendships along the way.

GIVING IS THE GREATEST GIFT OF ALL

As important as it is to know how and when a person was raised, his or her views on money, and why your organization is so important to him or her, it is also important to know why someone would part with hard-earned money. Exhibit 1.2 lists twelve main reasons that people give.

EXHIBIT 1.2. *Reasons Why People Give.*

1. Belief that giving is the greatest gift of all.
2. Belief that all the money in the world cannot buy happiness.
3. Belief that there will always be someone less fortunate who needs money.
4. Belief that charity begins at home.
5. Belief that it is the right thing to do.
6. Decision that accumulated assets have made it possible to give.
7. Desire to emulate others who give.
8. Experience of a life-transforming event, such as an accident, near-death experience, or winning the lottery.
9. Guilt, especially when the money was earned or received in less desirable ways.
10. Desire to reduce taxes.
11. Pressure from a friend, peer, or colleague to support a cause that is important to that person.
12. Need to be recognized.

In my experience, most people who give when asked in person do so almost instinctively. It is part of who they are and how they live. They want to make their world a better place for generations to come. People also give because they have a strong interest in sharing. Sharing feels good and makes us feel less selfish and self-focused. How people have been raised governs not only their views on money but whether and when they feel a need to help those less fortunate. Many people I have had the pleasure of working with have always given something, particularly to their religious institution. Others began giving as a result of a persuasive direct-mail campaign. Yet others have witnessed grave injustice, poverty, or illness that has motivated them to take action.

People give because they reach a point in their lives where they have the assets to make a gift and it will not impede their lifestyle. Their cushion of comfort makes it possible to support a nonprofit group or groups in a significant way. They saved and planned, and it just took the right time to trigger the gift. Sometimes a gift is spurred by an unexpected windfall, such as winning the lottery, getting a case settlement, or making a superior investment. This over-the-top increase in their personal wealth makes it possible for them to give effortlessly. Giving can also be triggered by a sudden, life-transforming experience, either for the person himself or herself or for a loved one. Anyone who has fundraised for a hospital in particular knows the truth of this statement. Many grateful patients give back because a special doctor, nurse, or ambulance team saved their lives or the life of a loved one.

Fundraisers also cannot rule out *emulation theory:* some people give because they want to be like someone else or, possibly, want to be perceived as having the assets and lifestyle of a prominent person. These folks will give at a certain level so they can be thought to be as prestigious or charitable as a noted and well-respected peer. This elevates their status in the community, particularly when the gift includes a large naming opportunity. This motivation makes people happy to give because it puts them on an even playing field with some prestigious people. May you have many of these people as your prospects!

Although we would all like to think that people support nonprofit causes entirely out of the kindness of their hearts, it would be very naïve to think that other motivations do not come into play. Reducing income, estate, and gift taxes and capital gains taxes are real motivators for some donors. I personally do not think this is a bad thing; in fact it is a blessing. If some donors could not reduce these taxes, then they would not make charitable gifts at all. It is our job as askers to fulfill their personal and philanthropic goals and desires. Tax breaks for giving to charitable organizations can make it possible for many donors to release precious financial assets to support causes that save children's lives, extend the quality of life for the elderly, or preserve acres of natural resources.

I have also known donors who have been disappointed with themselves for failing to recognize or act on issues that affected their families. Issues such as smoking, drug and alcohol addiction, and mental illness can traumatize any family. These people have thought long and hard about what they can do beyond helping their immediate family, and they usually support prevention programs aimed at the diseases or other problems that have affected them or a loved one. It is important to know the motivation of the people you are asking for money because that will *tell you why they want to give and what the act of giving will mean to them.*

The need to be recognized can also drive a person to give. Now at first glance this may appear to be another "negative" reason for giving. We may feel that people should give because they want to help others and they are able to do so. There are people, however, who are proud of what they have accomplished and have the assets to give. They may want to set an example for others like themselves so that these others will also give. This is not a bad reason to give; it is a celebratory reason to give. These donors can set the tone and pave the way for others to give. Most of them want to take on leadership gift volunteer roles. If you have these folks, clone them, and you'll never have a fundraising worry again.

All these reasons why people will give to your group are fabulous motivations. Tuck them in the back of your mind as you are preparing to ask for money. When you are about to ask someone for a gift, do not think of it as "giving up money" or "giving away money." Think of it as offering the prospect the greatest opportunity people have to *share*—because sharing isn't giving anything away, it's spreading it so more people can enjoy it. Think of asking for money as asking for "an investment," because investments usually last for years and those investments will make it possible for the nonprofit group to thrive and prosper for many years to come.

EVERY ORGANIZATION HAS ITS OWN SPARKLE
AND IS DESERVING OF A GIFT

There are over 1 million registered charities in the United States (GuideStar, 2004) and over 78,000 registered charities in Canada (Canada Revenue Agency, 2003). All these groups are raising money for worthy causes—preserving wildlife, assisting people with handicaps, increasing literacy, reducing homelessness, improving child care, supporting international causes, funding the performing arts, improving education, making health care accessible, promoting research, and defending the environment, to name only a few.

With so many groups to support, fundraisers may wonder why someone would want to support one group over another. Generally, people who have this concern are brand-new to the field, just taking their first plunge into the fundraising pool. The answer to this question is that every organization has what I call its unique *sparkle*. It has something that separates it from all the other nonprofit groups and that draws in donors, volunteers, leaders, fundraisers, and administrators like a magnet. It could be that a certain group is taking care of the homeless in a select section of the city, that a theater conducts monthly workshops for children after school hours, or that the rivers are free from waste because a group successfully lobbied local government. Sometimes it is leadership that provides the sparkle, turning a group from nothing to a huge success. More often than not, it is the select group of beneficiaries the organization serves that makes the group unique and gives it sparkle.

Anyone who has concerns that the vast universe of causes might hinder any ask should remember the following. As the asker, you, in your heart of hearts, must believe in the mission of your organization, be dedicated to speaking on your organization's behalf, be proactive and tenacious for the cause, and most of all, have faith in the organization, even when circumstances, whether within or outside your control, may be challenging. Your commitment to the group must be clearly demonstrated in every conversation and interaction you have with the person you are going to ask for money. If you believe in your group and the prospect has an initial inclination or strong desire to learn more about that group, then you are halfway there. In time your positive energy will convince the person being asked that, yes, your group is unique, that its sparkle is different from all the rest, and best of all, that giving, early and often, to this sensational organization is an opportunity not to be missed.

KNOWING THE ORGANIZATION INSIDE AND OUT

Just thinking about asking for money without knowing as much as humanly possible about the organization should be every fundraiser's worst nightmare. Inevitably, prospects will have many questions about the organization, and anyone asking for money should be well versed and knowledgeable about the group. There are a number of things any asker (fundraiser, other organization member, or volunteer) can do prior to asking for money in order to avoid the embarrassment of not knowing the essential facts about the group:

- Read as much as you can about the group in both internal and external publications.
- Meet the group's leaders, volunteers, and beneficiaries.
- Visit the group's facilities, programs, and so forth.
- Attend group events.
- Review current and past annual reports.
- Frequent the group's Web site.

Through these activities you will come to know a great deal about the mission of the group, its top funding priorities, its financial stability, and what it intends to accomplish now and in the future. That should arm you with enough information to make you feel well versed about the group.

ASKING MUST BE DONE IN PERSON

As important as it is to know as much as you can about the group prior to the ask, it is equally important that you do your asks of individuals *in person. People give to people;* they do not give to paper. You will have a markedly higher chance of getting money when the ask is done in person rather than on paper. People cannot see or hear your passion for the cause in a piece of paper. But they may sense from you personally that, yes, this is the right thing to do and it should be done *now*. A written proposal for an individual is fine *as a follow-up* to the ask; it cannot substitute for the initial ask. This is not the time to hide behind paper. It is the time to believe in your cause and to ask in person.

The same can be said about doing the ask over the telephone or in an e-mail. These *distance media* do not allow the personal exchange needed for the ask. When you use them, the ask is one step removed from what it should be, an in-person event. They diminish the quality time you need with your prospect to ask for money, and they can make your group's need appear less important than it is.

There are exceptions, certainly, when it may be impossible or highly inconvenient for you to ask in person. For instance, you may be working with a prospect and then he moves abroad or so far out of your area that you cannot see him in person to do the ask. In that case it is preferable to call the prospect, specifically state that you regret not being able to do this in person, and ask for the gift. *The ask can then be followed up with further telephone calls, correspondence, or e-mails*, but telephone asks and e-mail asks should be avoided at all other times. The bottom line is that except in unusual circumstances, *always* ask individuals in person for money.

SAYING NO TO THE GIFT IS NOT SAYING NO TO YOU

I have saved the best for last, that ultimate fear, the sense of rejection when a prospect says no to the ask. Equally heartwrenching is getting an extremely negative reaction to the ask. In Chapter Nine, I explore all the responses you may receive to the ask, including no and other negative reactions, and you will be offered ways to handle these responses. What is important at this point in addressing the fear of rejection is to know that you will at times receive no as an answer; that you will be in situations where it can be uncomfortable to ask, such as asking a friend, relative, colleague, or coworker; and that each person you ask will respond in her own unique way, sometimes more favorably and sometimes offering more of a challenge.

I have a few helpful hints on tackling this fear of rejection or apprehension about asking. These can work for the fundraiser, and they can also be used in training a nervous or very shy volunteer:

- When someone says no to the ask, he is not saying no to you.

- Many prospects are uncomfortable right after the ask, so just sit back, remain silent, and listen.

- If the situation feels awkward because you are friends with, are related to, or work with the prospect, state that up front, and emphasize the opportunity to support a great cause.

When people say no to the ask, they are not saying no to you, or, "Gee, your asking style needs some work so, no, I'm not going to give." They are saying no for other reasons, which you will learn as you further discuss with them why they cannot or will not make the gift at this time. Also, *no now does not mean no later.* Chances are, if you hang in with these prospects and continue cultivating them, they will eventually make a gift. It is all in the timing. That fact alone should shift the weight off you personally. The key is to avoid internalizing what is happening; avoid a focus on yourself. Focus on the cause, the organization's mission. Some people will say no, but there are many others that may and do say yes.

Many people get extremely uncomfortable right after the ask. All you have to do is sit back and listen. If you remain silent after the ask and let the prospect speak first, the prospect will let you know why she feels uncomfortable. Remember, this is not a reflection on you, and you should not interpret it as a negative reaction to anything you have said or done. It is about the prospect; how she feels at this moment about your group and whether she is in a position—financially, philanthropically, mentally, and emotionally—to give.

If you are in the position of asking a relative, coworker, best friend, or neighbor for money, recognize up front that, yes, this is uncomfortable. Say to the person:

"It feels a bit awkward asking a relative [or friend or coworker or colleague or neighbor] to support this group because we know each other so well. However, I believe in this organization and feel you share the same passion about supporting it as well. I could not pass up this opportunity with my close relative to ask you to join with others to support us now."

The sooner you get your discomfort out in the open, the sooner you can focus on the ask and the compelling need to raise money now for a great group.

CONCLUSION

Although asking for money can be anxiety producing, once you understand and can overcome the psychological barriers that can get in your way, you will feel empowered to ask. The more you practice these skills for overcoming fear and hesitation about making the ask, the easier and more fluid your ask will be. It is a thrilling moment, and, yes, a bit of a rush when the person looks you in the eye and says "Yes, I would like to make that gift. Now, let's talk about how and when I can do it." Just remember there is just as much joy, fun, and reward in asking as there is in receiving.

LOOKING AHEAD

Now that you have some coping tools to deal with the fear and hesitation that may cause any fundraiser to be apprehensive about asking for gifts, the next chapter will focus on judging the prospect's readiness for the ask. It is a natural extension of this chapter, given that many people hesitate about or postpone asking others for money because in their judgment the ask is coming too soon and they think that with more time the prospect will surely say yes. When they employ the one simple formula of the readiness test and take the time to match the right gift opportunity with each prospect, all fundraisers will be well equipped to place fears and hesitations aside because they will know when it is the right time to ask each prospect for the right type of gift.

Judging the Prospect's Readiness for the Ask

Some people (like me) want to give money away. I prefer a straightfor-
ward approach where you tell me what the opportunity is and why it fits
in with my strategic objectives. If you make a good case relative to the
other requests I get, you'll get a check.

—Steve Kirsch, Chairman, Kirsch Foundation, San Jose, California

IF I HAD A QUARTER FOR EVERY TIME THE ISSUE of prospect readiness comes up, I would be a wealthy lady. One of the hardest parts of the ask is knowing when your prospect is *ready* to be asked. Fundraisers (whether staff or volunteers) spend a long time with their prospects, getting to know them and their views on everything from politics to sports to entertainment, and just experiencing together the day-to-day events that shape people's lives. The last thing you want to do is either jump the gun and ask the prospect too early for money or, conversely, put the ask off for a long period of time because you do not know every fact and figure about the prospect. There is no exact right time to ask, but there are some guidelines that will help you determine, as best as humanly possible, when to ask your prospect for money. Before I lay out those guidelines, however, I want to prepare you to resist the tempting traps and pitfalls that can prevent fundraisers from making a sound judgment about whether a person is ready to be asked.

AVOIDING COMMON PITFALLS
WHEN JUDGING READINESS

A number of circumstances, sets of events, and facts can lead a fundraiser into believing that the time is right to ask a prospect for a gift. Although the trains of thought involved may seem logical at first glance, they are to be avoided. Exhibit 2.1 displays a short list of the logic fundraisers sometimes use to convince themselves that the time is right, when in fact not enough thought and reflection has been given to each prospect.

EXHIBIT 2.1. *Readiness Traps.*

1. Everyone we asked previously for a larger gift said yes, so naturally this prospect will say yes.

2. I heard this prospect just gave a local group a major gift and we do the same work but on a national basis, so we should ask for a major gift as well.

3. Our usual cultivation time is three months and that's how long we've been talking to this prospect, so she is ready to be asked.

4. This prospect has been "worked on" for years by numerous people in the organization; it has to be time to ask.

5. This prospect always brings up the topic of money and giving, so he needs to be asked now.

6. It is a known fact that this prospect has the assets for a sizable gift, and if we wait, she may give it to another group.

7. A board member [or volunteer] gave me this prospect's name and contact information and said he is an "excellent prospect" and that we should move quickly and ask.

8. We need to reach our fundraising goals, so I have to ask this prospect for a gift.

Every Prospect Is Different

Looking over this list of readiness traps, a few characteristics stand out. Circumstances, timing, fundraising goals, and evaluations, and also the fundraiser's spirited competitive edge, are driving the thought process and resulting in hasty decisions to ask. Such decisions are most likely to be met with many unpleasant consequences and lack of success. The whole key to judging readiness to be asked is to *treat each prospect separately and distinctly.* What works for one prospect does not in turn automatically work for another. No two prospects are alike, and they cannot be treated alike. This is important enough to be a guiding principle.

Guiding Principle 2

Every prospect must be treated separately and distinctly.

If prospects are not treated individually, a fundraiser cannot possibly know whether a particular prospect is ready to be asked.

It is unfortunately very easy to take the route of gauging your timing by your successes or failures with other prospects. For instance, if a fundraiser working for a diabetes foundation over the past two years has been enormously successful with asking donors who normally give $100 gifts to now give $500 or $1,000, that fundraiser may be tempted to now give other prospective donors less time before asking for the enhanced gift. After all, the fundraiser's success rate is quite high. In some situations that may work fine, and this discussion is by no means meant to discourage people from asking for upgraded or larger gifts. Fundraisers, however, really need to take a look at each person, making sure that each prospect knows enough about the organization and that it really is the right time to ask that particular person for a larger gift. I am not speaking of blanketing a target audience with direct-mail requests for upgraded gifts, of course. The focus here is on the individual, personal ask for a gift, and this always requires time and attention for each prospect.

This concept also holds true when an organization finds prospects who are supporting similar groups. It is all too easy for a fundraiser to snap to the conclusion that if Prospect A supports a local organization that has a mission similar to the mission of the fundraiser's group on a national level, then prospect A will support the national group as well. The fundraiser might think that a representative of the organization just needs to meet with Prospect A, convince her that the national group does so much more on a national level, and then ask for money. This is incorrect. People who contribute to similar groups should most certainly be thought of as prospects, but a fundraiser should not ask Prospect A for money until he knows that Prospect A has been educated about and is interested in the national group. Again I am speaking of personal solicitation not direct mail. Many groups' direct-mail lists consist of prospects who have given to similar causes but have yet to give to the group doing the mailing. Such direct-mail solicitation of donor acquisition lists is fine, but going in person at this stage to ask these prospects for money is not.

Cultivation Time Varies with Each Prospect

Just as there is no exact right time to ask, there is no exact length of time that determines how much cultivation each prospect needs before she is asked. Some prospects take a few months; others take years. Fundraisers need to take a look at their prospect list and make sure that each prospect is being cultivated to the degree required for that prospect. One cannot add up the cultivation time or actions taken and use that sum as a yardstick to measure the time to ask. For example, fundraiser Lou may have an overall list of fifty prospects and a short list of five top prospects whom he has seen or taken to events for the past year. Some of those five may be ready to be asked, but others may tell him that they love his organization but circumstances are not good for giving at this time. What a mistake it would be if Lou set up the asks according to the amount of time he and others spent with each prospect, rather than listening to what each prospect has told Lou about his or her level of commitment to the group.

Sometimes a fundraiser just joining a group discovers that certain prospects have been cultivated by everyone in the group for long periods of time or have been cultivated intermittently without being asked to give. This is more common than you might think. Fundraising staff, like many other professional staffs, have a fair share of turnover. The average length of time a fundraiser spends with any one organization is less than four years (Wagner, 2002). Groups that have higher turnovers in staff are especially vulnerable to an ebbing and flowing in their prospect cultivation. When the fundraising positions are filled, prospects are given attention, and when there are gaping holes in staffing, many prospects are dropped or, worse, ignored. Fundraisers new to the group can look at past records and contact reports for these prospects and surmise that with all this activity, steady or intermittent, certain prospects should be asked. Under certain circumstances this may well be true, but the new fundraiser still needs to get to know these prospects before asking. However, this often does not happen when the focus is on the *quantity of the contact,* not the *quality of the contact.* Prospects do not take too kindly to new fundraisers, people they don't know, who quickly ask them for money. Once this happens it will take a long time to start over and to form a long and lasting relationship. The rule is to take some time to get to know your prospects when entering a new fundraising position.

Wealth Does Not Always Translate into Giving

During the early stages of cultivation it is very likely that the prospect will begin to discuss money and gifts given to your group or other groups. This is a wonderful thing to embrace. It is not, however, an automatic high sign that it's all right to ask for a gift. The fundraiser needs to have a series of conversations with the prospect about what the prospect would like to give, when, and for what purpose. Again, under certain circumstances with certain prospects this may indeed be the ideal time to ask, but askers must have a firm grip on the size of the gift to ask for and the purpose of the gift. Otherwise they run the risk of asking for too little because they do not have enough information about the prospect and her ability to give.

In your fundraising career you will most certainly come across prospects who have either given modest gifts to your group or who have an affinity for your group and who also have enormous wealth. The CEO or president of the group or the person supervising the fundraising staff and volunteers may apply great pressure to "move on this prospect" because of the wealth indicator. The fundraiser still needs a well thought out strategy before these people can be asked. Such a strategy usually involves a series of high-end cultivation moves such as (1) arranging for the prospect to meet and socialize with the head of your organization and your board members, (2) placing the prospect on the board or a committee, (3) honoring the prospect at an organizational event, (4) introducing the prospect to the group's beneficiaries, (5) giving the prospect several private site tours of the group's facilities, (6) asking the prospect to host or attend a select high-end reception, and (7) keeping the prospect in close contact with the group's existing top donors. Such prospects are extremely bright. Most of them have earned their wealth through successful business ventures and are very busy people. They will not give until they are 100 percent convinced that your organization is worthy of their investment. It would be a big mistake for anyone in the organization to ask these wealthy prospects for money prematurely, perhaps out of a fear that they might consider giving to another group so "we have to ask first." They need time and attention, and you have to earn their trust, respect, and loyalty.

Board and committee members can and should be sources for uncovering people who have wealth and may be interested in your group. These board and committee members can and should broaden the group's base of support by attracting new people who may be interested in volunteering or giving to your group. Often board and committee members reveal their connections or information formally in committee meetings or peer-screening activities—where they are given a list of prospects and asked whether they know any of these individuals and might help in involving them more closely with the group—or informally in conversations with the group's CEO, president, or top fundraiser. These board and committee members should be thanked by the group's leadership and top fundraisers. This is not the time, however, to think about quickly asking these wealthy new prospects for money. If a board or committee member has this expectation, then it is up to the leaders or top fundraisers to inform and educate the board or committee member that *any wealthy prospect needs time, attention, and a strategy well before the ask.*

The only exception to this principle occurs when these new prospects are being considered for a board position and board guidelines require each member to give at a certain level each year. For instance, many universities, hospitals, and cultural organizations require board members to give anywhere from $10,000 a year to six- and seven-figure gifts a year. It would be entirely appropriate under these circumstances for the prospective board member to be asked to meet that requirement.

Fundraising Goals Should Not Force the Ask

Most organizations have yearly fundraising goals in addition to individual goals. These goals are to ensure that prospects are actively cultivated and asked for gifts. Monthly prospect management meetings should be held for the purpose of coming up with strategies for each prospect to achieve the stated goal. Fundraising goals are intended to motivate and energize the team to work together to meet or exceed the goal. Even if the organization has one fundraiser and a CEO, the two or three people that make up the organization need to meet, with volunteers whenever possible, to focus on the goal and each individual's respective role in achieving the goal.

The fear most staff fundraisers have is that if they don't meet their goals, whether for money or for a certain number of contacts or asks, they will be evaluated poorly or, worse, fired. Healthy and inspiring nonprofit groups need to stay clear of using such goals as the sole measure of the quality of work a fundraiser can bring to and share with the group. The most important things are that gift strategies have been developed for all the prospects; that the fundraisers, leaders, and volunteers agree on these strategies; that the strategies are being executed on a timely basis; and that all involved are working individually and collectively to reach the fundraising goal.

THE READINESS PROFILE

Now that we have explored what you should avoid when judging a prospect's readiness to give, it is time to learn the guidelines and principles that will help you define the right time to ask. Whether you are new to the fundraising field or have been actively involved in the splendor of fundraising, it is the personal interaction you have with your prospects, that dynamic connection, that makes this process so enjoyable. You will meet and get very close to people of all ages and from many geographical locations. Many will have definite opinions about giving and where they fit within your organization's hierarchy of giving. This is why the timing of the ask is crucial. The best time is the moment when there is a true understanding and appreciation that the prospect's gift will be instrumental and transforming for the organization.

Exhibit 2.2 outlines a number of preliminary things that every fundraiser should know prior to asking for the gift.

EXHIBIT 2.2. *Contents of a Prospect Readiness Profile.*

1. The prospect's addresses, employment history, age, education, family members, religion, hobbies, recreational activities, travel and vacation habits or preferences, outstanding honors, recognitions, memberships, committee work, and board appointments with your group or other groups

2. The prospect's giving history, including pledge payments paid and pledge payments unfulfilled to your group and others

3. Acknowledgment and stewardship for each gift the prospect has already made to your group

4. The prospect's wealth indicators, such as salary, stocks and bonds, company shares, real estate, family foundation, and inheritance

5. The prospect's attendance at your events (and the dates of that attendance)

6. Communications, marketing pieces, e-mail blasts, and direct mail the prospect receives from you

7. The prospect's contacts with any member, volunteer, or beneficiary of your organization (with details and dates)

8. Any publicity, good or bad, about the prospect or the prospect's business or family

9. The prospect's motivation to give or prospectively give to your group

10. The strategy behind asking the prospect now for a gift

Every person who is going to be asked for a gift should have his own up-to-date prospect profile in your group's database. (A list of the fundraising software any group can use to store and track this prospect profile information is listed in Resource A, and a good source to constantly check for new software providers is the *Chronicle of Philanthropy*.) The prospect's record should contain the basics: addresses for home or work, e-mail address, age, employment history, family members, giving history, outstanding pledges, religion, board or committee appointments, recognitions, and honors and a record of the organization's gift acknowledgments and stewardship for each gift already received. It should also contain information about other groups the prospect has supported or volunteered with or that have recognized or honored the prospect. The profile should reflect any organizational mailings, such as newsletters, magazines, and invitations, the prospect receives or does not receive; any prospect committee work; and prospect attendance at any of your events. Any publicity, good or bad, about the prospect or the prospect's business or family should be in the profile. Hard copy of any articles in the print media should be either scanned into the record or maintained as hard files.

Hard Data Research

As a result of prospect research, the profile should contain the prospect's wealth indicators, such as salary, stocks and bonds, company shares, real estate, a family foundation, and inheritance. These indicators are used to gauge the level of gift the prospect has the assets to make when and if she so desires. After all, one should not be asking for a certain gift amount when there is no indication that the prospect has the capacity to give at that level. These are the *hard data,* items that should be updated frequently so that the group has an accurate database.

Additionally, the organization with a large number of prospects may find it beneficial to do an electronic screening of a portion of its donor base or perhaps its entire database. Electronic screening uses a number of *filters,* such as a person's job title, where she lives, her public stock holdings, and her board or foundation affiliation, to rank the best prospects for the organization. It can be an enormous help, especially to organizations that have many prospects, to have some guidance on identifying the best prospects, the ones they should be focusing their time and attention on as potential givers. (A list of prospect research providers and of helpful research Web sites that can assist you in finding these hard data are listed in Resource B. The *Chronicle of Philanthropy, Advancing Philanthropy* [the magazine of the Association of Fundraising Professionals], and *Currents* [the magazine of the Council for Advancement and Support of Education] also have regular listings of prospect research providers and companies that can do electronic screening.)

Soft Data Research

Beyond these basics are what I call the *soft data,* the contact reports that fundraisers and administrators past and present have recorded in the group's database whenever contact was made with the prospect. These reports should contain details of conversations with prospects (either in person or on the telephone), letters or e-mails exchanged between anyone affiliated with your group and the prospect, and the contacts made during events. Exhibit 2.3 outlines the contents of a contact report.

In essence you want to capture the moment so that you do not lose any details useful for future reference. For instance, if the prospect attended an open house at your organization and spoke with the organization's president, that conversation should be recorded. Similarly, if the prospect met with a fundraiser and at the beginning of the meeting the prospect was sharing details about the most recent family vacation or a board retreat, those facts should be recorded in the contact report. All too often, wonderful conversations revealing important details about the prospect go undocumented, to the detriment of the group. Be vigilant with your contact reports, because when it comes time to ask someone for money, it is impossible to recall all these details. The contact reports serve as your *refreshers,* so that you can recall all the wonderful encounters and conversations you and others have had with the prospect.

These contact reports should contain any indicators the prospect has offered of his motivation to give. For instance, if a prospect had

EXHIBIT 2.3. *Essential Contents of a Contact Report.*

1. Significant portions of conversation about the prospect's life, work, hobbies, education, religious beliefs, and political and philosophical opinions

2. Whom the prospect knows or has met at your organization

3. The prospect's opinions about your group's events, newsletters, and outreach to supporters

4. What the person making the contact report said to the prospect

5. Any follow-up that needs to be done in the immediate future

6. The next step for the prospect

once received a scholarship to attend an independent school and later, during a conversation with the headmaster during an alumni event, had said, "If I could do anything for the school, it would be a scholarship," then you have the driving force behind the prospective gift. If the prospect who volunteers for a food pantry tells another volunteer that "volunteering here is the best part of my week," then you know it is the mission of the food pantry that draws the prospect to the group. Unfortunately, many people overlook the importance of knowing the prospect's motivation and, even worse, do not record these conversations that reveal the motivation to give.

As important as what the prospect has said is what the fundraiser has shared with the prospect. Any updates, reports on gifts, or regards from the CEO, board members, or volunteers must be entered. Remember, the purpose of the contact report is to *stay in the moment* with the prospect, so that anyone can pick up the file or go into the database and see the most current and accurate conversations with the prospect.

The most important elements in the contact report are

- The *follow-up* that needs to be done
- The *next steps*

What good is meeting with the prospect if he asked for certain things to be done and then that request is ignored? For instance, a fundraiser might meet with a prospect and the prospect might ask for information on the organization's bequest society. If fundraiser fails to record this request and no one follows through on it, the prospect is likely either to be upset or to assume the organization isn't interested. (Chapter Ten discusses the importance of the follow-up in depth.) The contact report should serve as a to-do list for the organization, so it can follow up on the prospect's immediate issues and concerns.

I am a strong advocate of the following procedure. Every contact report should have a section titled "Next Steps" that lists the next actions to take in the cultivation of the prospect. Without it, folks, you may as well have not seen the prospect. *Every* prospect needs follow-up, so the contact report needs to spell out what needs to be done— "Send more information about X," "He wants 'clarity on our giving levels,'" or similar directives to do any of the myriad things that pop into prospects' minds. Build this "Next Steps" section into your contact reports, and you will ensure that you follow up with *all* that needs to be done before, during, and after the ask.

A word of caution about highly confidential and personal information is necessary here. Highly confidential or highly personal information the prospect reveals needs careful consideration. Use your discretion and common sense in determining how much of this information you include in the contact report and how you phrase it. The guideline is that the prospect or donor has the right to see his file at your organization. If he walks into the organization and asks to see the file, will he be extremely upset and will he view as a breach of confidentiality the fact that certain information is recorded in the database? I suggest that highly sensitive information be stated in neutral terms. If the prospect is going through a very messy divorce, state simply that prospect has some family issues. I am not suggesting that you leave this important information out of your contact reports entirely. I am suggesting that you be extremely careful and sensitive about prospect and donor information that will be shared with others in your organization.

THE READINESS FORMULA

There is no one right way to judge a prospect's readiness to be asked for a gift. There are, however, some guidelines and parameters you can use to gauge this readiness. The following formula that I created has guided all my asks:

EDUCATION + INVOLVEMENT + CULTIVATION + INCLINATION + ASSETS = THE RIGHT TIME TO ASK

Over the years I have found that if I stick with this formula, I am pretty much on the mark to know when it is the right time to ask someone for a gift. As we examine each element of the readiness formula, keep in mind that prospects will have varying degrees of education and involvement and that each may require a different quality and quantity of cultivation. Generally, the elements of the readiness formula are proportionate to the size of the ask. In most cases the larger the gift ask, the more education, involvement, cultivation, and inclination a person must have before she will make a large gift to your group. Again, these elements are guidelines, not hard and fast rules, and you need to apply them one by one with each prospect to judge her readiness to give.

Education

Your prospect should be well educated about your group. The person you are about to ask for money should know some or all of the following:

- The group's mission
- How long the group has been in existence
- The name and background of the group's CEO or president
- The number of beneficiaries the group serves, and how the group serves its beneficiaries
- The group's financial status
- The size and effectiveness of the board and committees

- How much money the organization raises each year
- The size and areas of the fundraising team
- How the group communicates with prospects, donors, and beneficiaries, via newsletters, magazines, e-mails, a Web site, and so on
- The types of the group's campaigns or specific fund drives and their progress

The level of education needed will vary from prospect to prospect. Obviously, the larger the gift you ask for, the more education the prospect should have about your group. I call this the *sliding scale theory.* For instance, if you are going to ask someone for a five-, six-, or seven-figure gift for a capital campaign, then she has to be well briefed on all aspects of the group. People do not relinquish their hard-earned dollars in such amounts unless and until they are totally convinced that giving to your group is a sound investment. Conversely, if you are asking someone in person for an annual gift or to support a walk-a-thon or golf outing, the person you are asking should know about the good work your group does, how the money she is about to give will support the group's beneficiaries, and that you will report back to her on the success of the overall fundraising effort. But she probably does not need the high degree of cultivation required for larger gifts.

Involvement

Ideally all your prospects should have some level of involvement with your group. Some folks love to read all the literature you send them or to visit your Web site regularly. They then call or meet with the fundraiser to offer suggestions on areas of improvement, or they let the staff know what a great and creative job the organization is doing of keeping everyone informed. That is one level of involvement, and it is also a sign of high-level education about your group. On the next level are the people who come to all your group's special events. Every organization has a set of people, and you know who they are, who show up in response to every invitation. They love to mingle with the group leaders and are genuinely fond of the fundraising staff. Events are a way to keep them active in and informed about your group. The next level includes the people who volunteer for the group, as speakers, event hosts, or committee or board members, for example, and those who are honored by the group. This is high-end involvement. The sliding scale theory applies here as well. The larger the ask, the more involvement is required. For example, if you are considering asking someone for a major gift, it would be ideal if that person spoke before your beneficiaries or served on an advisory board. This level of commitment to helping your group paves the way for the person to then support the group in a significant way. On the opposite end of the scale, your good friends who read all your publications, visit your Web site, and attend a few events, but who have not been asked to speak before your group or to serve on a committee or board, may not be ready to make a major, planned, or capital campaign gift. They have not yet demonstrated a sufficiently high level of involvement. They may, however, be ready to make a larger annual gift or be willing to take a top-tier level of sponsorship for one of your special events.

Cultivation

Cultivation is a two-way street. It is the series of steps you take with each prospect to learn as much as you can about him, and he in turn needs to know as much as he can about your organization. It requires that the fundraiser, fundraising team, volunteers, and leaders carefully plan a series of activities that will educate and involve the prospect with the organization (see Chapter One, Exhibit 1.1). Prospect cultivation is essential for any fundraising program, because without cultivation the chances are highly unlikely that your prospects will give. Cultivation most assuredly will lead to big gifts (Warwick, 2000, pp. 244–245).

The more creative you can be with cultivation, the better. One of the best cultivation techniques is to learn the prospect's hobbies or recreational activities and, whenever you have the chance, to send him some article or small gift that reflects these interests. For instance, almost everyone has a prospect who is an avid golfer. If you see a humorous article or editorial about golf, clip it out, place a handwritten note on it, and send it to your prospect. If you are in an airport and you see a golf ball that is a clock with legs, and you have a budget for these small prospect gifts, buy it and send it to your prospect on his birthday. If sports are not the prospect's forte, turn to books. If you know what your prospect likes to read, send reviews on a favorite author. If your prospect loves a particular type of music, send music reviews, or a special CD on his birthday. The whole point to cultivation is that you get to know your prospect as best you can so that you will be in a position to know when it is the right time to ask for a gift.

The sliding scale theory is a bit different when it comes to cultivation. Generally, people who are going to be asked for a large gift need more cultivation. They need to know, trust, and like the leaders, volunteers, and fundraising team. They have to be convinced that they are about to give to an organization that is transformational and that will be successful well into the future. This is what I call *giving to a forward-moving train.* Prospects need to feel that the group is on track and moving well on the road to success. That said, I have worked with several prospects and donors who have given very large gifts who did not require much cultivation. Some prospects do not like you to "waste" the organization's money on them, so they decline invitations to receptions, lunches and dinners, or breakfast meetings, and they do not want you to send them anything with your group's logo on it. This is admirable, but it can make it more difficult for the fundraiser to cultivate these folks. In this situation I usually resort to periodic telephone calls, holiday and birthday cards, and e-mail where appropriate. This is the level of activity that makes these prospects comfortable. You must remember to use these, albeit distant, forms of communication to exchange information about your group and to gather information about your prospects. In your cards, for example, ask them how they are doing at home or at work, ask them to call you, or tell them you will call just to see how they are doing. This is not the ideal situation because naturally you would like more face-to-face time with these folks, but you have to tailor your cultivation activities to match the prospect's comfort level.

As long as you stay active with each prospect, and there is a steady stream of information flowing both ways between you and your prospect, your cultivation efforts will help you judge when it is the right time to ask. Perhaps the best benefit of cultivation is that it can provide fundraisers with constant feedback so that they know the prospect well, know that that the prospect's interests in the organization have not changed or strayed, and know that they are in the right position to fully appreciate the right time to ask for a gift.

Inclination

People can be educated, involved, and cultivated to their comfort level with your group, but without the inclination to give, they simply will not give. Inclination is akin to motivation. The prospect must have the motivation, the inspiration, to support your group. Now, if the fundraiser has done his or her homework educating, involving, and cultivating the prospect, all signs should lead to sparking the prospect's inclination to give. A good example is what happens when a group selects a particular prospect or donor to honor at a special event. It is a thrilling moment for the honoree, her family, and her colleagues as they experience the admiration and gratitude the group bestows. If the event is a fundraiser, then the honoree usually supports the group at the event by giving at a top sponsorship level. After these events most honorees are or should be in line to be asked for a follow-up major gift to the organization. These people are at their peak of inclination right after being honored. This event has brought them within the group's inner circle and as long as these prospects stay in close connection with the group, their inclination will be to make a gift at a significant level.

The reverse situation is that because each prospect has her own set of circumstances, good and bad, personal and professional, that she has to deal with day to day, it can appear that she should give but the inclination is simply not there. For instance, you might have a top prospect who could be a poster person for your group because she is so highly educated about it, has served on several committees, and has hosted and attended many of the group's functions. All the stars seem aligned for an ask, but then your prospect tells you that her health has taken a turn for the worse or that she is in the middle of moving her mom into an assisted living facility or that her company was just acquired by a larger firm and jobs and locations have yet to be settled. Despite the education, involvement, and cultivation this prospect has enjoyed, it is highly doubtful that she is inclined or motivated to give *at this point in time.* There are just too many complications in her life right now. Supporting your organization is not a priority for this prospect, hence, she has no inclination or motivation to give right now. It won't be until things settle down for her that you may be able to get this prospect back on track with your group through further cultivation, and rekindle her inclination to give to your group.

Assets

You cannot ask a person for a gift at a certain level if he does not have the assets to make a gift of that size. It does not get much clearer than that. The person you are about to ask for $25,000 to name a room in a rehabilitation unit must have the means to make that gift without depleting his bank accounts. As I stated in discussing the Readiness Profile, you can find out a great deal about a prospect's assets through prospect research. Prospect research can be done even in a one-person shop as long as you have a computer and access to the Internet. If you have the budget, check out some of the prospect research providers; they may save your group a ton of time and be well worth the investment for you (see Resource B).

Crucial asset information is knowing that a prospect is living well, that his family members are provided for, and that he does not have any large debts or outstanding pledge payments to other groups. Fundraisers do not want to be blindsided during an ask; they don't want the prospect to turn to them and say, "Sounds good, and I would love to do it, but I've committed $100,000 over several years to the Girl Scouts so my money is tied up right now," or, "I just lost my job, and the recent hurricane destroyed my summer home." The rule is that you need this background information to estimate how much money you think the prospect can give to the organization at this point in time.

Three notes of caution about using prospect research to judge the amount for an ask. First, prospect research does not reveal every single asset a prospect possesses. Your prospects probably have private holdings such as bank accounts, mutual funds, and stocks and bonds. Unless the prospect tells you how many shares of XYZ corporation he bought or traded or the size of his mutual fund holdings and bank accounts, you do not have the total asset portfolio for your prospect.

Second, the best prospect research is done in person through cultivation. During your meetings, conversations, and easygoing, quality time with your prospects, you will get to know and experience their lifestyles. You will know whether they spend their money on cars, boats, real estate, or vacations or on their children, stepchildren, and grandchildren. Many fundraisers make the quick assumption that if prospects have wealth, as evidenced by expensive homes and hobbies, then they have the assets to give large gifts. It could very well be that their assets are supporting their expensive lifestyles and that they do not have the additional money to make a large gift to your group. I know many a prospect who wants to live long and live well, and that does not translate into giving large gifts to nonprofit organizations.

Third, assets should not be mistaken for inclination. If your top prospects are sitting on piles of money and appreciated stocks and real estate and they have a modest lifestyle, this does not automatically translate into an inclination to share their wealth with your group. Someone at the leadership level in your group may well question why a person who has the capacity to give is not supporting the group. Quite simply, if this prospect has already been educated, involved, and cultivated and has the assets, then this prospect just might not be inclined or motivated to give. Some prospects never get to the point of being inclined to give. This could be why they have so much stored-up wealth! The bottom line is that fundraisers can do only so much with educating, involving, and cultivating; they cannot instill the inclination or motivation that will make prospects share their assets. Now you see how all the elements of the readiness test are dependent on each other.

Having Some but Not All of the Readiness Elements

What if you and the group's leaders or other members of your fundraising team think that a prospect has almost all of the readiness elements and you all really feel the time is right to ask. For instance, what if you know the prospect is educated about the organization, her involvement is minimal, but she has said in conversations with you and others that she may be inclined to do something more for your group. You sense through conversations and research that she has the assets to make a major or planned gift. Then, yes, ask this prospect for a gift. The readiness formula is just that, elements and guidelines for you to use. You do not need to know 100 percent for each element documented in your database. As long as you and your fundraising team have gone through the exercise of checking the elements of the readiness test, you should be in a good position to make the right decision.

The Match

It is of utmost importance to determine the area, program, or project a prospect would support if he decided to give in a significant way. This is called the *match,* matching the prospect's interests with your organization's opportunities. It is one of the most effective ways to raise large gifts (Irwin-Wells, 2002, p. 81). Sometimes the prospect's interest is obvious because you and others have been cultivating his particular area of interest. For example, a prospect raised by a single parent may want to give money to support a children's family service or an after-school program. A minority farmworker who received financial assistance from a farmer assistance program may want to support a minority farmer loan assistance program. A breast cancer survivor may want to target her gift to breast cancer research. These are a few examples of how easy but yet very important it is to find the match.

Some fundraisers fall into the trap of focusing largely on the organization's priorities or its need to achieve the fundraising goal for a particular project, and they try to convince the prospect to support those priorities or that project. I am not suggesting that these gift opportunities should not be fully discussed with the prospect—by all means, organizational needs and priorities should be shared with each prospect. I do caution any fundraiser that finding the prospect's match is crucial, even if at the end of this process the prospect wants to give the gift unrestricted. You can waste precious hours trying to steer the prospect to your group's funding needs *when your time could be better spent exploring all options and letting the prospect decide.*

At times a prospect will want to support something that does not currently exist in your group but that the prospect feels is a natural fit for your group or natural extension of a program that is in existence.

First, you need to make sure the idea fits within the organization's mission, strategic plan, and budget. The last thing you want to do is stray from your organization's mission or strategic plan or go over budget, even with the promise of a huge gift. Next, if the idea fits the mission, the person proposing it is a high-end prospect, and the gift proposed is very large, let the prospect know that you will discuss this idea with the organization's CEO, president, or board, as appropriate. Let the prospect know that you will get back to him as soon as possible. Here is an example of how this can work. An alumnus of your university wants to expand the master's degree program in nonprofit management by creating a center that will include a social entrepreneurship component. This prospect is willing to endow the center. After much discussion with the university president, provost, deans, and faculty, it is decided that the center would expand the existing program and would attract top leaders from the nonprofit business community to the program. It is a win-win situation for everyone, and best of all, you found the match.

THE PRE-ASK CONVERSATION

What if, after all the hard work of cultivation, you still do not have a good idea about what the prospect would support and hence do not have a good idea for a match. Remember, no two prospects are alike. Some folks will open up very easily, and others keep their thoughts private. In these situations I recommend using what I call *pre-ask* conversations. Pre-ask conversations involve open-ended questions that explore prospects' key interests in an organization. The technique is very simple, as these examples show:

"Brittney, you have mentioned on several occasions that science was your favorite subject in school. When and if you were to make an important gift to the library science center, is there any particular area you would like to support?"

"Stephanie, the kidney foundation is so grateful for all the support you and your family have given us this past year. We hope we have done a good job letting all of you know how important it is to have you as family members of our foundation. Is there an area within our foundation that you like the most, or do you just like the overall good work that we do?"

"Mark, we at the braille institute could not be happier to have you as such a wonderful volunteer. We hope that you were pleased with the opportunity to come and meet with our board to share your volunteering experience. Tell me, of all the things we do at the institute, what tugs at your heartstrings the most?"

These are open-ended questions that do not ask for money. Their purpose is to determine the prospect's key area of interest, so that when you do ask for money, you will know exactly what the prospect wants to support.

UNRESTRICTED GIFTS ARE OUR FRIENDS

Hearing that a large gift is unrestricted is music to any CEO's or president's ears. Such gifts give them the financial cushion they need to fund essential work within the organization and to do more and better things for the group. Many fundraisers, however, shy away from asking for unrestricted gifts, especially when seeking a major or capital campaign gift. Asking for an unrestricted gift for a group's special event, a phone-a-thon, or a block association fundraiser is easier because it is expected that these unrestricted gifts will be used to help the organization better serve its beneficiaries. When it comes to major or campaign gifts, however, many fundraisers feel they need to suggest funding something specific and tailored, otherwise the gift amount will be much lower. There is merit in this theory, because many prospects and donors who have a real connection with and fondness for a nonprofit group have a particular area that they are committed to support. Conversely, I have known prospects to make very large unrestricted gifts to an organization, especially if they are close to the CEO or president or the board leaders. These prospects have the utmost faith in and respect for the group's leadership and know that their unrestricted gift is in good hands. I share this experience with you because, if you have these types of prospects and existing donors, you should know that their gifts will be at the level they want and that the unrestricted element will not diminish the size of the gift. Embrace the unrestricted gifts; they are our friends, and you will score big points with the head of your organization because she or he will have the extra assets to either improve existing programs or to branch out with new and exciting initiatives.

ASKING FOR MONEY ON THE FIRST VISIT

What if you meet a prospect for the very first time and become convinced that this prospect is ready to be asked? If you are asking on behalf of a special event or project or for an annual or enhanced annual gift, and your meeting is going well, I would say, yes, by all means, ask. This is your opportunity to let the prospect know that you want her to join with others for this particular fund drive.

There are a couple of additional instances in which it may be appropriate to ask for money on the initial visit. First, the fundraiser may be on a joint visit with someone else from the organization, someone who has seen and worked with the prospect previously. Ideally, well before this prospect meeting, that person has shared the prospect profile with the fundraiser, and together they have tested the elements of the readiness formula. In this situation the fundraiser must still gauge the prospect's comfort level. It may be awkward for the prospect if someone she has not met is in the room when she is asked for a larger gift. Remember, when asking for significant gifts, a close and trusting relationship needs to exist between the asker (or asking team) and the prospect before the ask can be made.

The second instance arises when the fundraiser is new to the organization and has not yet met the prospect, but the prospect has been asked previously for a gift by a fundraiser who is no longer employed by or involved with the group. For instance, let's say a planned giving officer met several times with a prospect over the past year and showed her several illustrations of how to arrange a $10,000 charitable gift annuity with the group. That officer then left the group, and you were hired as the new planned giving officer. When you meet with this prospect for the first time, you should follow up on the $10,000 charitable gift annuity ask. After all, it is an outstanding proposal that needs to be in the forefront of the prospect's mind, and you should mention it in the first meeting to refocus the prospect on it.

Conversely, if you are seeking a major, planned, or capital campaign gift from a prospect you have never met before, I would caution you not to ask on the first visit. Think of the moment. You are just meeting the prospect for the first time. This meeting and future meetings are to be treasured, not rushed so that you can make the ask. You need to build a personal relationship with each prospect, and that happens through cultivation and takes time. How would you know on this first visit how much to ask for and for what organizational purpose? Where is the match?

CONCLUSION

The readiness formula should be applied to each prospect in order to decide whether the prospect is ready to be asked for a gift. After careful review of the prospect's readiness profile, fundraisers, volunteers, and leaders will be in a very good position to make sound decisions on the timing of the ask for each and every prospect. Although it is tempting to lump prospects into large categories and groups or to let ambitious fundraising goals and deadlines guide the timing of the ask, it is of utmost importance that *each prospect be treated separately and distinctly.* Avoid these pitfalls and traps at all costs.

Equally as important as gauging the right time to ask is to make sure a match exists between the prospect's interest and your group's opportunities. The match can be a specific project, program, or fund, or it can be an unrestricted gift. Fundraisers and volunteers should use cultivation time as well as pre-ask conversations to learn all they can about the prospect so that they will have a solid handle on the match. The right timing plus the match will most assuredly lead to many, many successful asks.

LOOKING AHEAD

Now that you have a good picture of the timing for the ask, the next step is to learn how to decide who should ask for the gift and how to determine the number of people who should be involved. In the next chapter we will explore some ground rules for selecting the ideal person or persons to make the ask, as well as the time commitments that need to be made by each asker, before, during, and after the ask.

Selecting the Right Person or Team to Do the Ask

CEOs and presidents of large corporations are constantly solicited for donations by a great many legitimate charities, both on corporate and personal levels. My personal contribution is based upon one of two criteria: Most importantly, I have an emotional attachment to the organization because it has touched my life in some fashion. The other reason is because someone important to me has solicited the gift because of their own emotional attachment. All other solicitations usually go unfulfilled.

—Hal J. Upbin, Chairman and CEO, Kellwood Company,
Chesterfield, Missouri

ONCE YOU KNOW THE TIMING IS RIGHT TO ask a particular prospect for a gift, your next big decision is selecting the person or team that will make the ask. In some instances this will be an easy choice; in other instances it will be harder because the organization's leaders, members of the fundraising team, and volunteers do not always agree on who should do the ask. Luckily, there are a number of organizational factors that will guide you during the selection process. As the initial step, it is always a good exercise for any organization to agree on its universe of potential askers. This takes a careful assessment of both the internal staff and the external volunteers and supporters and a review of the organization's fundraising strengths and limitations.

Determining Your Pool of Potential Askers

I highly recommend that you define your organization's pool of potential askers before you select one or more people to ask a prospect for a gift. These potential askers might be organization leaders, members of the fundraising team, administrators and staff, board members, and donors and volunteers. Once you have established the pool of prospects, the next step is to give these individuals a firm grip on the group's fundraising programs, past, present, and future. Once those in the pool of potential askers are fully apprised of the group's fundraising operation, the organization will have a good idea of who can do the ask as well as who is willing to do the ask. It should not be assumed that just because people are in leadership positions or board positions, they are automatically the ones who should be available 24/7 to do an ask.

Exhibit 3.1 lists the factors that will affect an organization's pool of potential askers.

The Size Factor

The size of the organization's leadership and fundraising teams could very well be the determining factor for the size of the pool of potential askers. If the organization is small—a grassroots group, for example—the staff running the group may consist of just two, three, or four people—the CEO or president and a fundraiser or two, with support staff. The leader plus the one or two fundraisers may be the universe of askers for that organization. On the opposite side of the spectrum a large organization—such as an international organization with offices or chapters in several countries—may have several layers of leadership plus numerous fundraisers associated with each office.

The size of the organization can also influence the number of administrators and other staff who may be considered potential askers. For instance, a medium-size community hospital may have terrific doctors, nurses, and paramedics who have personal and heartwarming relationships with grateful patients. These folks should definitely be considered part of the askers pool. A large legal foundation may have a number of attorneys on retainer who provide pro bono legal assistance to foundation beneficiaries, and these people should be considered part of the pool. All too often groups overlook the internal

EXHIBIT 3.1. *Factors That Shape the Pool of Potential Askers.*

1. The size of the organization's leadership and fundraising teams

2. The number of administrators and other staff members who may be appropriate for assisting with the ask

3. The size and activity level of the board

4. The size and activity level of the volunteer group

5. The number of donors who may be appropriate for assisting with the ask for multilevel gifts

6. The level of fundraising expertise and willingness to ask for gifts among the leadership team, fundraising team, administrators and staff, board members, volunteers, and donors

7. The age of the organization and its history of fundraising

8. The types and sizes of gifts the organization needs

9. The size of the prospect and donor base

10. The time that the potential askers can realistically devote to asking for gifts

administrators and staff beyond the fundraising area. Anyone inside the group who plays an active role with prospects, donors, or beneficiaries can and should be considered a potential asker or at least an asker's assistant.

In addition to looking at the internal paid staff, you must look at the size of the board, the volunteer force, and at select donors to determine the number of potential askers in your organization. I define *select donors* as people who have over time made a variety of gifts on several levels to your group and who love to speak about how wonderful it is to be part of your organization. Their stories are infectious, and people are drawn to them. These donors are energetic and charismatic and can share with prospects how important and meaningful it is for them to support your group. Board members and volunteers who are tried and true believers in your group can also function in this way.

The Level of Expertise

Once you know how many people your group might use to ask for gifts—including leaders, fundraisers, administrators and staff, board members, volunteers, and donors—the next step is to determine their *level of expertise in asking for gifts.* Your group may have been in existence for years, but it is the level of experience among the pool of askers currently associated with your group that matters. A group might have twenty to forty people who could ask for gifts, but if only a handful know how to ask, have asked, or are willing to ask, the number of people who can be counted on to do asks is relatively low. One cannot simply add up the numbers in the initial pool to determine how many people can and should ask for gifts on behalf of the organization. Many of these people may need training, including coaching in role playing, by the fundraising staff or consultants before they are ready to ask for gifts.

Just as important as their asking experience is their *willingness to do the ask.* The last thing a group wants is a pool of askers who are not comfortable asking or who would rather serve on seven committees than ask for money. Your core group of potential askers consists of those who have both experience in asking and the willingness to ask.

The Maturity of the Fundraising Program

It is important to know not only the birth date of your organization but also the history of the organization's fundraising program. A group's age is not necessarily an accurate guide to the maturity of the fundraising program. I have known nonprofit organizations that have been in existence for decades but whose fundraising staff has been in place only for the past ten to fifteen years. Once you know the longevity of the fundraising program, it is important to learn what fundraising strategies have been used. Has fundraising been done by direct mail only? Have asks been made only by the leaders? How many people have been asked? Have the leaders or board members asked prospects for major or planned gifts? Has the organization ever had a capital campaign, and if so, when, and what did it accomplish?

If you are going to assess the pool of potential askers at this point in time, the fundraising program's history of successes or challenges may be a key influence on individuals' willingness to ask. For instance, board members who were active with your group's previous capital campaign may feel "exhausted" and unwilling to ask for major or planned gifts or gifts for a future capital campaign. New board members may jump at the opportunity to ask for gifts once they learn that your group has untapped prospects, people who have never been asked to give. Volunteers who up to now have assisted with the annual fund program or who have run the group's special events may welcome the opportunity to visit prospects with the fundraising team and ask for gifts. Select donors may have had a rocky relationship with past leaders or fundraisers, and so even if the group is now on an upward swing, they may still be feeling soured by a lack of stewardship and attention.

Once you know the history of your group's fundraising program, it is essential to know where the group is headed. Is the organization a forward-moving train? Is it ready to ask for and accept endowed gifts or planned gifts? Have giving levels been established and adopted by the board? Is the organization considering, now or in the immediate future, a capital campaign? As much as the organization's history of fundraising can influence the willingness of the pool of potential askers to ask for gifts, the present and future fundraising activities are an equal influence. Some people may specifically ask to be placed on or taken off a board because the group is embarking on a capital campaign. Others may ask to serve on a finance committee because they have investment expertise and the group is now accepting endowed or planned gifts. These individuals may want to make sure that once they ask for and receive gifts, those gifts will be properly invested. This may seem beyond the obvious, but anyone considering asking for money on behalf of an organization needs to know the types of gifts the organization is accepting, the levels of gifts needed, how the gifts are invested, and how and when the gifts are distributed to the beneficiaries.

The Size of the Prospect and Donor Base

Everyone who has expertise in asking for gifts and is willing to ask should know the approximate size of the group's prospect and donor base and whether the group is actively seeking to expand this base. This will ensure that everyone has realistic expectations about the number of asks the group might do at this point in time. For example, a group may have solid leadership, an experienced fundraising staff, and an active board, but a comparatively small prospect base. In this instance those in the pool of potential askers need to know that they will be doing a modest number of asks now but that once the base of prospects and donors increases so will the number and level of asks.

The Time Factor

Last but not least you should consider time. You must make a realistic measure of the number of hours per month the pool of askers can devote to asking for gifts. All too often, nonprofit groups, large and small, set unrealistic monthly or quarterly goals for the number of people they will ask for gifts. They make this determination by looking at the number of askers and the number of prospects who should be asked, not at the quantity of time each asker actually has to make asks. Exhibit 3.2 presents some of the questions you can use when assessing the quantity of time each person has to devote to asking for gifts.

Even if you are the CEO or president of the group or a full-time fundraiser, you will have responsibilities other than making asks. The leaders have to run all the administrative and fiscal aspects of the organization. The full-time fundraisers have to staff committees, identify prospects, cultivate prospects, steward donors, attend internal meetings, write reports, manage staff, and run special events. Even if your title is director of major gifts, director of planned giving, or director of leadership gifts and your primary job is to see prospects and ask for money, you more than likely have these other activities that take great portions of your time. Volunteers and board members have other organizational responsibilities, such as attending board and committee meetings and attending the group's special events, as well as their outside personal and professional obligations.

I strongly suggest that once you know your pool of potential askers that you assess very carefully the amount of time each person has to ask for gifts. Keep in mind that not every ask will be local and that each ask needs preparation that also takes time. To get a good handle on this assessment, a few months before you start your fundraising year, prepare a chart listing the people in your pool of potential askers and the time they have each month to devote to asking for gifts. Exhibit 3.3 illustrates the simple format you might use.

EXHIBIT 3.2. *Questions for Determining How Much Time a Person Can Devote to the Ask.*

1. Is asking for gifts your full-time job?
2. What percentage of your time can you devote weekly, monthly, or quarterly to asking for gifts?
3. What other areas of fundraising are you responsible for?
4. What other committees do you serve on?
5. How much do you travel out of the area for business or pleasure in a year?
6. Do you experience heavy business or event months that would prevent you from having the time to ask for gifts?
7. Do you have the time to travel out of the area to ask for gifts?

EXHIBIT 3.3. *Chart to Track the Time Available for Asks.*

September

Name of Asker	Dates Available	Time Slots	Dates & Times Unavailable
CEO/president Myers			
Board member Lucas			
Committee member Henley			
Director of Development Williams			
Select donor Andrews			
Volunteer Baker			
Administrator Griffin			
Organization staff Michaelson			

I suggest that someone on the fundraising staff, the director of development, for instance, distribute a blank copy of this chart to each person listed on the chart at quarterly intervals, because I believe most people have a good picture of their business and personal calendar four months ahead of time. Give these people two weeks to fill their charts out with dates available and time slots as well as their dates not available and to send them to the director of development. Once the director has them all back, she can create a master list combining everyone's availability for each date and time period, and record this information, using either an Excel spreadsheet or calendar software such as On Time or Meeting Maker. When comparing the time individuals have available to the time needed for an ask, make sure you factor in the travel time needed to get to the meeting with the prospect, whether by mass transit, driving, flying, or walking. Although compiling this chart may seem time consuming, the completed chart serves many purposes. First and foremost, your group will have a clear idea of the number of hours its pool of askers can and will devote to asking for gifts. This can be a real eye-opener. Conversations with your askers pool may have led you to believe that these people have lots of time available. However, when they put pen to paper and look at their calendars, they may have many other commitments that severely diminish their availability.

Second, giving you this information commits your pool of askers to devote the time to ask for gifts. They must be serious about the time blocked out and avoid the temptation of scheduling other activities in these time slots. Additionally, having this information gives you a certain amount of time to give notice to an asker when the organization cannot schedule a prospect to be asked during a time slot the asker has offered. For instance, if a board member has told the group she is available on two designated afternoons but the organization cannot line up a prospect to be asked during those exact hours, then the asker needs to know a few days ahead that her time slot is now free.

Third, and most important, having this chart will help you to keep your group on track by arranging an appropriate stream of asks each month. There is nothing worse than having gaping holes in the calendar because a group has not asked for money in a month or two. This can easily happen, especially in the summer months and during holidays.

Knowing how many people are available to do an ask and the time that each has committed to do an ask is essential because this information will govern how many asks the organization can realistically do in person each month. If you have seven people who are willing to ask, but two are traveling for business during most of September, one is on vacation for the first two weeks of that month, and two cannot commit during the Jewish holidays, you do not have a critical mass of people to make asks that month. Your master chart tells you the number of asks your group can do each month so that no one has unrealistic expectations. Keep your charts up to date, remind your askers how important it is for your group to stick to the agreed-upon ask schedule each month, and you will have the ideal structure to organize your askers' time.

CHARACTERISTICS OF A GOOD ASKER

Even when a person has the time and is willing to ask for gifts on behalf of your organization, he may not possess the characteristics that make a good asker. Askers should meet the criteria displayed in Exhibit 3.4.

As we go over each one of these elements keep in mind the sliding scale rule. The larger the gift, the more important it is that the person doing the ask should possess all these characteristics. Large asks, for a major, planned, or capital campaign gift, for example, require that the person doing the ask have the background, confidence, and stature within your group to ask for a significant gift. Charismatic personality, energy, demonstrated commitment, and loyalty to your group are a must for any large ask. Conversely, it would not be the end of the world if the person asking for an annual gift or special event support possessed eight out of the ten characteristics. These smaller gifts are requested more frequently than larger gifts are, and even though, ideally, you would want any asker to posses the same qualities as someone asking for a transformational gift, the reality is that the ask for a smaller, albeit very important gift, will go very well as long as the person has a majority of these qualities.

Put Yourself in the Prospect's Shoes

I think the best way to analyze the elements of a good asker is to take the prospect's point of view. The person who is about to ask the prospect for money should be known, well liked, admired, and

EXHIBIT 3.4. *Ideal Characteristics of Any Asker.*

1. The person is known, liked, admired, and respected by the prospect.

2. The person played a major role in cultivating the prospect.

3. The person has given at the same level that is being asked of the prospect.

4. The person has given at a level in relation to his abilities that is comparable to the level being asked of the prospect in relation to her abilities.

5. The person is comfortable, relaxed, and confident with the prospect.

6. The person has demonstrated a strong commitment to the organization and is fully knowledgeable about the organization.

7. The person knows the details of the gift opportunity and can clearly articulate the need for support.

8. The person has the time to prepare for the ask, do the ask, and carry out the necessary follow-up to the ask to ensure receipt of the gift.

9. The person keeps everyone involved with the fundraising process fully informed on the details of an ask and the follow-through.

10. The person has fun doing an ask and can feel the rewards of asking for money for the organization.

respected by the prospect. Can you think of a more awkward situation than having someone the prospect dislikes or mistrusts ask for the gift? Mutual respect and admiration between the prospect and the asker should set the tone for the ask. The person doing the ask must have had some part, preferably a major one, in cultivating the prospect. Cultivation is the time when much is learned about and shared with the prospect. The meetings, events, correspondence, telephone calls, and e-mails are the foundation for crafting the right gift opportunity for your prospect. Yet I have known organizations to give part or all of the ask to a person who has had little cultivation time with the prospect. The results were not good. Put yourself in the prospect's shoes: how would you feel if someone with whom you have had very little contact asked you for a major gift for an organization? You would not be experiencing the close, meaningful, and personal setting that is needed for any individual ask. Strive to have all your askers play a major role in cultivating your prospects.

Give First, Then Ask

It is essential for anyone asking for money on behalf of an organization to follow the third guiding principle.

Guiding Principle 3
Anyone asking for a gift must make his or her own gift first.

Giving solidifies the asker's commitment to the organization. It is one thing to talk a good game; it is another to make a personal monetary commitment. No asker should be in the position of asking anyone else for any amount without giving first. Why should a prospect give if the person asking her has not given? People who have given first will always be more successful in asking for gifts because they have demonstrated their commitment to and investment in the group. The asker can easily say with conviction:

"Joan, join with me in this great investment."

"Russell, I support this group, and it is worthy and deserving of your support as well."

"Sandra, I have made a five-year pledge to this group because I wanted to invest in its future. Please join me and other top supporters and consider making a gift now. Our combined support will be no less than transformational."

Although fundraisers are in total agreement that one must give before one asks, there is always a great deal of discussion in the fundraising arena about how much a person should give before asking and when and if he should ask someone for a gift larger than the one he has given. There are no hard-and-fast rules on this issue, but there are some guidelines. First, whenever possible, have the asker give at the same level being asked of the prospect. It just carries more weight, more cachet, and it puts the asker on par with the prospect. That said, some of your most dedicated and ideal askers do not always have the assets to make large gifts. It would be a shame if these people were discouraged from asking for money on behalf of the group, because they could be your best cheerleaders for drawing in new supporters. In these instances, have the person give at a level that is comparable for him to the gift being asked (Irwin-Wells, 2002, p. 82). For instance, you may have a board member whose top gift is $50,000. This board member has served your organization for years, recruited new board members, and used her expertise to improve your group's financial investments. She knows and has cultivated a prospect who should be asked for a $100,000 gift, a high-end gift for that prospect. The board member should ask this prospect for that gift because she has made what is for her an equally meaningful high-end gift.

Confidence, Commitment, and Knowledge— The Winning Combination

Nothing can be more persuasive than being asked for a gift by a person who is confident, committed, dedicated, loyal, and organized and who has complete knowledge about the organization. Anyone asking for money should be confident in his tone of voice, body language, and eye contact. *The person asking for money is the organization* in the eyes of the prospect. The person being asked needs to see, feel, and hear a solid and convincing presentation. The asker should be able to recall everything he loves about the organization. The last thing you want is to have as your representative someone who is disheveled, rambling in his conversation, looking all over the room, and *talking at the prospect, not with the prospect.* When that happens, the assured result will be a total disconnect between the asker and the prospect, and it will take time to once again get the prospect to the point where she can be asked to seriously consider a gift.

The person doing the ask should know as much as he can about the organization and about the gift opportunity. If an engaged prospect asks some basic background questions, such as the size of the group's board, the fundraising goal for the year, or the number of beneficiaries the group serves, you do not want these very basic questions to go unanswered. This can kill the momentum of the ask, and more important, it makes it appear that the group's leaders and administrators do not have their act together. The same holds true for the gift opportunity. The asker needs to know inside and out the amount being asked, the purpose of the gift, the number of gifts received at this level, how the gift can be funded, how the gift funds will be invested, and why the gift is needed now. That is the total confidence package and presentation that is needed for every ask.

Working with the Team to Get the Gift

Asking for money is a multifaceted activity. One does not just ask, sit back, and wait for an answer. *It takes a commitment of time before, during, and after each ask to see the gift come to fruition.* Moreover, one does not ask and then walk away and let someone else work with the prospect until the gift is received or completely rejected. Prospects expect that the person who asked them for money will continue to meet and speak with them and discuss the gift opportunity with them. They do not take too kindly to being handed off to someone else after the ask is made. If a CEO, president, or board member does the ask or is part of the ask, most likely it will be acceptable to have a staff fundraiser or volunteer available to provide additional information or materials to the prospect. The prospect will also expect, however, to hear from the top askers again, following up on the ask. The asker must be aware that *the amount of time needed to continue to work with the prospect after each ask may be equal to the time that was needed for the preparation and actual ask.* If this follow-through is lacking, the gift opportunities will lie in limbo, with no resolution.

Asking for money is rarely a solo event. Even the smallest of nonprofit groups will have a few people who make up the fundraising team, even if that team consists of just the leader of the group and a volunteer or the leader and an investor. It is very important that the information obtained before, during, and after each ask is shared with the fundraising team. All too often people ask for money and then do not share how the ask went, the questions the prospect had, or the prospect's request for more time to consider the offer or for further information. The conversation during the ask, observations about the prospect's reaction to the ask, and the next steps to be taken after the ask need to be shared with the fundraising team and recorded in a contact report in the organization's database. An organization does not do one ask and then wait until there is closure on that ask before asking for another gift. Multiple asks will be going on simultaneously, and the best structure for keeping full and accurate records on each ask is the group's database, so that leaders and fundraisers can accurately recall at a later time all the dynamics that occurred during the ask and the next steps that need to take place to get the gift.

The Reward Is in the Ask

To ask for a gift is a privilege, a wonderful expression of commitment to and ownership of the organization. Getting a yes to an ask can be a rush, but asking for the gift can and should be just as rewarding. This should not be a dreaded activity or a tense time. It is a time to share and celebrate the group's achievements and what the group can achieve for future generations, with help, support, and love from others. Best of all the ask can and should be fun. If it is fun for the asker, it will be a fun and positive time for the prospect. Prospects should see and experience the joy their prospective gifts will bring to the group's beneficiaries. The more upbeat and energized the asker can be, the more open and willing the prospect will be to consider the gift.

DETERMINING WHEN ONE ASKER CAN CONDUCT AN ASK

One issue to consider when choosing askers is whether one person should make the ask or whether two or more would be better. Exhibit 3.5 presents a number of the factors to consider in deciding this important question.

EXHIBIT 3.5. *Questions for Determining the Number of Askers.*

1. Is the organization small or understaffed?

2. Is more than one person available to do the ask?

3. What size gift is being asked for?

4. Does the prospect expect one or more people to do the ask?

5. Can one person cover complex questions that may arise?

Staff Availability Governs the Number of People Who Make the Ask

The smaller the organization, the more likely it is that most of the asks will be done by one person. Many small to medium-size organizations simply do not have sufficient askers on hand to assign two or more to a single ask. As stated earlier in considering the time available for making asks, askers have many other functions to attend to. Under these circumstances, most of the asks other than the high-end asks will be done by the staff fundraiser or a volunteer. This will ensure that the asks get done and that the group is not waiting for the leaders to free up some time so that they can participate in each ask.

Top Asks Deserve Top Askers

The group's needs are best served when leaders save their time for asks that involve high-level gifts and high-profile prospects. Think about what constitutes a top gift for your group. Whether it is $10,000 or $1 million, someone representing the leadership needs to be involved in the ask for this gift. This leader could be the CEO, the president, the chair of the board, or an active and knowledgeable board member.

In addition to the amount of the gift, you need to consider the profile of the prospect. Even if you are asking for a modest or not-quite-top gift, an organization leader should do the ask when (1) the prospect has a high position in a company, (2) the prospect is a celebrity or has a high public profile, or (3) the prospect has the potential to be a longtime supporter and to support the group in a significant way down the line, even though the initial ask will be for a smaller amount. Wealthy and high-profile people with high-level positions expect that a leader of the organization will ask them for money. Many will not give unless it is the head of the organization that does the ask. I also think it is important to pay attention to those prospects who have tremendous potential to be longtime supporters and also have the assets to make a significant gift. These folks may not now be at the stage of making a large gift to your group. They may want to make a modest gift or a series of small gifts to test the organization, looking to see how it will invest and steward the smaller gift before they give a larger gift. Whenever possible, have a leader of your group involved with each ask, starting with the first one. It is important to these prospects that this leader know them and stay involved with them. Then a mutual understanding and expectation can develop that because this leader of the organization has the strongest relationship with them, in time they will make a larger gift when this leader asks.

For instance, an organization might be blessed with a board member who has been trying to get her local celebrity friend to be more involved with the group. The board member convinces the celebrity to just "drop in" at the group's yearly major fundraising gala, held at a major hotel. The group has secured the media to cover the event, and the celebrity is sure to get some good press if he attends. The celebrity makes a surprise guest appearance at the cocktail reception preceding the event, and the board member introduces the celebrity to the head of the group, other board members and top donors, and some of the group's beneficiaries. The next day the board member calls the celebrity, thanking him for "stopping by" and inviting him to tour the group's facilities and to spend time with the president and beneficiaries. The celebrity says he simply does not have the time this month but will consider it in the future and will send a check to support last night's fundraising gala.

It is imperative that this board member *continue to involve the celebrity and not hand him off to the fundraising staff.* The staff can assist with all the background work, scheduling appointments and giving the board member updates to send directly to the celebrity, but it is the board member who needs consistent contact with the celebrity and who eventually may find the time is right to ask the celebrity for a large gift.

Complex Gifts Require Knowledgeable Askers

In deciding whether one person should do the ask, it is important to examine the complexity of the ask. Some gift opportunities are intricate, such as planned gifts, endowments, or an outright gift that may involve funding many areas. The asker needs to be knowledgeable and well versed in all aspects of the gift proposal. If the asker is seeking support for a special event or yearly fundraiser, then he needs to know if the money will be used to support general operating expenses, scholarships, or a capital project or if it will be used to increase the size of the group's endowment. If the ask is for a charitable gift annuity, then the asker needs to know the organization's minimum gift level for annuities and how annuities can be funded, and he should bring several illustrations showing the differences for tax purposes between an annuity funded with cash and one funded with appreciated securities. If a prospect is interested in having her gift fund several projects within the organization, then the asker must know the details of each and every project and also any restrictions, such as the minimum gift accepted for each project. Look at the complexity of the gift and make sure the person doing the ask is equipped to present the gift opportunity and can reasonably cover the potential questions that may arise.

USING THE TEAM APPROACH

Whenever possible use two people; this number is ideal for any ask. This team can be more effective because two people "have twice the talents and strengths of one" (Irwin-Wells, 2002, p. 83). Team members can use their individual strengths when making the ask and can feed off each other's energy and enthusiasm. While one member of the team is speaking, the other member can and should be a human sponge, absorbing the prospect's eye contact, body language, and tone of voice and judging the prospect's level of comfort. I always use the expression "four eyes are better than two." With two people making the ask, there is less chance that the team will miss something the prospect said, suggested through intonation, or expressed through body language. The bottom line is simply that there is strength in numbers, so every chance you get to do a joint ask, take it.

The best way to experience the benefits of a team ask is to do an ask by yourself; then do one with another asker. As long as you both are prepared and well scripted (a topic covered in depth in Chapter Five), it will be crystal clear that your comfort level and confidence rise when you do the ask with a partner. This is a wonderful exercise to try. Do an ask with a partner. Right after the ask, sit down, and go over all the details that you and your partner heard and saw. I guarantee you that your notes will be comparable for some parts of the ask, but for others you and your partner will have different versions.

For example, a director of development and a director of direct mail might jointly visit a prospect at her home to ask for an enhanced gift. This prospect has been a consistent giver through direct mail at the $200 level, but has the potential to make a larger gift of $1,000, which would place her in the group's Benefactor's Circle. It has been agreed that the director of direct mail will start the dialogue, thanking the prospect for previous important contributions to the direct mailings, and then the director of development will spell out the need for increased gifts to this fund so that the group can do three specific new things to help its beneficiaries. The director of development then asks the prospect for the $1,000 gift. The prospect responds that she needs some time to consider her finances, and the director of development agrees to call the prospect within two weeks.

After the visit the directors sit down and compare notes. The director of direct mail had noticed piles of magazines, unopened letters, and other direct appeals on the prospect's desk. He was also a bit distracted by the prospect's dog, who had wanted to play with him. The director of development missed all that because she was carrying most of the conversation, but she did see lots of construction taking place in the prospect's backyard. She wondered whether the cost of these renovations might be a factor in the prospect's need to think over whether to give a $1,000 gift now. The director of direct mail had missed all that because from his vantage point he could not see the backyard. This small example illustrates how two people can paint a much more complete and accurate picture of the ask, a picture necessary to appropriate follow-up.

The team approach also has the advantage of letting the prospect know that she is important to the organization. Even when the ask is not a top ask for the group, the fact that two people are doing the ask says that the group thinks very highly of the prospect. It sends the message that the organization does not take the ask lightly and that this is an important moment for the prospect and the organization. The prospect will feel elevated because time and attention have been devoted to her, and that sets the stage for a very effective ask.

A Board Member as Part of the Team

If you have board members who satisfy most of the ideal characteristics of a good asker (Exhibit 3.4), then whenever possible have one of these board members on the asking team. Board members lend prestige to the ask. Their volunteerism and financial support for your organization will be among the most powerful and influential factors in any ask. Their presence alone heightens the level and importance of the ask.

Asking board members to go on the road and ask for gifts with other members of your organization also serves to give the board members a realistic view of the group's prospect pool. It is one thing to sit in a meeting, removed from prospects, and think that it is an easy task to ask for money. It is another to be a part of that process. Some board members may think their group has such a rich pool of prospects that it should be raising more money. This is easy to say in a meeting; it is not so easy to experience when these wealthy prospects say no to the ask or take months or years before unleashing a large gift to the group. Board members need this dose of reality so that they can better understand and appreciate the fundraising process.

Because board members together with the CEO or president are the leadership for a group, they need a little tender loving care as they embark on the wonderful journey of asking people for money. I have some words of wisdom on this subject. First, obviously, be conscientious about board members' time. The organization should not be asking them to do more than they can handle. Using the chart displayed in Exhibit 3.3 should ensure that each board member does not volunteer to do more asks than she or he can handle and that the organization has realistic expectations of each board member's time. Second, nothing succeeds like a quick success. During board members' early asks, try to have them ask prospects who are likely to say yes to the ask. A yes will empower them and make them feel as though they are good at asking, and they will then be more willing to do asks for a longer period of time because their rate of success is pretty good (Lysakowski, 2004). Third, have the fundraising staff do all the administrative work required on each ask, such as scheduling appointments, preparing letters to the prospects from the board members, and reminding the board members when it is time for them to call or visit a prospect to keep the ask viable. Some board members use their own support staff for these activities, which is terrific. In other cases, however, make sure the fundraising staff stay on top of the cultivation process; otherwise the ask will never be scheduled and there will be no follow-up. Fourth, to the extent your organization has the budget for it, offer training on how to ask for money, preferably from an outside consultant. Even the most seasoned board member, one who has asked for gifts for your group and other groups, can always benefit from training and role playing. Moreover, beyond knowing the prospects and the organization inside and out, board members also need to know the larger picture of the philanthropic climate. How are other organizations doing? Is giving on the rise, stalemated, or declining? Which groups are doing better than others? Which constituencies are doing better than others? Consultants or members of the fundraising team should carve out some time, before or during a board meeting or at a retreat perhaps, to focus on the skills and techniques of the ask, role playing for the ask, and updates on current national and global fundraising trends.

Lastly, many of your board members will be closely connected to the community and will have influential friends and family who can widen your group's base of support. Many board members, however, are hesitant to ask for gifts from people who are close to them; it seems awkward and uncomfortable to them. Share the following statistic with them as a motivator for them to ask their colleagues, friends, and family to be more involved with your group and in turn to give. In a recent survey, 1,751 U.S. consumers were asked about their motivations for giving: *87 percent said that a personal request from a friend or family member* was among their top three motivators for giving. And more than half the respondents, 58.4 percent, *ranked this as their top reason for giving* (PNN Online, 2004). Surely this will help to encourage many board members to take the leap and to ask those closest to them to support your group. Ask your board members to include their circle of close friends in this effort. Not to do so is a missed opportunity for your organization to expand its donor base.

Administrators and Staff as Part of the Team

Your group may have administrators or staff who could make an excellent contribution to the asking team. For instance, hospitals, assisted living facilities, nursing homes, and senior centers all have staffs of doctors, nurses, therapists, volunteers, and administrative personnel who interact with patients and clients every day. Some of these folks form a bonding and long-lasting relationship with their patients and clients. These patients and clients can and should be top prospects, and the doctors, nurses, therapists, volunteers, and administrative staff who have relationships with these prospects should be part of the cultivation and the ask. Many patients, for example, give because of one person in a facility who cared attentively for their medical and emotional needs. Leaving these people out of the ask would be a big mistake.

Colleges and universities have administrators and staff who played an instrumental role with the alumni when they were students. Beyond the president, deans, faculty, fundraising staff, and other alumni, there are guidance counselors, placement officers, co-op and internship directors, the provost, department chairs, the financial aid and scholarship director, and psychological counselors who might be included in an ask if the alumna or alumnus being cultivated had a special bond with that person. Remember, before, during, and after the ask, the more you can involve people who made a difference in the life of the prospect, the better chance you will have of getting the gift.

Select Donors as Part of the Team

In addition to all the other kinds of askers discussed here, you will have a group of top donors to consider. Some of these people may be appropriate for a joint ask, and some may not. The fact that they have made a significant gift or series of such gifts is not a signal that they should automatically be made part of any ask. However, if they possess most of the ideal characteristics of a good asker, as spelled out earlier, and if they know and have a personal relationship with the prospect, then, yes, they should be involved with the ask. Conversely, I caution nonprofit groups not to include a donor on the team making the ask when that donor has not cultivated or does not have a past, positive history with the prospect. Again, the point of the ask is to make the prospect as comfortable as possible. The ask should be an *extension* of the trust and faith the prospect has in your group. If you involve someone in the ask who does not exude that feeling of confidence and trust and who is not close to the prospect, the prospect will lose interest in what the askers have to say, and the ask will not be seriously considered.

Consultants as Part of the Team

Many groups employ consultants to boost their annual fund, help them create strategic fundraising and marketing plans, or help them run a comprehensive capital campaign, to name just a few of the projects for which consultants are hired. If your prospect knows, trusts, and has worked with your consultant on behalf of your group, it may be a good strategy to have the consultant be part of the ask. I think this works particularly well in capital campaigns when your consultant has done your feasibility study and has personally interviewed your prospects. If the consultant continues on, helping you form the case statement, arranging and attending campaign cabinet meetings, and assisting with identifying your top campaign prospects, then the consultant may be the ideal person to assist with these asks because he or she has formed relationships with these campaign prospects. However, I would *always* have someone from the organization be present with the consultant during the ask. It simply sends the wrong signal to have the consultant go it alone, and I firmly believe that many consultants would discourage a group from having just the consultant present during the ask. It is likely to make the prospect think, "Who is running this organization?" or, "This group does not think enough of me and did not have the time to personally ask me for money." Always have someone from your organization accompany the consultant on the ask.

Another caveat is not to overload or overwhelm the prospect by having too many people present during the ask. Two is a comfortable number. Three may be over the top for most prospects. Some prospects may feel outnumbered, ganged up on, or that the sheer number of bodies in the room is a total turn off. Other prospects may feel elated that so many from the group, including the consultant, are here just for the prospect. Gauge each prospect's level of comfort when determining the number of people who should be involved in the ask. Of course, if the prospect would want or expects the consultant to be part of the ask, then by all means use that talent for the ask.

CONCLUSION

Selecting the right person or team to do the ask begins with a close look at the organization's pool of potential askers. The size of the organization's leadership team, fundraising team, and volunteer group; individuals' level of expertise in asking for gifts; the time that each person can devote to asks; the maturity of the fundraising program; and the size of the prospect and donor base are the factors to consider. Potential askers may also include the organization's administrators, staff, and consultants. In order to be considered part of the asking pool and part of the asking team, an asker must have a strong personal relationship with the prospect, must have assisted with cultivation, and from the prospect's point of view, must be a natural part of the ask.

Once the pool of potential askers has been established, the next step is to see if each of these people has some, none, or all of the characteristics that make a good asker. He or she should be well known, respected, and confident and should have played an important and active role in cultivation, have given a gift comparable to or identical to the gift being asked for, and have demonstrated strong commitment to the organization. He or she should also have knowledge and expertise about the gift opportunity, have the desire to keep everyone involved in the ask apprised of all communication, and be able to have *fun in the process.*

Whenever possible two people should do the ask, because asking teams are more effective. They possess double the strength and talent, and while one person is speaking the other can observe everything that is taking place during the ask. Top asks require the top leaders of the organization, so if the organization is small or short staffed and the team approach is not possible, make sure that the leaders' time is used wisely for large asks or asks made to important, influential, and affluent prospects.

LOOKING AHEAD

Now that you have some strategies for selecting the right person or persons to do the ask, the next chapter will focus on gauging the right number of prospects to be worked with for each type of ask. It will give some parameters for selecting the right number of prospects to work with in any size organization, so that you have a strong and robust pipeline of prospects at all times. And it will discuss the importance of the setting for the ask and the tone of the ask as well as the need to be in tune with the prospect's body language and to check out the asker's body language. Particular emphasis is placed on the four essential elements of the ask as well as the crucial need to stay silent after the ask.

4

Preparing for the Ask

When someone asks me for money I look at the effort and perseverance
of the presentation, a sound business plan and accountability of results.

—B. Thomas Golisano, Chairman and CEO, Paychex, Inc.,
Rochester, New York

T HIS CHAPTER FOCUSES ON ALL THE PREPARATION
the asker and asking team need to do before the ask. Setting the
right tone by selecting the right location and being extremely conscientious about portraying positive body language are key. Careful
preparation of the prospect's profile and all the elements of the gift
proposal are also a must. A particularly useful exercise is to make sure
that each ask is scripted. Scripts set forth the time frame for the ask,
who speaks and who listens during the ask, and the four essential elements of any ask: the warm-up, the actual ask, the prospect's comments and concerns, and the close and follow-up.

Preparation is everything when it comes time to asking for money.
This is not the time when you want the atmosphere to be hectic or distracting, and you do not want your askers to be unprepared or to walk
through the motions of the ask. Many of your askers will be your
fundraisers. However, as the size of your ask increases, it will require the
participation of your CEO, president, board members, and volunteers,
all of whom live very busy lives. It can take a lot of effort to get them to
leave behind the contents of the last meeting, forget the disturbing

e-mail they just received, and postpone returning yesterday's telephone calls so that they can be on time to ask your prospects for money. It is the fundraiser's job to make sure that the asker or the asking team is well prepared in advance of the ask.

THE RIGHT TONE FOR THE ASK

Preparation for the ask begins with setting the right tone, as outlined in Exhibit 4.1.

Selecting the right place to do the ask takes more work than you might think. The objective is to find a place that is quiet, calming, and with no distractions. The place should be somewhere the prospect and the asker both feel comfortable.

Location, Location, Location

The ideal places are usually the prospect's home or office, a private room at the organization, the CEO's or president's office, a conference room, or a private club. I say that these are *usually* good places to do the ask for the following reason. Not every prospect's home is a calm place, especially if she has young children, works at home, is repairing or reconstructing an area, or is taking care of an elderly parent who lives with her. You do not want these potential distracters when you ask for money. The same can be said for asking the prospect in an office setting. If your prior encounters at her office have been interrupted by messages from an assistant or urgent telephone calls, then her office is not a good choice.

EXHIBIT 4.1. *Preparing the Right Atmosphere for the Ask.*

1. Select a calm and quiet location.
2. Bring energy, enthusiasm, and charisma to the meeting.
3. Present a confident and professional image.
4. Be extremely aware of your body language.
5. Speak in a clear and convincing voice.

Doing the ask at your organization—for example, in the CEO's or president's office, a conference room, a study, or a library—may be an excellent choice, especially if the prospect has been in these areas before and likes coming to your facilities. In that case the prospect and the askers will be very comfortable with these surroundings and will have a more controlled atmosphere. The askers can ensure that there are no interruptions because the organization's site is within their control.

A private room in a private club may accomplish the same goals, especially if the prospect has been cultivated in this atmosphere and enjoys the private club scene. It is important that the askers notify the club staff in advance that they do not want to be disturbed at a certain point in time during the meeting. For instance, if it is a meeting that involves a meal, after the plates are cleared and the coffee pouring ceases, the wait staff should disappear so that the askers can focus the prospect's attention on the gift opportunity. The other word of caution about private clubs is to make sure the prospect likes being taken to private clubs. Some prospects feel they belong in a elevated level of society and should be there. Many may belong to a club or two, and in that case you should not think twice about doing the ask in a private club. Other prospects, however, may feel that a club is pretentious and that the organization should not "waste its money" on private club fees. The rule here is to *know what makes your prospect comfortable* and select that venue.

There is much discussion about whether people should be asked for money in a restaurant or café. *Unless your prospect is available only during breakfast, lunch, or dinner or expects you to take her out,* I would avoid doing the ask when food is involved. It gets complicated and unpredictable for several reasons. First, even if you tell the wait staff in advance that you want some uninterrupted time with your prospect, there is no guarantee they will remember and give you some time. After all, it is their job to attend to your table, and now you are asking them to leave you alone! Second, you probably cannot predict the level of conversation that will take place around you during your ask. We all have had the experience of having a very loud and lively table next to us, and it is very distracting. You do not want to be competing for your prospect's attention, and you do not want to be raising your voice over another conversation so that your prospect can hear you. Third, you have to navigate the awkward moment when the check arrives. I have gone to a restaurant well in advance of the meeting and have given the manager explicit instructions that the wait staff give me the check. I have even supplied my credit card in advance of the meeting so that the wait staff can give me the check with my credit card and all I have to do is sign. Sometimes this works, but at other times the dreaded black leather folder containing the check is left smack in the middle of the table and the prospect and I end up practically arm wrestling for the check. If at all possible, spare yourself this anxiety, and select a place to do the ask that is not a restaurant or café.

Positive and Professional Demeanor

During any meeting one or more persons govern the tone of the meeting. In a sales meeting, for instance, the person who reports that the team has reached or surpassed its marketing projections is filled with excitement and pride. All eyes and attention are on this one person. Ditto for meetings that involve the ask. The prospect will generally mirror the energy level and level of professionalism set by the asker or askers. This is why it is so important for the asker or asking team to have high energy, be enthusiastic, be upbeat and positive, establish strong eye contact, and present a polished and professional image (Hartsook, 2001). It starts with appearance. Even when you are asking for a gift from a studio artist, a florist, a retiree, or someone else who generally does not wear a suit or dress clothes every day, you and the others doing the ask must look professional, crisp, and polished. This requires careful attention to hair, nails, shoes, and an appropriate handbag or briefcase. Would you want someone who looks like he slept in his clothes or who had missing buttons or stains on his clothes asking for money on behalf of your group? Wear appropriate business attire with the appropriate accessories, and you can never go wrong.

Your energy and enthusiasm should be contagious. After all, this is the big moment. The moment when the asker and asking team will be doing the final *sell* of a fabulous opportunity for your prospect. The asker needs to be as charismatic and positive as possible so that the prospect will in turn be pumped up to hear the details about the gift. Mind you it is easier said than done for each ask to have the ideal aura. Realistically, not everyone has a good day every day, and we all have personal and professional issues that sometimes prevent us from feeling our best. When that occurs, I recommend two things to get you back on track and feeling more positive. I learned this when I was a practicing attorney, scared to death to do a trial or oral argument against an experienced opposing counsel. The first tactic is to think of yourself not as you but as someone you admire. I used to imagine that I was a famous actress or politician. I focused on what that person would do and say in this moment. If you focus on someone you admire and try to adopt their star-power qualities, it will help you get out of your own head, your own funk, and be more positive and likeable. The second tactic is to do or concentrate on the things that make you happy. Put on your favorite CD, dance, sing (only if you have a good voice), buy yourself flowers, or visualize yourself as winning an Olympic competition. It just may force you to smile and, in turn, feel better for the ask.

Positive Body Language and Tone of Voice

An asker can say all the right things but still sabotage the ask because his body language or tone of voice is sending the wrong message. During an ask, each person doing the ask has to stand tall, sit upright, have his shoulders back, and his head and eyes fixed on the prospect. The asker's body position is very important because it can send so many different signals. The asker does not want to appear nervous by looking around the room, looking past the prospect, reading from notes, reading the whole proposal, or rearranging the pillows on the sofa. The asker also does not want to appear overly comfortable by slouching on a chair or sofa or leaning way back with his hands folded over his head or stomach. This body positioning can be visually distracting to the prospect. One of the reasons why it is always good to have two people on the ask is to learn about one's body language. Askers may have no idea how distracting they look when they get comfortable in a cushy armchair. If only one person is doing the ask, how can he receive feedback about his asking style and effectiveness? All askers need to be aware of their body language messages and should respond positively to feedback if improvement is needed.

Just as your body language can send a good or distracting message, your tone of voice can do the same. For instance, if an asker is nervous, she may tend to lower her voice, to cough in between sentences, or to get a dry mouth and be desperate for a glass of water. All this can be very distracting to the prospect and can undermine the importance of the ask. Voice and body language go hand in hand. When people lower their voices, they also generally lower their heads. Now not only will it be hard for the prospect to hear what the asker is saying but all eye contact has been lost as well. The asker's voice should be clear and convincing. It should resonate with confidence in and dedication to the mission of the organization. If it does, strong body language will follow, and then you will have the complete package for a strong ask.

While we are discussing appearances, you should make sure that askers are not chewing gum or taking way too long with a breath mint or hard candy. It may seem silly to mention this; however, many people want to make sure their breath will not knock the prospect over, so right before they ring the prospect's doorbell they pop in a piece of gum or a mint. While you are traveling to see the prospect is the time to check your breath, so that by the time you arrive that activity is over. Gum chewing or positioning a mint while you are speaking is very distracting for the prospect and diminishes the quality of the ask.

THE REVIEW PRIOR TO THE ASK

Before each ask the person or persons doing the ask must do two things: (1) review the prospect's file and (2) review all aspects of the gift proposal. The prospect's readiness profile, discussed in Chapter Three, plus all the prospect contact and cultivation activity recorded in the organization's fundraising database needs to be reviewed. It is impossible for anyone to remember all the details about each prospect without this review, and the asker or asking team really does need total recall about the prospect before asking that person for money. This will also help each person doing the ask to weave in bits and pieces of previous conversations during the warm-up to the ask, which we will discuss in detail later in this chapter. Reviewing the prospect's profile will put each asker right in the moment with the prospect's life, which is exactly where an asker wants to be when making the ask.

The Twelve Essential Facts for Any Gift Proposal

Equally as important as reviewing the prospect's file is reviewing and having thorough knowledge of the prospect's gift proposal. Some proposals will be easy, such as asking for support for an event or special project or for a larger gift to the annual fund. Others will be more complex, such as a major gift proposal that requests support for three programs or a planned gift or capital campaign ask. The more complex the gift, the more time each asker will need to allow well before the ask to review all the details of the proposal. Exhibit 4.2 displays certain *musts*, what every asker needs to know about the proposal.

The reasons the gift is the perfect match for the prospect's interests and the purpose and benefits of the gift are the basics of any proposal. What is most important here, as discussed previously in Chapter Three, is that the gift opportunity matches a key interest of the prospect. The asker or asking team needs to be fully familiar with the way in which an area of funding matches perfectly with the goals, desires, and interests of the prospect. For instance, if a prospect was

---

EXHIBIT 4.2. *Essential Facts Every Asker Needs to Know About the Gift Proposal.*

1. Why this gift is the perfect match for this prospect.
2. The purpose of the gift.
3. The benefits of the gift.
4. How the gift can be funded.
5. The assets the organization will accept to fund the gift.
6. The timing with which the gift can be paid.
7. The maximum years over which the pledge can be paid.
8. The possible income, capital gains, estate, and gift tax benefits of the gift.
9. Why the gift opportunity "costs" this much.
10. Other donors who have made gifts at this level.
11. The number of gifts the organization has received or will ask for at this amount.
12. The suggested recognition that will be given for the gift.

---

the chair or served for a number of years on your annual fund committee, the ask should include an annual fund component *and each asker needs to be aware that this previous service is the reason for an annual fund ask.* If a prospect has remarked several times during the cultivation period that "if and when I make a gift, it will in all likelihood be a charitable gift annuity," which would bring the prospect needed quarterly income, then the ask has to be for a charitable gift annuity that includes income to this prospect and each asker needs to know that he is following the prospect's explicit request for this type of planned gift.

The asker or asking team also needs to be prepared to fully articulate the purpose of the gift and the benefits. Why is this gift needed now? What will it do for the organization now and later? These are basic questions many prospects will ask, and each asker needs to have a solid knowledge basis for answering both of them. Surprisingly, many people who ask others for money are not 100 percent sure how and when it is distributed to beneficiaries and how that whole process works. It is strongly suggested that well before the ask, the people doing the ask review the organization's annual reports, magazine, strategic plan, campaign case statement, and Web site and compile a series of bullet points that address how this gift will benefit the organization and how it will be distributed to its beneficiaries.

The Money Points for the Proposal

The next set of issues centers on the financing of the gift. First, the asker or asking team should have some idea of how the prospect is likely to fund the gift. Previous conversations with the prospect are the best source for this information. Obviously, if the prospect has substantial stock holdings, there is a strong possibility that stock will fund all or part of the gift. If the prospect is thinking of retaining the stock, expecting it to appreciate further, then cash assets or real estate may be the funding vehicle.

Second, it is always good to think out well in advance what one will say when the prospect asks about funding the gift. For example, if the prospect asks, "What types of assets does the organization accept to fund an endowed gift?" then the asker or asking team needs to know at what level endowed gifts start for the organization. Is it

$2,500, $5,000, $10,000, $50,000, or more? At what level can stock be used to fund the gift? Would that level be $5,000, less than that, or more than that? It is not enough to know the parameters of the gift; knowing how it can be funded is crucial to getting the gift earlier rather than later.

A third issue with funding is the timing of the gift. If there are no obstacles to the prospect's funding the gift now, that is ideal. However, circumstances in the prospect's personal or professional life may dictate that even though the prospect wants to make the gift, it will actually be done sometime in the future. Prospects will make gifts when they are good and ready and when the timing is beneficial to them financially. They may ask, however, if the organization is in urgent need of the funds now or if it is all right if the gift is given in the next calendar year. Of course, every organization wants the money in hand, but the asker or asking team needs to be flexible and ready to accommodate the prospect's timing for the gift. Each asker needs to know the organization's timeline for pledge payments. Is it three years, five years, or seven to ten years because it contains a capital campaign component? It is crucial that askers do not immediately agree to extend the timeline for a pledge simply because they would rather have some gift than no gift. What if the prospect for a $10,000 gift says, "I like the idea and want to do it, only I want the breathing room to do it over ten years." If your organization's gift acceptance policy allows a gift of this size to be spread out over a maximum of five years, the asker or asking team needs to explain to the prospect that the organization is guided by that policy and that ten years is too long for a pledge at this level.

Fourth, each asker needs to know that tax consequences play a major role in determining the amounts as well as the timing of gifts. This is especially true with planned gifts (and we will visit these gifts in depth in Chapter Seven). Income, capital gains, estate, and gift taxes can govern the amount, how the gift will be funded, and when it will be funded. Charitable gifts can be a real winner for many prospects, relieving them of heavy taxes they might otherwise encounter. Askers need to be brought up to speed so they can sell the benefits of tax relief associated with charitable gifts.

A fifth issue is what I call the *price* of the gift. Certain prospects think a gift opportunity is like everything else, negotiable. *Do not lower the gift level.* People at your organization have thought long and hard to establish gift levels and to determine what a project or program costs. It will do the organization great harm if the gift of a named endowed fund is $50,000, but your prospect wants you to consider the same gift for him at the $25,000 level and you agree to that change. You have now opened a can of worms, and you will not be able reseal it as tightly as it was sealed before. *You devalue a gift and all its benefits once its price is lowered.* Stick to your guns, and convince the prospect that $50,000 is the amount needed to fund this gift.

The Prestige of the Proposal

Giving can bring a sense of cachet, of being considered among the wealthy. As stated in Chapter One, many people give to emulate others and to be recognized. The asker and asking team need to know how many others have given at this level. No one likes to be a lone wolf when it comes to making a gift of a certain amount. Remember, there is strength in numbers. If you have donors who have given at the level you are asking of the prospect, let the prospect know. I would give the prospect a tally of these amounts without donor identities. Following the Code of Ethical Principles and Standards of Professional Practice of the Association of Fundraising Professionals (2004a), only when a donor has given you permission to use her or his name *can you reveal the amount that donor has given or pledged* and use that information to gather additional support (see Resource C).

The topic of recognition for the gift may seem premature at this stage, but I assure you it is not. Many prospects want to know what recognition they will receive if they give at a certain level: for example, they may wish to know whether there are naming opportunities and the details about them. Every asker needs to have solid answers to such questions. Can you imagine how awkward it would be if the prospect says, "You know, I always wanted to do something for my parents. Can I name a room after them if I make this gift?" and the asker has to reply, "Gee, I really don't know. I'll have to get back to you on that one." The rule is that you should know what forms of recognition are available and at what levels when you do the ask.

Examples of Lack of Preparation Before the Ask

My final note about proposal preparation is to take corrective action if the asker or asking team downplays the importance of this preparation, perhaps by making remarks like the following:

"I've known Ed for years; we went to school together. We have nothing to worry about."

"Jackie and I go way back. We have such great history and chemistry, we don't need to belabor these details."

"You have my time for the ask, not to review a pound of paper."

"I founded this program; don't you think I know it inside and out?"

"They won't ask for these kinds of details; after all, they'll need a lot of time to decide and that's when we can think about how they will fund it."

"Look at this portfolio. I wish I had this kind of money. This is a slam dunk."

Statements like these can set the wrong tone for any preparation for the ask and can give askers the illusion that they have a safety net. It is up to the fundraiser or fundraising team to emphasize the importance of preparation. To drive home the need to prepare, use examples of asks that failed because there was not enough preparation. If you do not do this, the ask will not go well, and I assure you that your asker will turn to you and say, "Why didn't you prepare me?" "I felt like a fool because I didn't have the answers," or "I don't think they will do this gift because they had so many questions, and hey, I'm not the expert here." The bottom line is that *there is no substitute for preparing for the ask, reviewing the prospect's profile, and thoroughly understanding the gift proposal.*

THE SCRIPT FOR EACH ASK

Part of preparing for each ask is to develop a script. A script is a road map that askers should use to rehearse the ask so that they are well prepared to do it. Some people may resist the idea of using a script, claiming that it is too formal, they know the prospect well, and a script diminishes the personal closeness needed for the ask. Remind these askers that the script is for rehearsal purposes and that when it comes time to do the actual ask, the script will be in their heads; they are not reading from paper. Exhibit 4.3 outlines the essential components of the script.

Time Frame for the Ask

Everyone has to have a clear understanding of the amount of time needed for the ask. If a time frame is not placed on the ask, you run the risk of using your precious time with the prospect for catching up and, in the worst case, never getting to the ask because your allotted time with the prospect has expired.

As a rule I believe that the ask should not take more than twenty-five minutes total. I divide the time as follows:

- The warm-up: five minutes
- The ask: six minutes
- The prospect's response: ten minutes
- The close and follow up: four minutes

If you have an hour with the prospect, terrific, but again, do not use the first half hour for small talk. Stick with the time frame I have just outlined, and then, if you have time left over after all the points of the ask are covered, go back to catching up with the prospect.

EXHIBIT 4.3. *Essential Components of the Script.*

1. Time frame for the ask
2. The warm-up
3. The ask
4. The anticipated response
5. The close and follow-up
6. Who speaks and who listens during the ask

The Warm-Up

The warm-up, or pleasant conversation time, is needed to break the ice. You do not want to enter the prospect's home or office, shake hands while saying hello, and then blurt out the ask. You need some time with your prospect to get back in touch. For instance, if the last time you met with the prospect he told you he and his wife were taking a cruise around the Mediterranean Sea, ask about the cruise. If the prospect's daughter just had a baby boy, ask how the family is doing and if he has any pictures of the grandson. This drives home the point made earlier about the need to review the prospect's profile in advance. Askers cannot possibly remember all the details of every prospect without this review, and they do need to know these details so they can easily weave them into the warm-up.

The most important point about the warm-up is that the prospect is reacquainted with the asker or asking team. It can and should be a bonding moment. Five minutes should be plenty of time to relax, smile, and share a story or two so that everyone is comfortable. This is exactly the right atmosphere in which to begin the ask.

The Ask

The ask has several essential components, as listed in Exhibit 4.4.

It is important that each ask be scripted because that is your insurance that each component of the ask will be covered.

EXHIBIT 4.4. *Essential Components of the Ask.*

1. Making a compelling case for the organization and the need for support
2. Using transitional statements that specifically reference the prospect's interest or prior support, or both
3. Asking for a specific amount and for a specific purpose
4. Detailing the benefits of the gift
5. Remaining silent

THE COMPELLING CASE The first thing the asker or asking team needs to do is to make a compelling case for the organization. This will focus the prospect on the purpose of the meeting, and it rekindles the prospect's interest in and dedication to your group. It also lays out why the organization needs support now and at what level. If there is no urgency or no organizational goal that needs to be met and funded, what difference does it make whether the prospect gives the gift now or years later? The answer is no difference, which is why the asker needs to emphasize the reasons why the group needs funding now.

EXAMPLES OF STATING A COMPELLING CASE The following are some suggested statements for conveying a compelling case for your organization:

"Jack, our college was just ranked in the Top 10 Best Values in *Money* magazine. We feel the timing could not be better for us to launch a comprehensive campaign. Let me share with you some of the goals for the campaign."

"Bridget, our women's clinic just received a substantial foundation grant that must be matched by private sources. We have such a loyal following, we are extremely confident we can meet this matching sum over the next three years."

"Anthony, our young writers series attracted over 200 youths this summer. Although the conference was underwritten, we want to take this to the next level and hold conferences twice a year and give scholarship aid to deserving participants."

"Lisa, our biomedical research institute just completed a five-year strategic plan. We had twenty experts from around the world help us draft this plan, which calls for raising over $15 million in public and private sources. Among our top priorities is to increase our endowment so that we can guarantee our critical research will last well into the future."

When making the compelling case, the asker or asking team needs to be direct and to provide context in the form of the big picture for the organization. The prospect will then be in a position to find out how she fits into the just-described new plans for the organization.

TRANSITIONAL STATEMENTS Askers use transitional statements to focus on the prospect's key area or interest with the group.

Such a statement is a natural handoff from a compelling case statement because it homes in on the specific areas that pertain to the prospect and the ask. In the examples of compelling case statements given earlier, for example, the asker is positioned to explain to Jack what the campaign will do for the college, what the areas of funding are, and how Jack's interest in scholarships would fit squarely within the campaign goals. Bridget is in a position to hear the details of the foundation's matching grant and how her prospective gift to the women's clinic will help meet the match for that grant. Anthony can now be asked either to help support another conference or to contribute to the newly formed scholarship fund for the young writer series. Lisa is ready to hear an overview of the strategic plan; ideally, right then and there she will also be handed a copy to take home, and she will be ready to be asked to support the biomedical research endowment. In other words, the asker has the prospect's attention, and it is time to transition to prospect participation. The transitional statement is a precursor to the actual ask. Remember, you do not want to blurt out the request for money too quickly; the prospect may feel attacked and uncomfortable. You want to make a natural and smooth transition to the ask.

EXAMPLES OF TRANSITIONAL STATEMENTS   Here are some examples of transitional statements that askers can use to focus the conversation with the prospect on the ask:

"Amy, you have been an exemplary donor, and your gifts have inspired so many others to support us. We cannot thank you enough. The last time we met, you expressed an interest in helping us acquire better vans to transport our disabled residents. We have an opportunity that matches your interest, and we would like to share it with you now."

"Josh, having been a trustee for a number of years, you can appreciate and celebrate how far we have come over the past five years, but as you also know, there is much work left to do. We share your concern that there is not enough space in our facility to help the number of homeless we serve. We are coming to you first with our idea on how we can expand and meet these growing needs. Permit me to share the plan with you."

"Leslie, your support for our mentoring program has put us on the map as the model for these community programs. We have the chance to take the program to a national level that is exciting and equally challenging. Let me take a few minutes to share with you what needs to be done to make that dream come true."

"Scott, volunteers are our best publicists, and we would not be here today without your leadership and dedication. We are truly blessed to have you as such an important part of our group. You have said on several occasions that our group needs to have a more powerful voice in government. With your help we can make that a reality. Let us explain."

These transitions let the prospect know that the organization did its homework, that it listened to the prospect and matched his interest with the right gift opportunity to meet his desire to support the organization. You have the prospect's full and complete attention, which is *exactly* where you want to be at this point in time. The prospect will be curious to know exactly what the organization has in mind. And now it is the ideal time for the ask.

THE ASK AMOUNT AND PURPOSE Each ask must state the amount and the purpose of the gift. This bears repeating because it is a guiding principle.

Guiding Principle 4

Ask for a specific amount for a specific purpose.

This principle may seem painfully obvious, but many, many asks are done without requesting a specific amount. If you do not ask the prospect for a specific amount, she may supply her idea of an appropriate sum, and it may be well below what you are anticipating or dreaming she will give. Why make this an unnecessary guessing game or mystery? Stating a specific amount gives the prospect an idea of how the organization views her participation (Irwin-Wells, 2002, p. 86). It sends the signal that the organization thought long and hard about how she could play an important role with the special event; the fund drives for the annual fund, major gift, or planned giving areas; or the capital campaign. Failing to request a specific amount can diminish the personal value of the gift. It can leave the prospect with the feeling that "it doesn't matter whether the group gets a check from me or from someone else."

As important as asking for a specific amount is asking for a specific purpose. Simply asking the prospect for $2,500 to support the organization will probably not do much good. She is likely to want to know more precisely what the money will be used for. If the ask is for an unrestricted gift, then let the prospect know the group needs unrestricted funds to cover operational expenses. If the gift is for a restricted fund, then let the prospect know that it will be placed, for example, in the endowment fund and will generate approximately 5 percent interest to be used for the scholarship fund. The bottom line is that the *ask must be specific and straightforward.*

EXAMPLES OF SPECIFIC ASKS WITH SPECIFIC AMOUNTS Here are a few examples of specific asks that state the purpose of the gift and the gift amount:

"Glenn, we would like you to consider a gift of $25,000 for a named endowed scholarship at your school. We can work with you and whomever you desire on the terms of the scholarship."

"Alex, we invite you to consider an investment of $1,000 to help sponsor our community fair."

"Fred, we ask this only of our top donors. We would like you to join with other top donors and consider a leadership gift of $1 million to support the construction of our new surgical wing."

The ask should be articulate, crisp, and concise. Two simple sentences are all you need to make an effective ask, one that states the ask amount and the purpose of the gift.

BENEFITS OF THE GIFT This is a prime time for launching into the benefits of the gift. Notice that the asker or asking team needs to speak about the *benefits of the gift,* not the *financial needs of the organization.* Prospects want to hear how the gift will help others, not how the organization will reach its fundraising goals. If a prospect is asked to make a scholarship gift, it is much more effective to say that the students need and deserve the opportunity for a great education than it is to stress the goal of increasing the scholarship fund. Remember, even if the gift will construct a new wing, add an additional studio, or pay for new laptops, ultimately the gift will help people. Let the prospect know how many beneficiaries the gift will help and the difference the gift will make to the beneficiaries. If you have written testimonials from beneficiaries or pictures of beneficiaries, bring them with you and share them with the prospect.

Benefits are also a two-way street. The gift not only aids the beneficiaries but also satisfies the prospect's interests. The prospect gains the knowledge that the gift will fulfill his aspirations to help the organization. If the gift also helps the prospect to meet his own financial goals, make sure this point is highlighted. For instance, if the prospect can donate his second home, which he wanted to sell anyway, and can get many tax benefits from doing so, then the asker or asking team has to celebrate with the prospect that this is a win-win situation for him and for the organization's beneficiaries.

REMAINING SILENT   The cardinal rule after any ask is that the asker or asking team *must remain silent.* The next person to speak *should be the prospect.* This is extremely hard for askers to do. The asker or asking team is usually very excited and filled with energy, and the temptation is to keep the conversation going by elaborating on the details and benefits of the gift opportunity. However, if you speak now you run the risk of second-guessing the prospect's reaction, and then you will not hear in the prospect's own words how she feels in this moment after being asked to invest in your organization. It is the prospect's immediate reaction that lets you know, right away, your next strategy. We will explore in great depth in Chapter Nine the myriad reactions prospects have to being asked for money, and what to do and say to keep the gift opportunity on track. For now, it is important to know that in order to get the prospect's thoughts, ideas, and concerns, the asker or asking team needs to be silent after the ask is made. A suggested way to emphasize this point is to place *a great big blank space* in each asker's written script right after the ask. This is what I call a *visual pause in time.* It serves as a visual reminder that silence is a good thing and a necessary thing at this point in time.

The more you listen to the prospect, the more the prospect will listen in return (Panas, 2004, p. 81). Silence gives you a golden opportunity to hear the prospect's concerns, to hear the questions she may have, to hear her silence and hesitations indicating something is getting in the way of yes, and to hear about the financial and personal issues that may influence her decision.

Many people may think that listening is relinquishing control because as long as you are talking you can steer and shape the direction of the conversation. However, listening can be one of the most effective ways to maintain control. Think back to a committee meeting or speaker series you attended when the person doing the presentation stopped, paused, and reflected silently for what felt like an extremely long time. Everyone in the room was probably fixated on the speaker, waiting in great anticipation of what the speaker was going to say or do. It is by means of this very same *silent control* through listening that you will gain the insight you need to uncover how your prospect really feels about the chance to support your group in the special way you have suggested.

The Prospect's Response

As mentioned, Chapter Nine deals in depth with how to respond to the many different reactions and responses the asker or asking team will get. As I stated in Chapter One, many people do not like to ask others for money because they fear the prospect's reaction and worry that they will not be able to handle the prospect's questions and concerns. Prospects will have a variety of reactions, verbal and nonverbal, and the asker or asking team needs to do some homework to anticipate the prospect's reaction. Out of the twenty-five minutes allotted to the ask, I suggest that you devote the most time, at least ten minutes, to dealing with this reaction, because it is the *pivotal part of the ask*. If the prospect has more time and the questions and concerns are complex, then give him all the time he can spare so that he can state his concerns and you can address them the best way possible. It is not necessary that everything be covered in this initial meeting, and in most instances a lot more information needs to be explored and exchanged before the prospect can make a final decision.

The Close and Follow-Up

After the prospect's concerns and issues have been aired and addressed as best as possible during the ask, the asker or asking team needs to bring the meeting to closure. The close contains several key elements (Exhibit 4.5).

EXHIBIT 4.5. *Key Elements of the Close.*

1. Thank the prospect for taking the time to share this exciting opportunity.

2. Thank the prospect for listening to you.

3. Restate the gift opportunity and its benefits.

4. Give the prospect a date when you will get back to her with further information in response to her questions or concerns.

5. Ask the prospect if he has any additional comments or concerns.

6. Speak with the prospect as though the prospect will make the gift.

7. Where appropriate, ask the prospect, if and when the gift is made, how she would like to be recognized.

8. Set the date and time when the asker or asking team will meet with the prospect again.

Thank the prospect for his time, not only for allowing the asker or asking team to share the exciting gift proposal but also for listening. As difficult as it was for the asker to stay silent after the ask, it was probably just as hard for the prospect to listen to an entire presentation without interrupting or stopping the ask midstream.

The asker must also restate the gift opportunity and then one or two of the benefits. It is not necessary to repeat every point made, just highlight one or two. This will ensure that both asker and prospect heard and understood all the elements of the gift proposal.

If the prospect raised a question that could not be addressed during the ask or if he requested back-up information, tell him when you can get the information to him. This shows the prospect that the asker or asking team has listened carefully and that together they are moving the proposal forward. Set a realistic but short time frame. If the request requires expertise and research, then a week or two is OK. If, however, you have the materials, data, statistics, or other information readily available at your organization, then I suggest you tell the prospect you will send it in a day or two. No more than two weeks at the very most should go by without getting something back to the prospect.

This is also a good time to ask the prospect if there is anything else he needs to know or if he has any other comments or concerns not raised previously. It is important that the asker or asking team pause here in silence again to let the prospect mull over all the information that has just been shared. If the prospect needs more information, then repeat the pledge to get the information or answers to the prospect as quickly as possible.

A positive voice is a very powerful and effective tool. Speak with the prospect as if he has said yes to the gift or will do so very soon. This will keep the meeting on a steady upbeat and continue the enthusiasm and momentum. It is very easy to lose this momentum during the final portion of the ask. It can be draining and straining, but you cannot lose any steam now. This is why it helps if your voice is upbeat, energetic, and positive, because that will carry the tone of the meeting.

Telling the prospect about the recognition opportunities associated with the gift can be done during the discussion of the gift benefits or at the close of the ask. I think it is important that the asker or asking team be flexible in discussing recognition benefits. Sometimes prospects want to focus just on the mechanics of the gift, such as how and when it can be funded, or on the ways in which the gift will bring about change and help a good cause. They are not ready to hear about recognition because they have not yet said yes or because recognition does not interest them. In other instances recognition for the gift may be part of the *total benefits package* for the gift, so the asker or asking team should share those benefits with the prospect during the ask. For example, if you feel the prospect is leaning toward supporting your special event, tell him that his name or company name can be in the program, on a banner, or in a public announcement. If the prospect is leaning toward being a backer for an artist's opening show, tell him how the press releases for the upcoming show will list the investors. If the prospect has been asked for a specific major or capital campaign gift and your organization has recognition levels or naming opportunities at that level, let the prospect know. Whatever his response you will learn something, because discussing recognition benefits during either the ask or the close gives you a sense of how serious the prospect is about making the gift. If the prospect chimes in during the conversation with a question about naming opportunities for your organization's rooms, wings, lobbies, or solariums, that is a good sign because you have the prospect's wheels spinning in a positive direction about the gift. If, however, the prospect says, "That's getting ahead of us now," or, "It is premature to discuss this," then it shows that the prospect will really need much time before deciding on the gift.

The last element of the close is the most important. *Do not leave the room until you have set a date and time to meet again with the prospect.* Some prospects may be unwilling to commit to the next meeting. All too often they will say, "I'll get back to you on that," "I don't have my calendar with me now," or, "I need some time, so I don't want to set a date yet." These are all perfectly understandable reasons not to set a date, but to the extent one can be set, at least in terms of days, weeks, or the next month, do so. It will be much harder to pin down a date with the prospect once you have left the meeting. Without being pushy or overly forceful, set a date or prospective time frame when you can meet, ideally in person. This will keep the ask in the forefront of the prospect's mind. Chapter Ten focuses in more detail on setting up a meeting or telephone call immediately after the ask to ensure that weeks or months do not go by without appropriate communication with the prospect about the ask.

Once you are back in your office, send the prospect a thank-you letter, keeping it as personal and in the moment as possible (see Resource D for an example). Reference elements of your conversation with the prospect, and if you have set a date for the next meeting, reiterate the time and place. If you have not set a date, tell the prospect that you will call soon to set one. Most of all thank him, thank him, and thank him again for all he does for your organization and for his time and interest in your group.

Finally, be sure to record the meeting for the ask in a contact report, using your fundraising software, and to gather and send any additional information, data, statistics, or research the prospect requested.

Who Speaks and Who Listens

The last part of scripting the ask is to make sure each asker knows what she or he is to say and cover in the ask. If one person is doing the ask, then there is no question about who will carry out all the elements.

However, when two or more people are part of the ask, there is a risk that one will trip over the other in giving information or that each may think the other is going to do the actual ask. It is very important that the asking team have in writing which asker covers which areas. Here is an example of how easy it is to script who speaks and who listens:

> *Joyce:* Does the warm-up and compelling case statement (5 minutes).
>
> *Keith:* Does the transitional phrases and the ask (6 minutes).
>
> *Joyce and Keith:* REMAIN SILENT UNTIL THE PROSPECT SPEAKS.
>
> [*Leave a space here.*]
>
> *Joyce and Keith:* Address the prospect's concerns. Keith will cover all aspects of the gift proposal; Joyce will cover all questions about the organization (10 minutes).
>
> *Keith:* Restates the gift opportunities and benefits, including recognition; asks if the prospect has any final questions or comments; and proposes a date and time to meet or speak to follow up on the ask (4 minutes).

That is all you really need. Do take the time to write it down. It is one thing to all be happy and smiley in a meeting before the ask and to agree to divide up the time and tasks for the ask; it is another to see this agreement visually. Remember, your volunteers lead very busy lives, and it is very easy to forget who does what and when. Furthermore, the asking team may be prepped a day, a few days, or a week before the ask, and it is not surprising that people forget these important details by the time of the ask. So write down the timing details in the script, and you will have crafted a masterpiece!

The Four Questions

One final stage of preparation is necessary. In addition to carrying out the activities described earlier, anyone asking for money needs to answer the following four questions. These questions take a bit of soul searching.

1. Do you like who you are?
2. Do you like what you do?
3. Do you like whom you do it for?
4. Do you like whom you do it with?

Notice that the questions go from easy to answer to more difficult to answer. People asking for money need to like themselves. That means they have a sense of self-esteem, self-confidence, and a positive attitude, all of which the prospect needs to see and experience.

People who ask for money should like to ask. If this is something they loathe, hate, or fear, their rate of success on the ask will be quite low. Why would people want to do something they dislike? How effective can they possibly be if they wake up in the morning and dread going to work because they have an appointment to see a prospect and would rather sit quietly at their desks?

Ideally, people asking for money are also working or volunteering for an organization that they like, admire, and enjoy, and they want to be a part of its success. If they are working or volunteering for a group that they are lukewarm about, their asks will be half-hearted and their presentation style will be mediocre at best. If you are one of the latter, find a place you can call home, where you embrace each day with all its challenges, and even if you and others cannot save the world today, you always have tomorrow.

Last but not least is the question I love to ask because it is the hardest. Do you like the people you work with—superiors, volunteers, donors, coworkers, and administrative staff? People may have the best jobs in the world yet struggle with "difficult personalities" at work that can eat away at their time and their tolerance. Office politics are very difficult to leave behind when people are asking others for money. Usually some of these "difficult" people are ones that an asker may need to work with before, during, and after the ask.

I raise these four questions for a good reason. When you ask people for money, *you are Saran wrap, you are not aluminum foil!* I just love that metaphor. Prospects can see right through you. Askers cannot mask or leave behind the fact that they are not quite happy in their jobs, that they feel their efforts are going unnoticed or unappreciated, or that their coworkers are "stealing" their prospects and that that is a game they would rather not play. I am not suggesting that everyone has to have a good day every day or that people who are not 100 percent contented with their jobs because of where they work or whom they work with should leave. I am suggesting that askers need to put themselves in each prospect's shoes. Who are prospects seeing and hearing when they are being asked for money? They want to see and hear someone who represents the organization as a forward-moving train, not as one that has not left the station. This exercise of answering the four questions is a reality check. If you have answered yes to all four, then nothing can come between you and your success with each and every ask.

CONCLUSION

Every ask needs detailed preparation, starting with selecting the right location, one that is calm and that permits everyone in the room to hear the others without distractions. Each asker needs to be energetic, to speak with a clear and convincing tone, and to make sure that his or her body language is sending positive messages. People who ask prospects for money should review each prospect's profile to refresh themselves on prospect facts and should also review the details of the gift proposal.

Every ask should have a script for the asker or asking team. The script should be written and should lay out the time frame, the warm-up, the essential components of the actual ask, the anticipated responses, the close and follow-up, and who speaks and when. It is essential that the script specify that the asker or asking team *ask for a specific amount for a specific purpose* and that once the ask is made *the asker or asking team remain silent.*

Once the prospect's issues and concerns have been addressed as well as they can be during the ask, the asker or asking team needs to thank the prospect, restate the gift opportunity and benefits, set a date by which any requested additional information will be sent, and most important, set the date and time for the next meeting with the prospect.

The follow-up entails sending the prospect a thank-you letter, recording the ask activity in a contact report (using the group's fundraising software), and gathering and sending any requested additional information for the prospect.

When anyone asks for money on behalf of an organization, *that person is the organization.* How askers feel about themselves, their work, and the people they work with and for is critical to the effectiveness of the ask. Prospects want to be asked by positive, upbeat, and confident people, not by people who are half-hearted about the organization or who make it apparent that this job may not be the best fit for them. Select a place that you love, adore, and are proud to be a part of for your professional or volunteer work, and I guarantee you that you will be very effective with each and every ask.

LOOKING AHEAD

Now that you have a firm grasp on all the preparation for the ask, it is time to get down to the actual ask. The next chapter deals with asking for a special event or community project gift or for an enhanced annual gift. Through studying case studies and examples of how to take a good ask and make it the *best ask,* you will become well prepared to make these asks.

Asking for Special Event or Community Project Gifts and Increased Annual Gifts

*I ask because it is important for people to take ownership of our neigh-
borhood. I'm setting the tone that when you give it is very powerful. It
starts in one little corner in our neighborhood and spreads and influ-
ences others to give.*

—Kathy Donaldson, President, Bedford, Barrow,
Commerce Block Association, Inc., Greenwich Village, New York

*When I ask I am armored with the belief that giving is a privilege and
honor that always gives back more than is owed.*

—Terri Howell, Volunteer, Bedford, Barrow,
Commerce Block Association, Inc., Greenwich Village, New York

NOW THAT WE HAVE THE PREPARATION FOR
the ask covered, it is time to focus on the varying degrees of the
ask, starting with the request to fund a special event or community
project or to give an enhanced annual gift. Raise your hand if you
have ever volunteered to help a group raise money for a walk-a-thon,

bike-a-thon, golf outing, black-tie dinner, or office fund drive; to sell daisies or popcorn for groups that fight disease; to be a *backer*, or investor, for a new theater production or art exhibit; or to support local elementary school and high school sports. Chances are that at some point in time, everyone has been or will be asked to raise money for all these causes and more.

I have divided this chapter into two parts. The first part addresses how *volunteers* who are not normally fundraisers can ask for money. Throughout this chapter the term *volunteer* means the person who is not a professional or staff fundraiser, not an official part of a special event team in an established organization, and not a director of development or major gifts officer who needs to raise money via a special event. So this discussion is for members of that broader audience whose full- or part-time jobs do not involve fundraising; rather, these people are admirably volunteering to support the community or another good cause. Many of these volunteers find they simply do not know how to ask a friend, neighbor, colleague, coworker, or business owner to support a school's lacrosse team or a religious organization's raffle. They want to help the nonprofit organization be successful and they would like to feel they are a part of that success, but they put the ask off to the last minute because they do not know how to approach people for money. To meet their needs, the first part of this chapter explores three specific instances of asking, with scripts that volunteers can use to get money from friends, coworkers, and the business community.

The second part addresses how both fundraisers and volunteers can ask people who have made steady annual gifts to an organization for an *enhanced annual gift*. It explores what the annual gift is, who the annual fund donors are, and how to *upgrade* these folks. The emphasis is on the guidelines each asker can use to determine the manageable number of annual fund donors that he or she can ask *in person* to increase their annual fund gift. In addition, this part of the chapter covers the *pitch* and a unique angle for selling the annual fund that should be part of any asker's script.

I have two reasons for pairing the ask for enhanced annual fund gifts with the ask for money for special events or community projects. First, many groups raise a substantial portion of their unrestricted money through both special events and the annual fund, so these two activities have a natural affinity within many organizations. Second, many groups use volunteers for both these types of asks. These volunteers may include an organization's donors, beneficiaries, board and committee members, and administrative staff, and all these individuals will need to be prepared for their fundraising work, whether they do it on their own in the instance of raising money for events and projects or alongside organizational fundraisers, who will also need training, in the instance of asking for enhanced annual fund gifts. Later chapters build to the complexity of asking for larger gifts, such as major, planned, and capital campaign gifts.

THE ASK FOR A SPECIAL EVENT OR COMMUNITY PROJECT

Let us look at three specific, realistic instances in which a volunteer may need to seek the help of a friend, colleague, neighbor, or businessperson: asking for money to support a local sports team, asking for money to support a block association's annual community event, and asking for a monetary investment in a cabaret production so that it can be produced at various venues nationally. These principles, guidelines, and scripts can be applied and adapted to any special event, community project, or call for investors. For each example, I show a volunteer's initial satisfactory but average ask, and then I demonstrate how to make this ask much more effective. This process illustrates how easy it is to turn a mediocre ask into a highly effective ask.

The first example concerns a township that needs to fund its female soccer league. The team needs $5,000 to cover the costs of playing field rental, uniforms, referees, training, and insurance. Frank, who heads the parents' group in charge of the league, has come to Mr. and Mrs. B, whose two daughters are both in the league, to ask two things: (1) would they be willing to make an "investment" in the league by giving $250? and, (2) would they ask their friends and local businesses to be sponsors and to take ads for the league tournament?

> *Frank:* How are you, Mr. and Mrs. B? I saw both of you at the last practice, but you left before I had a chance to chat with you.
>
> *Mr. B:* Yes, we had to leave a bit early.

Frank: I would like to speak with you folks about a couple of things. Is now a good time?

Mrs. B: Sure.

Frank: Well, you know that the township has been cutting our league's funding little by little each year, while the number of teams in the league has increased. I think the kids and the parents agree that soccer is one of the best sports mentally and physically.

This year we need $5,000 to cover the cost for the upkeep of the field, uniforms, referees, trainers, and whopping insurance costs. Your daughters really enjoy themselves, and it's a pleasure to have them in the league. Would you be willing to help us out?

What is wrong with this ask? Frank did not ask for a specific amount. Asking someone, "Can you help out?" or, "Would you give what you can?" or, "Can we count on your support?" does not give the prospect any idea of what the asker really wants. Is he asking for the prospect's money? Is he asking the prospect to ask others for money? This example illustrates that any asker must ask for a *specific amount*. Although Frank did say that the money would be used for the field, uniforms, referees, trainers, and insurance, he did not ask Mr. and Mrs. B for a specific amount. Here is what Frank could have said:

Frank: Well, you know that the township has been cutting our funding little by little each year, while the number of teams in the league has increased. I think the kids and the parents agree that soccer is one of the best sports mentally and physically.

This year, we need $5,000 to cover the cost for the upkeep of the field, uniforms, referees, trainers, and whopping insurance costs. Your daughters really enjoy themselves, and it's a pleasure to have them in the league. Mr. and Mrs. B, would you consider making a $250 gift for our league? We have only a handful of families we can ask, and your gift would spark other families to give. Your gift would strengthen not only the league but also our community.

This ask is direct, it contains a stated amount, and it contains a stated benefit (that the contribution will help not only the league but also the community). There is no guessing about what Frank is asking Mr. and Mrs. B to do. The ball is now in Mr. and Mrs. B's court, and they have to respond to Frank.

Let's assume that Mr. and Mrs. B say that they will give $250 or will seriously consider giving to the league. Frank's next task is to ask them to ask friends and local businesspeople to be league sponsors or to take ads in the printed program for the tournament.

> *Frank:* I'm so glad you will consider making this very generous gift of $250. We also need sponsors and people to take ads in our tournament program. You both have been in this area for years; surely you know people who would want to help out.

The fact that prospects or donors know certain other people or have strong business connections does not necessarily mean that they want to ask these other people, feel comfortable asking them, or know how to ask them. Think of all the details that are missing. Frank did not supply enough guidance about the levels of sponsorship or advertising; the numbers of sponsors and ads needed at the various levels; the time frame or deadline for signing up; the friends, families, or businesspeople who have already been approached; and what help Mr. and Mrs. B will have with these asks. Here is how Frank could have covered these details:

> *Frank:* I'm so glad you will consider making this very generous gift of $250. We also need sponsors and people to take ads in our tournament program. I'd be happy to sit down with you at your convenience to go over the details. We have a list of local businesses we'd like to approach, forms to give them, and scripts for you to make it easy to ask for their support. We have a volunteer who is coordinating lists of the businesses and people being asked so that we not all tripping over ourselves. Of course if you know personal friends or business owners who might help, it would be great to add them to the list to the extent you feel comfortable. We'd like to do this over the next three months. We have six families

who have already agreed to help us this way. Before I go any
further, do you think you could give us just a little bit of
your time to help us raise money for sponsorships or ads? I
promise we will do everything we can to streamline the
process and be considerate of your time.

Look at how much more has been covered in this last script for
the ask. Frank clearly lays out the fact that this is an organized approach, that there is a volunteer to help, and that all Mr. and Mrs. B
need to do is to consider how much time they have to help with asking for sponsorships and ads. When asking people to ask others for
money, you must make their asks as easy and effortless for them as
possible. Specify what you can do and what is expected of them to do.
A time frame within which they will be expected to complete their
tasks is essential; otherwise, your volunteers may agree to ask friends
and colleagues for money but months will go by without their making the first ask. Lastly, you need to emphasize that they will not be
doing this alone, that other people like them have already agreed to
help or will be asked to help. There is strength in numbers, and volunteers need and want to be involved in an activity that has a strong
volunteer base, because together they will be successful.

The next example concerns the need to raise money for a community block party. Each year a neighborhood block association has a
block party with the goal of raising $100,000 or more. Half of that
money is distributed to organizations within the community, and the
other half is used to preserve the trees in the neighborhood. The event
is run entirely by volunteers. Although the table and chairs, music,
and beverages are underwritten by sponsors (whose names are displayed on huge banners), the challenge each year is to get the merchants to donate items for raffle prizes. Volunteer Lori has an
assignment to get a minimum of ninety donated items in the six
weeks before the block party. She sets out to ask a restaurant owner to
donate a lunch or dinner:

Lori: Hi, how are you today? I'm looking for the manager or possibly the owner.

Glenn: I'm the manager. What's up?

Lori: I'm from the block association, and we want your restaurant to donate a lunch or dinner for our raffle.

This is a good start, but there is not enough information. Lori did not tell Glenn the purpose of the raffle. Why should the restaurant give away a lunch or dinner? What type of fundraiser is this block party? If the restaurant does make this gift, what will it get in return? The ask must include all these items. Businesses want two things, customers and publicity. When asking them for money, the asker must clearly state how they can benefit by making the gift and what their gift will mean for the community. Let's try another approach:

Lori: Hi, I'm Lori, and I'm from the block association. Do you know about *your* block association?

Glenn: I've seen some posters, but no, not really.

Lori: The association is made up of volunteers who live in our community. Many of them are your customers. To date we have over 300 volunteers. Our big fundraiser is the block party. We have been holding this event for about thirty years. We raise money to empower organizations based in our community and to preserve our trees and green spaces.

Glenn: Nice idea.

Lori: We are asking all our local merchants, such as your restaurant, to participate in this important event because you are an important part of *our community.* We would like you to donate a free lunch or dinner so that we can use it as a raffle prize. This is a great restaurant; my friends and I come here all the time. We would love to have your restaurant participate. Will you do it?

This ask displays a number of good points. First, the asker cannot assume that the businessperson knows about her group or her fundraiser, so a degree of knowledge is passed along in this ask. Second, whenever possible, the asker should give a bit of the history of the group and the fundraiser. In this example the block party has a great history and tradition, and the association has a solid base of volunteers.

Third, an asker should put herself in a businessperson's shoes. That person will have to be convinced that the event will be a success before he will make a gift. Telling businesspeople about the group's past success with this event, the number of participants who attend, and the number of volunteers who help to make it a success will win them over. Fourth, the asker should remind the business owner that he is an important part of the community. It is a partnership, a give-and-take; businesspeople should want to support the association because the people who live in the community and volunteer for the event frequently patronize community businesses. Lastly, the asker should use the word *we*, not *I*, and strong phrases like *your association* and *our community*. Business owners must be told and reminded that they and community residents are in this together and that there are mutual benefits in supporting events like a local block party. Their support will help people and good causes in the neighborhood, and it will generate a solid community reputation for their businesses that will bring in more customers. All I would add to Lori's last remark is this:

> *Lori:* And with your permission we would like to list your restaurant as a contributor to this great event, both on the flyers that we pass out during the block party as well as in the hundreds of newsletters we send to members of our community. This would be great publicity for your restaurant.

It is easy to think the business owner knows that some publicity will be involved, but make sure you let her or him know the details. Now you have the solid ask you can use when asking merchants to support your community project.

The last example is for people who need to raise money for a noncharitable cause, such as opening a new art gallery, starting up a company, or as in this example, asking people to be limited partners for a cabaret production. In this example, two women, enormously committed to the theater and the call to promote and celebrate famous women performers, have created a cabaret show. Over the past two years they have devoted all their time to recruiting the talent, getting donated space for the performances, and making all the costumes. The show has been a big hit, and they want to take it on the road, primarily by asking people to be limited partners. Their goal is to raise $55,000 to cover additional expenses for the show for one year, then to bring in agents who will license the show in various venues such as cruise ships and co-ops and condominiums, particularly in Florida, that have small theater spaces. They are convinced that once it catches on the show will be very profitable for its investors. Sheri, one of the co-founders, approaches Larry, whom she knows through a friend. Larry has attended three performances of the cabaret show.

> *Sheri:* Larry, thanks for meeting me and thanks for coming to three of our shows.
>
> *Larry:* Oh, they were great. I especially liked the last one when you had famous actors introduce each act. How did you get them to do that?
>
> *Sheri:* Believe it or not, we just asked and they said yes.
>
> *Larry:* You must be good at this.
>
> *Sheri:* As a matter of fact I am, which is why I want to speak with you.
>
> *Larry:* Oh.
>
> *Sheri:* Larry, our show has been an enormous success and now we have the opportunity to expand the show to other venues. We are asking people, engaged people like you, Larry, to become limited partners in the show. Share the dream. Larry, will you do it?

This is a good start, but let us see how we can improve the ask. Sheri gets off to a good start by thanking Larry for supporting the show. After all, if he has seen three productions he has a real interest in this cabaret. The focus then shifts to the ask. Although Sheri tells Larry that investors are needed if the show is to continue in other venues, she does not state the following crucial information: (1) the other venues for the show, (2) the time frame within which all this is to happen, (3) the total amount that has to be raised, (4) the amount that has been raised to date, (5) the other people who have been asked or will be asked, (6) the amount Larry is being asked for, (7) the approximate time when Larry can expect a return on his investment, and (8) the rights and liabilities of a limited partner. One cannot assume that just because Larry is an avid cabaret attendee he will naturally want to give money above what he has paid for each ticket or has any interest in investing in the show. Let's see how we can retool this ask so that it probes his interest one step at a time:

Sheri: Larry, our show has been an enormous success, and now we have the opportunity to expand the show to other venues. Can I have a moment of your time to explain?

Larry: Sure.

Sheri: For the last two years, my business partner and cofounder and I have pretty much done everything for the show, from recruiting the talent to securing donated stage space, designing the costumes, marketing and advertising, getting sponsors, and producing the show.

For the past nine months, with the help of an attorney, we have been strategizing, working to see how we could expand the show so that it is produced in other places and makes a profit. We came up with the idea to offer a handful of select people who know and love our show—such as yourself, Larry—a way to be a part of this exciting new direction for the show. Before I go any further, Larry, we think you share our dream that it is important for famous theatrical female performers to be timelessly honored. We believe we do this better than anyone. Would you agree?

Larry: Oh yes. As you know, I've seen three shows and they are great. What do you mean by be a part of the show's new direction?

Sheri: Larry, we are asking terrific supporters like you to invest in our show. We need a total of only $55,000 to run the show with some enhancements this year. During this year my cofounding partner and I will invite agents to come in and see the show so that we can license our show to other venues.

Larry: What do you mean by invest?

Sheri: We are asking people to be limited partners. The investments start at $2,500. Larry, would you consider being one of our private, passionate investors by investing $2,500 or more in your show?

This ask has much more give-and-take and tests Larry's engagement while constantly supplying him with information. It gives him the history of the production and its future direction, the reason why the investment is needed. An important concept in this ask is that Sheri speaks with Larry as if he "shares the dream." Whenever anyone is asked for money it is about fulfilling dreams, hopes, and aspirations. Another important word in this ask is *passion*. Whenever possible, an ask should use the word *passion*. Sheri asks Larry if he would be a *passionate* investor. People will give when they feel passionately enough about the cause. To further refine this ask, Sheri needs to state how much has been raised, the time frame for getting all the investors on board, and what benefits the investors can expect:

> *Sheri:* We are asking people to be limited partners. The investments start at $2,500. To date we have raised $35,000, and we have investment opportunities for a few more people. The first show opens in two months, so we have about six weeks left to get our full complement of investors, which I am most confident will happen. As a show *investor and insider* you will have an opportunity to help create the show. Your investment will bring a sense of pride and commitment that goes far beyond what you experience as a ticket holder. You, Larry, will not just watch our success, you will be part of our success. I am sure you have questions and that you will need time to think this over and to review the limited partnership agreement, which I would be happy to do with you, your attorney, or your financial adviser. But right now, Larry, how do you feel about this chance to invest in a rising theatrical production?

This last ask covers all the details Larry needs to know at this point. Most important, Larry now has a good idea of how his investment would fit into the big picture, which is very important to people. Again, people do not want to be the sole investor, nor do they want to think that the asker has a plethora of people who could be asked so that it makes no difference whether any one person says yes or no. In this ask, Larry's investment could be one of the final few that complete the funding, and that can be very empowering to people.

When people make gifts or investments that make a dream possible, it is intoxicating and instills a sense of pride and accomplishment.

This ask also confirms that Larry will have more questions. It does not deemphasize the need to make a decision; rather it acknowledges that the decision is an important one, especially because it involves reviewing a limited partnership agreement. Sheri also does something that every asker should incorporate into any ask. She asks Larry how he "feels" about the opportunity she has offered him. Every asker needs to get to this point, because once the prospect is feeling 100 percent pleased about the possibility of making the investment or giving the gift, then it is not a matter of whether the person will do so; it is only a matter of when the person will do so.

THE ASK FOR THE ENHANCED ANNUAL GIFT

For many groups the annual giving program is the foundation of the organization's fundraising. It is where the greatest volume of people becomes involved with the group through either volunteering or giving. The gifts to the annual fund support the organization's general operating fund and can help it continue with its projects and programs by filling the gap between projected need and existing financial resources (Dove, Lindauer, and Madvig, 2001, p. 7). These unrestricted funds give the leaders the latitude and breathing space to run the organization. Any annual giving program also involves identifying and recruiting new prospects as well as renewing and upgrading current donors (Greenfield, 2002).

The goals for the annual fund program are (1) to renew donors at a higher level than their last gift; (2) to minimize the number of lapsed donors: (3) to win back lapsed donors; (4) to acquire new prospects; (5) to engage donors in participating in all aspects of the organization; (6) to recognize donors for their giving, usually through gift clubs or levels; (7) to coordinate prospects with the major, planned, and capital campaign gift areas; and (8) to turn annual fund donors into major, planned, and capital campaign gift donors. Groups can use direct mail and phone-a-thons to achieve many of these goals, but as in the rest of this book, we focus here exclusively on fundraising in which *individuals* do the ask. The enhanced annual fund gift requires a personal ask (Dove, Lindauer, and Madvig, 2001, p. 8). It is possible to get increased annual fund gifts via mail and phone-a-thon appeals; however, the success rate is greater when the ask is done in person. Further, the probability that high-end annual fund donors will become major, planned, and capital campaign gift prospects is greater when they have been lifted out of a pool of annual fund donors, treated separately and distinctly as a special group, and *asked in person.*

Ensuring Systems Are in Place for the Ask

Exhibit 5.1 contains a checklist that each organization should analyze before embarking on the task of asking donors in person for larger annual fund gifts.

Each organization should have a definition of what constitutes an annual gift. This will be largely dependent on the organization's definition of a major gift. For instance, if a major gift is $2,500, then a gift in any amount up to $2,500 should be considered an annual fund gift. If a major gift is $25,000, then a gift in any amount up to $25,000 is an annual fund gift. Within the annual fund each organization should have a tier system, so that larger donors can be treated

---

EXHIBIT 5.1. *Checklist for the In-Person Ask for an Increased Annual Gift.*

1. Levels for what constitutes an annual fund gift and a major gift have been established.
2. Gift tiers within the annual fund program have been established.
3. Recognition guidelines for each annual gift level have been established.
4. Budget for traveling to, meeting with, and thanking donors for their annual gift has been approved.
5. System to accept and acknowledge gifts and pledges is in place.
6. System to send pledge reminders is in place.

---

with more time and attention. For instance, at Pace University gifts of $100 to $249 place the donors in the Century Club; $250 to $499 gifts place them in the Silver Century Club; $500 to $999 gifts place them in the Gold Century Club; $1,000 to $2,005 gifts place them in the Provost Club; and a $2,006 gift places them in the President's 2006 Centennial Society (this gift memorializes the fact that in the year 2006 Pace University will be 100 years old). Donors become President's Fellows for $2,007 to $4,999 gifts; $5,000 to $9,999 gifts place them in the President's Circle; and gifts of $10,000 or more place them in the President's Ambassador Club.

There are several good reasons for creating these tiers. First, your group will then have the opportunity to cluster donors by their giving level and to recognize them as a group. Remember, donors see strength in donor numbers. Second, the tiers offer an open invitation and *incentive* for donors at one level to become donors at the next higher level. They have a logical place to move up to, otherwise their giving might well remain stagnant, and an asker can point to all the additional benefits and recognition the donor will receive by moving up. Third, having these tiers gives the asker some parameters to work with when asking a donor to increase the annual gift. When there are established levels, the fundraiser is not randomly making up a suggested enhanced level, but inviting the prospect to participate in a system of meaningful gifts and recognition that the organization has given some time and attention to creating.

Once an organization establishes these levels, it also needs a system to acknowledge and steward the donors at each level. You can adjust and adapt the following suggested gift acknowledgment system to the tiers set by your own organization. For instance, all donors of gifts up to $500 could receive an immediate acknowledgment in the form of a receipt. This is usually accompanied by or followed up with a personal note or letter from the fundraiser who was working with the donor. Donors of gifts of $500 to $2,000 could receive a telephone call, followed up with a thank-you letter from the top person in the development office. Donors of gifts of $2,000 and above could be acknowledged by the organization president or CEO. This is just an example, and it can be adjusted to fit any organization with gifts at any level. *The important point is that the organization has established gift levels and has a procedure in place to acknowledge gifts at each level.*

A reliable fundraising software program is a *must* for generating thank-you letters and pledge reminders. This sounds elementary, but there are organizations that have not checked that their current system can perform these functions with any degree of consistency. All it takes is one donor calling to say, "I gave $500, not $100," and you know you have a problem with the system (and also with a disgruntled donor). An investment in a good fundraising system that can accurately record gifts and generate pledge reminders is essential.

In addition to managing the calls and thank-you letters for each annual gift, the organization must manage the recognition benefits the donors receive for making gifts at certain levels. At Pace University, for example, recognition benefits are as follows:

Century Club: $100–$249

- Club membership card
- Name listed in the annual report
- Recognition in the annual report for gifts designated in memory of or in honor of a loved one or other special person

Silver Century Club: $250–$499

- All the benefits above, plus
- Priority reservation for one distinguished lecture or special school-sponsored program

Gold Century Club: $500–$999

- All the benefits above, plus
- Invitation to the president's annual leadership reception

Provost Club: $1,000–$2,005

- All the benefits above, plus
- Invitation to provost-hosted receptions prior to select university events and gallery openings

President's 2006 Centennial Society: $2,006

- All the benefits above, plus
- Embossed membership card
- Membership listing in the annual report

- Invitations to semiannual Centennial Society cocktail parties and receptions
- Advance notice of the Alumni Federation national and international trips

President's Fellows: $2007–$4,999

- All the benefits above

President's Circle: $5,000–$9,999

- All the benefits above, plus
- Opportunity to join special trips and events hosted by the president
- Priority reservations for Alumni Federation national and international trips

President's Ambassador Club: $10,000 and up

- All the benefits above, plus
- Invitation to a pretrip "welcome party" with the president and tour leader for Alumni Federation international trips
- Opportunity to attend an "evening on the town" with the president and his or her spouse

After you have set the gift levels that apply to your organization, spell out what donors will receive at each level. Recognition may simply be thanking the donor on the telephone or sending a personal thank-you letter. This is the best and most meaningful way to recognize donors and should not be underestimated. However, to the extent you can add a little something extra, such as a special invitation, do so. Some donors will love and take advantage of these little extras and some will never use them, but you will have a solid recognition plan in place that pleases all your donors in some way.

Calculating the Number of Increased Annual Gift Asks an Asker Can Make

We are at the point now of determining the number of prospects a fundraiser or volunteer can comfortably and effectively work with when asking for a larger annual gift. Figuring this out takes a series of steps, starting with an analysis of the group's base of annual fund donors (Exhibit 5.2).

First, determine the number of people who make annual fund gifts. If your group is at the beginning of its fundraising program or if it is relatively small, it probably has a small number of annual fund donors, and it should be manageable to work with a majority of the total number of donors and to ask each of them in person for a larger annual gift. If, however, your group has a medium or large number of annual fund donors, then that pool of donors needs to be segmented.

As stated previously, groups should have tiers within the annual fund, arranged according to gift size, so that donors can be appropriately stewarded at each level. The suggested way to segment the annual fund pool is to find out how many donors are in each tier, and focus on the top tier, working your way down to the next tier. For instance, take a look at the number of donors your group has who are nearest to the highest tier. If your group's definition of an annual gift is anything up to $5,000 (and amounts above that are major gifts), then examine how many annual fund donors have made gifts of $4,000 and above, $3,000 and above, $2,000 and above, $1,000 and above, $500 and above, $250 and above, and $100 and above. This will give you a very good idea of the number of donors you can work with, starting with

---

EXHIBIT 5.2. *Analysis of the Pool of Annual Fund Donors.*

1. How many donors make annual fund gifts?
2. What is the breakdown of annual fund donors by annual fund tier?
3. How many donors have made annual fund gifts that are close to the highest tier?
4. How many donors have given to the annual fund for the last two consecutive years or longer?
5. At what levels did these consecutive annual fund donors make gifts?

---

the top tier. If the number of people who have made gifts at the $4,000 and above level is too small, then combine those people with the people in the $3,000 and above tier to give the askers a workable number of people to ask in person for increased annual gifts. Conversely, if the number of people who have given $4,000 and above is too large for your askers to handle, then break that tier down further, and look at the number of people who have given $4,500 and above.

Even if your group's highest annual gift is $100, you can do the same exercise of segmenting your pool. The exact size of your highest annual fund gift does not matter; you can apply the same principles whether your high-end annual fund gift is $100 or $10,000. The point here is to break down the pool of annual fund donors at each level until your group has a manageable number of prospects who can be asked in person for a larger annual fund gift.

Recognizing the Importance of Consistent Givers

Another group of annual fund donors that should not be overlooked is the consistent givers. This brings us to another guiding principle.

Guiding Principle 5

Consistent givers can and will make larger gifts.

Many annual fund programs have a loyal following of people who love the group's mission and regularly send in checks, usually at the same level. These people can and should be upgraded as soon as possible in person. A suggested way to organize this activity is to take a look at how many people have given consistently over the last several years and at what level. Take the top-tier consistent givers and work your way down to the next tier and then the next. Even if a majority of your consistent givers are in the lower annual fund tiers, *do not ignore them or place them on the back burner for in-person asks.* I consider the likelihood that they will give increased gifts to be as good as or better than that of prospects who have made a one-time, high-end annual fund gift. By their consecutive giving they have demonstrated loyalty and commitment to your group. Their giving pattern is a strong indication that they will be open and receptive to giving a larger gift, particularly if they are asked *in person*. Asking in person sends the signal that they have been recognized for their loyalty to your group and that their consistent giving has not gone unnoticed.

An Example of the Ask for the Increased Annual Gift

Because fundraisers and volunteers now know the number of prospects they can manage and ask each month, it is time *to do the ask*. Fundraisers and volunteers need to be totally familiar with the prospect's profile, particularly the giving history, and with the gift opportunity, which in this instance is getting the prospect to the next tier in the annual fund program. The best way to learn how to ask for these types of gifts is by example. Let's use the example of a donor named Renee Cooper, fifty years old, who over the past three years made two gifts of $500 to a foundation for the blind and, most recently, a gift of $750, which was matched by her employer. This last gift was made eight months ago. The goal is to have Renee make a gift of $2,500, which will place her in the next giving level, the Angel Society. Tim Burton, a fundraiser for the foundation, calls Renee and asks to see her to give her an in-person update on the foundation and to speak about a special giving opportunity. Renee agrees to see Tim because she has some questions about the way her last gift was acknowledged.

Tim: Ms. Cooper, I am Tim Burton from the foundation. Thank you so much for agreeing to see me.

Renee: Oh, call me Renee. I feel so old when people call me Ms. or madam.

Tim: Will do. So how have you been?

Renee: All too busy but what else is new? I just had some major renovation at home that is taking ages to complete. I fear I will never have a kitchen again.

Tim: Oh, I know how that goes. I had what I thought were "minor" repairs to mine awhile ago, and they ended up taking months because the contractor keep squeezing in other jobs.

Renee, I want to be considerate of your time, so, first, let me thank you from all of us at the foundation for your loyal and generous gifts. They make the difference in quality of life for all who need our services.

Renee: [*Smiles.*] I give what I can. I know it's not a lot, but I think about how I take my eyesight for granted every day, and I really want to help people with impaired eyesight any way I can.

Tim: Can I take you on the road with me and let others hear you say that?

Renee: No, I'm much too busy and that's just my personal outlook on my giving.

Tim: Renee, you could have supported so many other groups, what motivated you to support the foundation?

Renee: I have a good friend I have known since college. She was in some of my classes, and I admired her because she never let her eyesight, she was partially blind, interfere with anything she wanted to do and accomplish in life. I am committed to giving what I can to help people like her to have all the joys and opportunities the rest of us have that we, unfortunately, take for granted most of the time.

Tim: This is a wonderful story and a testament to how important you are to our foundation. Maybe in time you would consider letting us do a little feature on you in one of our newsletters, magazines, or for a DVD we are producing for our friends and potential supporters. They would love to hear your story. We can talk about that if you have an interest and of course the time.

Renee: I'll think about it.

Tim: That would be great. Renee, you mentioned on the telephone that you had a concern with your last acknowledgment. How can I help you?

Renee: Oh, my company has a matching gift program and I thought I put in a matching gift form, but your letter didn't mention anything about the match.

Tim: I see. Let me check on my end to see what happened, and with your permission we can contact your company's finance director to see if the form was processed or sent to our correct address.

Renee: Sure, and let me know, because I would really like to get this resolved.

Tim: No problem. Renee, as I mentioned on the telephone, I am here to share with you some information about a special giving opportunity. At the foundation we have an Angel Society. People who make gifts of $2,500 are members of this society. We are trying to increase the number of people who make gifts at this level because our organization needs a larger amount of unrestricted funding to meet the needs of our beneficiaries. As you may know, the cost of providing our quality services escalates each year, and we want to maintain only the highest-quality services for our beneficiaries. For example, we are servicing 25 percent more men, women, and children than last year, so we have an important financial need and responsibility to help these deserving people.

Renee: I can imagine it costs a lot for the specialty care you provide, but doesn't the government give you some money?

Tim: Unfortunately, no. While we do receive some foundation grants, our individual giving program provides the most support. You may not know that private foundations can shift their funding priorities, so we may be lucky and receive a grant one year, but there is no guarantee we will receive it again the next. That is why private support, from good people like you, Renee, is invaluable to us.

Renee: That makes sense.

Tim: We do have an important benefit that we offer our members of our Angel Society. They receive an invitation for a special event where we gather everyone who has made a gift at this level and celebrate their wonderful generosity. Many of our beneficiaries attend, and it is really a special moment.

> Renee, can we turn to you now and ask you to join with others and consider your next gift to be at this important $2,500 Angel Society level?

[*Silence. The next one to speak is Renee.*]

That is how simple it is to ask for the enhanced annual gift. The most important point is that the asker must state the *beneficiaries' need and the donor benefit* of making a gift at this level. In the example there is a real need for additional funding because the organization now has many more people who need quality services. The benefits for Renee are that (1) she can feel satisfaction because her gift will directly help many men, women, and children who are blind; (2) there is strength in numbers and when her gift is combined with other gifts at that level it will be powerful and influential in the foundation's future; and (3) she will have an opportunity to meet others who think and feel the way she does about helping the foundation.

CONCLUSION

Asking for money to support a special event or community project entails a thorough explanation of the history of the event or project, why the funding is needed, when the funding is needed, and why the prospect should give or invest. The person being asked is important to the community, and the gift or investment solidifies commitment and support to the neighborhood. The asker must take time to engage the prospect throughout the ask by sharing benefits of the gift or investment. Most important, the asker must state the amount of the ask, how much has been raised to date, how many other people have been asked, and the deadline for raising the funds.

Annual giving is for many organizations the most important form of giving because it not only covers general operating expenses but also can keep important projects and programs up and running. Annual funds can go flat, however, unless attention is being paid to asking annual fund givers for increased gifts each year. The best way to capture enhanced annual gifts is by asking in person.

Asking for the enhanced annual fund gift entails asking for a specific amount, then sharing all the benefits of that gift for the organization and the donor. Establishing tiers of annual fund giving can be a good way to increase annual gifts. Tiers set the next logical amount for an ask and keep prospects on track to increase their gifts each year. Logically, an organization will want to work first to increase the gifts of those annual fund donors who have made gifts closest to the top tier, because they are most likely to become top-tier donors. At the same time, organizations should pay equal attention to consistent givers, because they are the most loyal and dedicated donors. They can be overlooked because the size of their yearly gift may not make them a top-end annual fund donor; however, their combined gifts over the years place them among the best prospects for not only enhanced annual fund gifts but also major, planned, and capital campaign gifts.

Looking Ahead

The next level of giving after enhanced annual fund gifts is major gifts. Major gifts occupy a place of their own in organizations of any size because they are large gifts that can start a new project or program, provide the solid funding needed to maintain these projects or programs well into the future, or cover large operational costs. Donors who make major gifts want to be an important part of an organization's rich philanthropic tradition, and their investment is a special expression of their commitment and loyalty. The next chapter addresses what constitutes a major gift for any organization and illustrates several solid major gift asks.

CHAPTER

Asking for Major Gifts

I view my contributions as a small repayment on the loan called
abundance which I've been blessed with. It is my desire to make a
difference in the communities that I'm a part of and so I am deliberate
about giving my time, talents and monetary contributions.

—Bridget-Anne Hampden, Retired CIO, Wachovia Corporation,
Charlotte, North Carolina

THE NEXT STEP UP FROM ASKING FOR AN
enhanced annual fund gift is asking for a major gift. Every organization defines *major gift* differently. For a small organization a
major gift might be $500 and above, for a medium-size organization
it might be $25,000 and above, and for a large organization it might
be $250,000 and above. The numbers do not matter. It is the princi-
ples behind knowing how to ask for major gifts that are important.
This chapter covers the importance of major gifts in any nonprofit
organization, regardless of the size of those gifts. It defines the ways in
which major gifts differ from other types of gifts, provides a checklist
of what needs to be in place for any successful major gifts program,
and gives examples of numerous specific major gift asks, first illustrat-
ing weak or mediocre asks and then refining the language and approach of each one and highlighting the differences. The resulting
solid major gift asks can be adapted to meet the needs of any group
raising major gifts.

DEFINING A MAJOR GIFT

What makes a gift a major gift? One could easily say it is the size of a gift that puts it in the major gift category. This is true, but it is only part of the equation. Major gifts are well thought out *personal decisions*. A major gift is a person's special expression of faith in an organization. The major gift prospect wants to be an important part of the organization's rich philanthropic tradition and wants to make an investment to ensure that this tradition continues. Once the gift is made it is one of the highest compliments and attributes that an organization can receive. The implicit message is that the donor truly admires, respects, and has utmost faith in the leadership and direction of the organization.

Major gifts are almost always asked for in person and are rarely received in the mail without any prior personal contact by someone associated with the organization. Likewise, major gifts are rarely asked for via e-mail because that does not meet the purpose of establishing a *personal relationship* with the prospect. With letters and e-mail it is impossible to see the person's expression when the ask is made, and one cannot detect the *tone* of the response. It is so important to see how enthusiastic or, conversely, uninterested a prospect is immediately after each ask.

Major gifts take lots of time to come to fruition. The organization must make a concerted and consistent effort to cultivate each major gift prospect, a process that can take months and even years, so that the prospect respects and trusts the asker and has utmost admiration for the organization. It takes time to find the match between the prospect's interest in the organization and the right gift opportunity, and it also takes time to assess the prospect's financial capability in order to propose the right gift at the right giving level. Major gift asks must *speak to the prospect's funding priorities and must fit within the prospect's financial comfort zone.* Many people would love to support a group in a significant way; however, their financial means and priorities may mean that they cannot act on their desire to make a major gift at this time.

Major gifts are in a league of their own because they allow the organization to accomplish things that cannot be done without substantial funding. They ensure that the group will be able to perpetuate its mission and its strategic goals and objectives well beyond individual donors' lifetimes. Once an organization starts receiving major gifts it has the power to attract more major gifts. This process builds and builds with such rhythm that the organization is solidified and strengthened not only fiscally but also spiritually, because it has so many supporters who believe in its good work.

Most of an organization's major funding will come from 10 percent or fewer of its major donors. Think about these numbers, and you will see why major gifts are so important. A significant portion of any organization's budget comes from major gifts. These gifts can empower the organization and bring it to new heights. Every organization should place emphasis, time, and attention on acquiring these types of gifts. A successful major gifts program takes an organized approach and a clear understanding of the tasks and responsibilities of the group's major gift fundraisers and volunteers.

DEFINING MAJOR GIFT PROSPECTS

Like the prospects for enhanced annual fund gifts, major gift prospects come from a defined pool of givers. First, the organization needs to define what constitutes a major gift. Typically, major gift prospects are those people who have made a top-end annual fund gift or who are known to have the potential to make a major gift. For instance, if a group's major gift level is $25,000 and up and a majority of its high-end annual fund gifts are $1,000 to $5,000, then the pool of major gift prospects includes all those people who have made gifts at the $1,000 to $5,000 level. Additionally, prospect research may reveal prospects who have the potential to make a gift of $25,000 or more regardless of their prior giving. Lastly, keep in mind that consistent donors, those who have made steady gifts over the years, are spectacular major gift prospects. They are often overlooked because a snapshot yearly review shows their annual giving level to be, say, $500, which may not place them in the major gift prospect pool. Their *total* giving to the organization, however, may make them major gift prospects. Recapping then, an organization's major gift prospect pool should comprise (1) all donors who have made a high-end annual fund gift, (2) individuals who have the potential to make major gifts regardless of prior giving history, and (3) steady and consistent cumulative donors whose total giving puts them beyond the top annual fund level and near or at the major gift level.

ESSENTIALS OF ANY MAJOR GIFTS PROGRAM

Before any major gift asks can be made certain prerequisites must be in place (Matheny, 1999, p. 2). The goal is to have these elements in place first, so that when major gift asks are made everything runs smoothly from the time the gift is pledged to the time it is received and stewarded. Exhibit 6.1 outlines the essential elements of any major gifts program.

Develop a Strategic Plan to Steer the Process

The organization needs a strategic plan, preferably one that covers three to five years, that sets out the goals and purpose of the major gifts program. For example, one organization's strategic plan might state that the organization will increase its endowment by a specific percentage each year so that at the end of five years the organization will have over $100 million. Another organization's plan might recognize that major gifts are needed to start new programs in new geographical areas and might set a goal of raising a specific amount of new major gift dollars in three years to fulfill that goal. It is possible to raise major gift money without a strategic plan, and many organizations do so, but whenever possible convince the leadership that your group will be far more successful if it has a plan that it can share with prospects and donors. *Major gifts will arrive quicker when the organization has a plan because a plan supplies purpose and a timeline* which connotes a sense of urgency, and that in turn can and will motivate prospects to give now rather than later.

Have a Base Pool of Prospects

Small or newly formed organizations may have no identified major gift prospects or only a small base of these prospects. These organizations should spend a bit of time identifying major gift prospects, with the help of leaders and volunteers. The best way to

EXHIBIT 6.1. *Essential Elements of Any Major Gifts Program.*

1. An organizational three- to five-year strategic plan with major gift goals

2. A base of major gift prospects or a plan to identify new major gift prospects

3. An appointed internal leader to run prospect management meetings; assign prospects to staff, leaders, and volunteers; and coordinate program elements

4. Computer capabilities to store and track prospect activity, proposals, gifts, and pledges

5. A budget for traveling to, cultivating, and thanking prospects and donors

6. Legal counsel to draft and review gift agreements

7. A finance department or outside financial organization to invest major gifts and create and send financial reports to donors

8. Planned giving expertise or retained planned giving advisers

9. Marketing materials to promote and advertise major gift opportunities as well as to showcase major donors

10. A board-adopted gift acceptance policy

---

find prospects when none exist within the organization is to recruit a wide range of volunteers who will work with the organization to attract more volunteers. In time this core group of volunteers should be asked for a major gift and also asked to identify others who might support the mission of the organization.

I also have a word of caution for organizations with a small donor base: if they still have only a handful of one-time donors, this may not be the best time to formulate a major gifts program. It will take some time to expand the base of supporters, engage and involve them, and then work their gifts up to the major gift level. However, this is not to say that these organizations could not receive a major gift or two while this process is taking place.

Appoint a Leader to Coordinate the Program and Avoid Territorialism

Once the organization has identified its pool of major gift prospects, it must assign one person to coordinate prospects. It must do this *even if it has only one fundraiser.* There will be many frustrations and wasted effort if the program is not coordinated or managed properly. In small organizations with a single development officer, that person should make sure that the major gift prospects are being seen and asked for gifts either by the person herself or by the president or volunteers. Conversely, in medium-size and large groups, the vice president for development, the director of leadership gifts, or the director of development should have responsibility for overseeing the assignment of prospects to staff, leaders, and volunteers and for making sure that these folks are working with their assigned prospects to the point of asking them for major gifts. It is very important to have open communication on who is working with each prospect and whether there is steady activity with each prospect to the point of asking for a major gift.

When askers begin feeling territorial about prospects it is a major problem for major gift fundraising, regardless of the size of the organization. In a two-person shop the president or CEO may never let the development officer see major gift prospects or even know about the contact the leader has had with these prospects. Medium-size and large organizations with regional, national, or international offices struggle with this issue all the time. Territorialism occurs in the absence of an agreed-upon, formal method of assigning prospects. The last thing any organization needs is several people working independently with prospects so that Officer A has no idea that Director B has an appointment with a prospect that Officer A has been trying to reach. It happens all the time, but it can be minimized and avoided through open and honest communication with everyone involved about who is working with major gift prospects.

Prospect management meetings, even in the smallest of shops, can be the ideal place for coordinating major gift activity. When these meetings are attended by everyone working with major gift prospects then everyone should be on board with the program and should know each prospect assignment, the gift level suggested for each prospect, the target area for support, and most important, who has primary and secondary responsibility for each prospect.

Employ Reliable Computer Software

Every organization needs a reliable computer system to store and track all prospect activity, proposals, pledges, and gifts. The emphasis is on the word *reliable*. Systems are only as good as the people inputting the data, and the person in charge of prospect assignment and coordination must also emphasize the need for askers to supply information about all prospect activity, proposals, pledges, and gifts accurately and on a timely basis. One way to encourage this is to distribute a tally sheet at monthly prospect management meetings, with each asker's face-to-face visits, proposals, and gifts recorded. If someone has zero activity without adequate justification, that is a red flag that this fundraiser needs to get out and visit with prospects and ask them for gifts.

Recognize That It Takes Money to Raise Money

Major gift fundraising requires a budget to cover travel, long-distance telephone costs, entertainment expenses, and gift stewardship and recognition. This budget naturally varies not only by the size of the organization but also to the degree that leaders understand and appreciate the need for this investment. Many organizations will not create a budget until they see or have a guarantee that it will bring in major gifts. However, you cannot properly cultivate major gift prospects in the first place if you do not have the resources to do so. If the organization has a strategic plan and major gifts are a factor in what the organization seeks to accomplish, then there can be very little debate that funds will be needed for major gift fundraising. One issue to be very sensitive to is what I call the *roller-coaster budget*. The organization gives the development office the funds it needs to cover expenses in the first year, but then cuts the budget in subsequent years owing to external pressures such as the performance of the economy. This is something one cannot predict, but if the organization has a strategic plan that sets definite goals, that may help to spare the major gifts program budget from large cuts.

Retain Legal Counsel as Necessary

At some point in time an organization may need help and guidance from legal counsel. Inevitably, some donor will want to do something creative with some stock or an insurance policy, or he will ask the organization to take ownership of a property for a number of years and place all sorts of contingencies on the transaction. Line up professional legal counsel *before* these issues arise, so you are ready to answer questions promptly and to create or review complex gift agreements. If your organization has in-house counsel who are available to the fundraisers and experienced with the complexities that can arise with major gift fundraising, then you are in good shape. If your group does not have this resource, the leaders should consider investing in outside counsel on a consulting basis, so that the organization is prepared to work with donors and their creative and complex ways to make major gifts.

Establish a Strong Finance System

Every organization should have a person or department in charge of handling the organization's finances, including accepting and investing major gifts. This seems beyond obvious, but it is not unknown for a group to have a finance department that deposits and invests each gift but is not set up to report the income generated on the gift, a figure that major gift donors will need to know. For instance, if a donor makes a $50,000 endowed scholarship gift, the organization should steward this gift by annually reporting to the donor the amount the gift earned, the amount that was available and awarded for scholarships, and any earned interest that went back into principal. It can be an absolute nightmare if the fundraiser has to figure this out or if there is a breakdown in communication between the fundraising department and finance. Coordinate these efforts, because major gift donors deserve timely notices on how their gifts are being invested and distributed.

Have Planned Giving Expertise Available

Oftentimes a major gift will include a planned giving component. This is called a *blend gift*. For instance, if a fundraiser has asked a prospect for an outright major gift of $100,000, and the prospect has thought about it and would like to give $25,000 outright but the rest as a deferred charitable gift annuity, then the fundraiser needs access to planned giving expertise, from a staff member, a volunteer, or a consultant. The ideal situation is for all your major gift fundraisers to have at least a working knowledge of how bequests, charitable annuities, trusts, and gifts of life insurance work, the levels at which these gifts can be funded, and the benefits, both to the donor taxwise and to the organization. This will keep the major gift fundraising process in constant forward motion. The major gift fundraiser can then work with planned giving staff, volunteers, or outside counsel until the gift is complete. The point is that *the organization needs to be ready to handle the blend gift,* one that includes a major gift and a planned gift.

Prepare Marketing Materials to Enhance the Program

Every organization should have some marketing materials, such as brochures, newsletters, magazines, DVDs, or flyers that market and advertise major gift opportunities. A picture is worth a thousand words, and donor testimonials on the benefits of making gifts to your organization are worth a million words. As part of the major gifts program, money should be designated for these important communication pieces. They can clarify the mission of your organization, make your organization come alive to prospects through dynamic and heartfelt pictures of beneficiaries and donors, and most important, convey in pictures and words the important role that major gifts will play in taking the organization from one level to the next.

Develop a Gift Acceptance Policy

A board-adopted gift acceptance policy is one of the most important parts of any major gifts program, as outlined in Exhibit 6.2.

It never ceases to amaze me how many organizations do not have gift acceptance policies. *Regardless of the size of the organization, a gift acceptance policy is a must.* For example, inevitably you will have a donor who wants to give a gift-in-kind that has nothing to do with the mission of your organization. You might be fundraising for a hospital, for instance, and a steady and well-known donor might want ten miniature houses that he has built to be a permanent display in the hospital's lobby. However, if the hospital's gift acceptance policy details the gifts-in-kind that the hospital will accept, all you have to

EXHIBIT 6.2.   *Reasons Why a Gift Acceptance Policy Is Important.*

1. It prevents misunderstandings between the donor and the prospect.
2. It ensures equal treatment of donors.
3. It makes the organization more accountable internally and externally.
4. It fosters sound fiscal management.
5. It establishes gift levels and gift recognition for each level.
6. It serves to protect the organization's charitable status.
7. It helps the organization avoid public relations disasters.
8. It educates the board and committee members on major gift fundraising.
9. It helps the organization adapt to changing times, through the regular recommendations of the gift acceptance committee.
10. It makes everyone aware of gift guidelines.

do to refuse this gift is show the donor the policy. Without such a policy that donor might feel you were treating him arbitrarily, and he might not make any future, more desirable gifts. Often donors who feel they have been treated unfairly will demand that the head of the organization meet with them and explain why the gift is not acceptable to the organization. Some donors even take the issue to the media, which can be a public relations disaster for a group.

You will also encounter many instances in which donors want to make a gift below a stated level yet receive all the rights and benefits of that level. For instance, your group may offer charitable gift annuities starting at $25,000, and a donor may want to set up an annuity with your group but may want to do it with $10,000. Without a written policy, it may appear that the organization is selecting which donors can make which gifts at which level. A gift acceptance policy keeps all donors on an even playing field.

The gift acceptance policy also ensures that staff, board, and committee members and volunteers are totally apprised of gift levels and gift recognition. Anyone fundraising on behalf of an organization needs to know the details of the gift acceptance policy. Everyone also needs to know that this policy can be amended and the details can change if the board has established a gift acceptance committee that periodically reviews the policy to make sure it is in alignment with the organization's finances and future direction. For instance, a policy that is ten years old may establish gift levels that currently seem extraordinarily low, and the committee might now recommend to the board that these levels be increased. Whether your gift acceptance policy needs to be simple, moderately detailed, or extremely complex, your board should establish a gift acceptance committee, have the committee draft a policy, and keep that policy up to date by having the committee review it yearly.

Examples of good gift acceptance policies can be obtained from the Association of Fundraising's Resource Center by calling (800) 666-FUND or by visiting www.afpnet.org and clicking on "Resource Center." This is a good way to get a look at a gift acceptance policy designed for a group that mirrors the size and mission of your organization.

MAJOR GIFT ASKS

We are now at the point when the asker or asking team is ready to ask for major gifts. *How* one does the ask has a lot to do with its success or failure. The best way to illustrate effective major gift asks is to begin with asks that are just OK; they're not ineffective, but they are less effective than they could be because they are missing some elements or they use words that are lackluster and not engaging.

The goal of the major gift ask is to communicate a *sense of inclusion,* that the prospect is part of a successful and winning team. *The asker cannot speak at the prospect; the asker must speak with the prospect.* The prospect should feel special, important to the organization, part of a small and powerful group whose investment with the organization will reap benefits for many years to come. So next I will take these just OK examples and add some polish, pizzazz, and punch that will dramatically change the level of engagement and inclusion between the asker and the prospect.

Examples of Just OK Major Gift Asks

Here are eight examples of major gift asks that could be used but that do not go out of their way to include the prospect or to make the prospect feel elevated or special.

1. "Al, our opera company is not in good shape, and if we don't raise enough funds this year, we will have to cut out half of our performances. I'm asking good people like you to give us $5,000 this year. Can you do it?"

2. "Lorraine, don't you just love the aquarium? You might have heard that we are adding a tropical fish exhibit in two years, and you know that will cost us a bit. I have been asking people to give $10,000 or more so we have the money for these fish. What do you think?"

3. "Carolyn, the church's foyer has been in horrible shape for years. Have you noticed the chunks of plaster that are about to come free from the ceiling? This is hardly the condition that is fitting for our parishioners. Reverend Tom and I have been asking families for $25,000 or more, and we're in a hurry to raise the money. Can we count on your family for support?"

4. "Dick and Mary, in this economy, charitable gift annuities are one of the best ways to make a gift and to receive an income along the way. The medical center is raising money for several new capital improvements. How does a $25,000 charitable gift annuity sound to you right now? It would help the center in this time of need."

5. "Denise, isn't the visiting nurse association the best? You can help us make it even better by giving $50,000 so that I can send more nurses abroad for specialty training."

6. "Ken, I hope you have been enjoying all the plays at the theater. We can add more to the series but only if I raise enough money. I figured that if just a few people give $100,000 I can do it. How does that sound to you?"

7. "Holly, as you know we are in full swing with the campaign to increase our endowment. Compared to our benchmark private academies, we rank the lowest. Can you believe that? The only way to fix that is to get money for our endowment. So can you give $250,000 for our endowment? After all, you would not want your alma mater to be last among its benchmarks."

8. "Ben, you always said you wanted your name in lights, and I have just the thing to make that happen. The international house is expanding its lecture series, and you can endow it for $500,000 and have your name on it."

These examples may seem a bit exaggerated; however, many a nervous or unfocused asker has used similar language. Let's examine them one by one to see what is missing. In the first example, the asker paints the opera in nothing but a negative light. Avoid using phrases like "not in good shape." If the organization is having a tough time, say, for example, "We have our challenges, but with your help, our future will be bright again." This first ask is a total turnoff, and it will take a lot of positive energy to get Al reengaged and feeling good about the opera company.

In the second example, the ask focuses on the need of the aquarium for the money, not on what the addition of tropical fish will do for the aquarium. An ask cannot be solely focused on the need for money. That presents the organization as being in a desperate position, and that is not the way you want your prospects thinking about your organization. Done correctly, this ask would state why the money is needed now when the tropical fish exhibit will not be up and running for two years, and it would state how this new exhibit will drastically boost this aquarium's membership and status among competing aquariums.

The third example suggests even more dramatically that the organization is in bad shape. Surely Carolyn has noticed that the foyer could use improvement. The asker should focus on prominence of the foyer for churchgoers, and why it is important that families share in the building's improvement costs.

The fourth example is a request for a planned gift, a topic covered in length in Chapter Seven. It is included here because, inevitably, a major gift that includes a planned gift will come your way. In this example, Dick and Mary are being asked for a charitable gift annuity. Like any planned gift, annuities are technical and may require some form of estate planning. The ask is sufficient; however, it could be greatly improved if the asker recognized that gift annuities are more complex than major gifts and take time and attention, and if the asker expounded on the need for capital improvements at the medical center.

Even if this has been discussed in previous conversation, it needs to be repeated and emphasized at the time of the ask.

The fifth example is what I call a *blurter,* a get-it-over-quickly ask. Fifty thousand dollars is a significant gift, and the ask for it requires more refinement. The asker could greatly improve this ask by describing one or two accomplishments of the visiting nurse association, in order to focus Denise on the good qualities of the association and spell out the need for more specialty training. Why do the nurses have to be trained abroad? What will happen if they do not receive this training. Anticipate the prospect's questions, and incorporate the answers in the ask.

The sixth example falls victim to using *I* instead of *we.* Notice how the asker takes way too much on himself or herself by stating, "only if I raise enough money," and, "I figured that if just a few people give $100,000 I can do it." Surely the asker is not in this venture alone. It is always much more effective to use *we* in any ask. This brings us to one more guiding principle:

Guiding Principle 6

Always use *we* instead of *I* in any ask. *We* connotes that the ask is being done with all the strength and backing of the organization.

When anyone is asking for money for an organization, the money will go to help the group's beneficiaries, so why use *I? I* gives the prospect the impression that the ask is all about the asker, when indeed the ask is all about doing something for the good of the organization, which is made up of many people—administrators, staff, volunteers, and beneficiaries. *We* gives strength, power, and confidence to any ask. *I* dilutes the ask, suggesting that it is an individual and self-centered effort when in fact it should be a joint, unified, and all-inclusive effort.

The seventh example tries to shame or embarrass the prospect, Holly, into making the gift. Giving benchmark statistics can be a real plus when the ask is done correctly. Here the asker is asking Holly for what feels like a bailout gift. Give us $250,000 so that we will not finish last in our endowment among our benchmark academies. What this ask should do is state the case for the importance of the endowment to the academy. How will a larger endowment improve the academy beyond moving it up in the ranking of comparable schools? Again, even if this campaign to increase the endowment has been previously discussed with Holly, reiterate these points in the ask to make it a full and complete package. Do not assume prospects remember all the details from previous visits and conversations. Some do; many do not because they live very busy lives and often support several organizations. Do not leave anything to chance. Lay out a full and complete ask by covering all the details, even if the prospect has received literature in the past or has been briefed or updated on the specific topic of the ask.

The last example, number 8, appeals to the prospect's ego. Many prospects will want a naming opportunity for a large gift, but even when the asker is extremely close to the prospect, this is not the way to ask for a $500,000 gift with a naming opportunity. The asker should start by describing how the lecture series is expanding, and mentioning any speakers of particular note associated with the series. This approach will include the prospect and make him a part of this great enhancement for the international house. Further, the asker should state why there is the need to expand the program. Has it become so popular that it needs to expand? Have foreign speakers of interest been easier to recruit or have they requested to be part of the lecture series? The asker should include the prospect by discussing all aspects of the need, purpose, and benefits associated with the gift; otherwise the asker runs the risk that the prospect will be disengaged, uninterested, and neutral about the gift opportunity.

Examples of Highly Effective Major Gift Asks

Let's take a look at how we can improve each of these eight ask examples:

1. "Al, as you know, our opera company has had its share of challenges over the past few years—from rental agreements to possible strikes to some vocal disagreements among the board that made the headline news for awhile. We believe that we have weathered these storms, and we are poised to get the opera company that we all love and

enjoy back on the right track. And this is the reason for our meeting. We have an invitation for you to make a real difference in your community opera company. We ask you now to consider a $5,000 yearly pledge for the next five years so that we together can get back on track and bring our opera company to new heights. We know this may be a stretch for you, but we are asking all our top donors to make this kind of stretch gift right now."

2. "Lorraine, we think you will agree that we have very ambitious plans for our aquarium. We plan within the next two years to have our tropical fish area up and running. How exciting and long overdue. The new tropical fish exhibit is projected to increase membership by 25 percent and attendance by 35 percent. As you know, our surrounding metropolitan cities that have aquariums have plans to expand in various areas, and to be competitive our aquarium has to keep up with this growth. It has been so great to see you and the kids at all our special member-only events, and we think you and your family would agree that tropical fish are a real draw for all ages, and as we recall, one that matches your family's particular interest in the aquarium. We ask you now to join with others by making a $10,000 gift to make this dream come true."

3. "Carolyn, it goes without saying that our church really needs to make major cosmetic improvements to the foyer. The foyer is the first area our parishioners and guests see, and we are sure you agree that this is not the kind of first impression we wish to make. We have always pulled together as a family for the good of our church, and in that light we ask you to consider a gift of $25,000 to support reconstruction of our church's foyer. We know you have many other obligations, but please know how much your gift would do for our church, our parishioners, and guests."

4. "Dick and Mary, from our previous conversations you may be aware that we are in the middle of an important fund drive to do several capital improvements—namely, to renovate our patient waiting area and to increase the size of our radiology department and improve its equipment. We have done studies over the past two years and have found that these areas are where a majority of our patients spend long periods of time, and these areas need to be upgraded and expanded to keep up with the demand. You mentioned that if and when you were to make a gift to the center it would be a gift annuity. We ask you now to

join with other supporters and make a $25,000 charitable gift annuity to support the medical center's capital improvements. Gift annuities are a great way to support your medical center and its patients, doctors, nurses, and staff. You seem to be pretty knowledgeable about gift annuities, but we would be happy to sit down with you, your attorney, or your financial planner at any time to discuss this type of gift. But right now, how do you feel about this exciting gift opportunity?"

5. "Denise, we think you feel as passionately as we do about the new direction and leadership of the visiting nurse association. Just in the past year we have a new dynamic president, and she has done a great job of raising local and national awareness of the nursing shortage and how our visiting nurse association has addressed this issue head on. Part of the new leadership's strategic plan is to enhance the skill level of nurses by increasing the number of nurses we send abroad. There is so much to be learned from leading medical experts around the world and the exchange of expertise is nothing but first-rate. We do need to raise $750,000 to make this exciting venture happen. We turn to you now as a devoted and loyal donor, and ask you to consider a gift of $50,000 to increase the number of nurses we can send abroad for specialty training."

6. "Ken, we have you and other loyal supporters to thank for the tremendous, quick success of your community theater. Almost every show this year was a sellout and we are sure you enjoyed seeing the good reviews we received for our major productions. We have a plan to begin a new-playwright series for which we would have a committee that would read new plays, select three, and produce them in our theater. You mentioned previously that bringing in juried playwright series, such as the one we are suggesting, would be a big boost for our theater. As with any new program, there are start-up costs as well as the cost of production, all of which are detailed in materials I can give you now or at the end of this meeting. What is most important to us now is that you be a part of our exciting new-play series. Ken, would like you to be part of a core group of supporters and consider an investment of $25,000 a year for the next five years to support our new-play series at your theater?"

7. "Holly, from our previous conversations we know how important it is to our academy to increase the size of its endowment. A larger endowment will make it possible for us to offer more scholarships, to recruit faculty nationally, and to have a nest egg for projects

and programs in the future that will strengthen the academy's curriculum. We are sure that as a leading financial analyst in the community you can appreciate the need for our organization to be fiscally sound. We have done studies with our benchmark academies, and at the present time we are on the low end of where we need to be. We have every bit of confidence that with your help and the help of other key leaders, we can turn this around. We believe that we need twenty families to commit gifts of $500,000 or more over the next five years in order to accomplish our goal. These leadership gifts will boost our endowment so that our organization is fiscally sound for years to come. Will you consider this gift opportunity and join with others to make the academy stronger for present and future students?"

8. "Ben, we think you would agree that expanding our lecture series at international house is an exciting project and worthy of your support. Last year we had to turn down several big-name world leaders who wanted to be a part of our series. We believe that the community is increasingly turning to us for information, alternative perspectives, and balanced opinions on all global affairs. Not expanding the series would mean not meeting the needs of our constituents. We invite you to join with fellow supporters by making a $500,000 gift that would endow the lecture series. This is an exciting time for international house, and we wanted you and your family to be a prominent part of our success. Of course we would be honored if we could name the program after you, your family, or your company. We will work closely with you to see if we can make that happen. How do you feel about this opportunity and the success of the organization that you have helped to build?"

These examples are much stronger, prospect focused, informative, inclusive, energetic, passionate, and positive than the first eight examples were. Notice how each one uses *we* instead of *I*. When you are doing an ask, you *are* the organization. You carry all the strength and power of the organization when you use the word *we*.

The words the asker or asking team uses are crucial because the ask should be as personal and sincere as possible. Under these circumstances prospects will really listen and will give the ask careful attention. Notice in the improved examples that the prospects are *invited* to *join* and to make an *investment* with others. In example 1, Al has an *invitation* to make a real difference in the community. In example 6, Ken is asked to make an *investment* of $25,000 a year over five years for the new-play series. The examples do not include words like *contribution* or *donation*. I think those words are archaic, dull, and one-dimensional. They neither inspire nor capture the prospect's attention, but inspiring the prospect is exactly what needs to be done when one is asking for a large gift.

The language in the improved examples suggests that it would be a missed opportunity if the prospect did not make the gift to support the organization, because the organization is positioned as a forward-moving train. In example 5, the asker remarks on the new dynamic leader for the visiting nurse association. In example 8, the asker reports that there is so much demand for the guest lecturers from around the world that international house must expand its lecture series. No one wants to be left out or left behind, so it is a good idea always to position the organization as successful, dynamic, and something everyone can feel good about.

The ask should be about fulfilling dreams and conveying passion. Without those two elements, why would anyone give money to a group? Notice in example 2 that Lorraine's gift to the aquarium would "make [a] dream come true." In example 5 the asker states that Denise feels "as passionately as [the group does] about the new direction and leadership of the visiting nurse association." Put these two elements into your asks because they tell prospects why they should feel good about your group and why they should give the gift opportunity serious consideration.

CONCLUSION

Major gifts are well thought out personal decisions that have the power to transform and empower the organization. Every fundraising program should have a major gifts program that defines the major gift prospect pool, the gift amount that constitutes a major gift, and the number of prospects each staff member and volunteer can adequately handle. In addition, certain internal mechanisms—such as a strategic plan; reliable computer software to track prospect activity, gifts, and pledges; and a board-adopted gift acceptance policy—must be in place in order for the major gifts program to be successful.

How one performs the ask is crucial when trying to capture major gifts. The ask needs to be personal, inclusive, and sincere; to use *we* instead of *I;* and to emphasize *inviting* people to *join with others* and to make an *investment* that matches their interest in the organization with an exceptional opportunity they will not want to miss. The ask should be phrased and delivered with compassion and conviction so that it conveys passion and fulfills dreams.

LOOKING AHEAD

The next chapter focuses on asking for planned gifts. Planned gifts are important for any organization because they are legacies. People who make planned gifts are saying that they want to be forever associated with the organization; that they, and in most instances their families, want to help the organization for years to come; and that this special and long-lasting gift is meant to ensure that the organization will succeed and thrive for years to come. The next chapter covers the profiles of planned-giving prospects and uses specific examples to illustrate how to ask for several types of planned gifts.

7

Asking for Planned Gifts

A lawyer friend was once asked to make a significant gift to a charity by the managing partner in his firm. He dutifully wrote the check and as he handed it over, he said: "you don't know how much this hurts." His partner took the check, glanced at it, and proceeded to tear it into tiny pieces. He then looked my friend straight in the eye and said: "Give generously to others when it makes you feel good, not when it hurts." With this lesson in mind, when I ask others to give generously, I make it clear that I am offering them the opportunity for the ultimate feel-good experience.

—Allan J. Pekor, Chairman, Lennar Financial Services, Inc.,
Miami, Florida

PLANNED GIFTS CAN AND SHOULD PLAY AN enormous role in nonprofit organizations of any size. Prospects think long and hard before making these significant gifts. Planned gifts are a way of forever binding the prospect, and in many instances the prospect's family, with the organization. When people make planned gifts they are saying they want to ensure that the organization will thrive and grow well into the future.

Planned gifts take the longest time to acquire. Charitable gift planning requires knowledge not only of the prospect's philanthropic interests and history of giving but also of his economic circumstances and needs, now and in the future. The planned giving ask must focus on the benefits, both economic and philanthropic, that can be derived from these important and complex gifts and not on the technical jargon, which can confuse and complicate the ask. This chapter will cover the importance of planned gifts to the organization and to the donors, the types of people who make planned gifts, and the prospect pool for planned gifts. As with a major gifts program, a number of elements should be in place before the organization embarks on a formal planned giving program. These prerequisites will safeguard the organization against asking for and acquiring planned gifts before it is ready to accept them.

A key factor in the success of a planned giving program is that it must be *coordinated and integrated with the organization's other fundraising programs,* such as the annual and major gifts programs and capital campaigns. It is vitally important that leaders, staff, and volunteers are fully knowledgeable about which prospects are considering a planned gift and who is assigned as the primary asker for these prospects. The organization should also try to ensure that prospects' annual giving continues while they are considering a planned gift.

Organizations considering a planned giving program should start out simply. They should begin with a bequest program and then build up to accepting charitable gift annuities and deferred annuities, life insurance policies, charitable trusts, and gifts from retirement plans. This chapter overviews the most popular planned gifts: bequests, annuities, and trusts, detailing the benefits of each and the types of prospects best suited to each type of gift. Internal and external marketing plans for these planned gifts should be in place, to ensure that the organization's prospect base is fully aware of these gift opportunities.

Lastly, this chapter gives examples of how any organization can ask for a bequest, a charitable gift annuity, and a charitable remainder trust, so that the reader will have sample dialogues to learn from and language to use and adapt when asking for planned gifts. Emphasis is placed on homing in on the prospect's economic needs, now and in the future, identifying family members who need to be beneficiaries of the gift, selecting the right planned giving vehicle, and selecting the right assets to make the gift and also meet the economic needs and philanthropic desires of each prospect.

THE IMPORTANCE OF PLANNED GIFTS
FOR THE ORGANIZATION

Some of the largest gifts an organization will receive will be planned gifts. People may think long and hard about the organization, what it has meant to them and their families, but often they do not have the outright cash assets to make a significant gift. They want to do something special, something meaningful for the organization, so they consider other ways of making a significant contribution. Although many prospects have heard that their assets can help the organization, they do not know how they can use these assets to benefit the organization without compromising their own economic needs. This is why the organization needs knowledgeable and experienced planned giving directors or officers or retained consultants to assist in explaining the planned giving options to each prospect so that the best vehicle is selected. Planned gifts are based firmly on long and lasting personal relationships with prospects, and they establish *an invaluable pipeline of future money.*

Planned gifts take many forms. Among the most popular are bequests by will, charitable gift annuities and deferred annuities, life insurance, and charitable remainder trusts. Setting them up ranges from the relatively simple action of naming a group in a will to drawing up contract agreements for an annuity or deferred annuity to drafting complex contracts and stipulations for charitable trusts. Planned gifts involve not only the donor and the organization but also legal council and financial advisers. The process begins with a prospect's interest in learning more about planned giving opportunities. This is followed by a series of discussions between the prospect and a planned giving representative, and sometimes a legal or financial adviser is also brought in. As will be illustrated later in this chapter, it is always advisable for the planned giving officer to share several planned giving illustrations with the prospect, showing several options for funding the gift, in order to give the prospect the widest range of options. Additionally, planned giving prospects should be strongly encouraged to share this information with their financial and legal advisers.

Statistics and research highlight the importance of planned gifts. For example, a recent survey by the Social Welfare Research Institute

predicted that of the nearly $43.5 trillion that is expected to pass be-
tween generations by the middle of this century, $444 billion will go
to charitable trusts ("Non-Cash Gifts," 2004). Most of that amount
will be noncash gifts, such as real estate, art, and patents. Additionally, according to the Giving USA Foundation (2004), gifts through
bequests in 2003 totaled $21.60 billion, a 12.8 percent increase over
2002. Bequest gifts represented 9 percent of the total giving in 2003.
These are staggering numbers and they all involve planned gifts. This
emphasizes the need for any organization, regardless of its size, to
have at the very least a bequest society so that prospects and donors
are encouraged to place the group in their wills. With the expected
enormous transfer of wealth from one generation to the next over the
next fifty years, every group should be on board to have a solid
planned giving program in place to capture these large planned gifts.

THE IMPORTANCE OF PLANNED GIFTS FOR DONORS

People who make planned gifts want to forever associate themselves,
their families, and their loved ones with the organization. They may
be motivated by social, religious, or cultural convictions and have a
strong commitment to better society and to strengthen the community through civic engagement (Barrett and Ware, 2002, p. 14). Their
gift communicates their values for future generations. They want to
leave a long and lasting legacy and impression with the group, and
their planned gift assures them that they will be remembered
throughout the lifetime of the organization. A planned gift perpetu-
ates values beyond the donor's life and can set an example for others
to make similar planned gifts. For instance, many people make
planned gifts to set an example for their family and for future generations to give in this way. Others desire to have the planned gift honor
the memory of a loved one.

There are also strong monetary reasons why people make
planned gifts. First, planned gifts can relieve many donors of large income, estate, and gift taxes and capital gains taxes. Some people consider this a negative reason to make a planned gift; however,
remember that when people make planned gifts they always consider
their personal financial situations and the assets that make the most
sense for funding the planned gift. They are maximizing the gift

through careful tax planning. Using appreciated assets to fund a gift that gives the donor the maximum tax benefits is simply good financial planning and is a *win-win* situation for the donor and the organization. Second, some people may just wish to share their good fortune of working hard, making the right investments, inheriting large estates, or getting a sudden windfall, and planned gifts are more attractive and flexible than money given outright to the group. Third, many people who make planned gifts do so because, even though they can part with appreciated assets or property, they would like a steady stream of income. They may be retired and the income generated from these gifts may make them comfortable and their lives more stable. Others may wish to have the assured income because they face uncertain investments or poor health. Charitable gift annuities and charitable trusts are excellent vehicles to use to accomplish these goals.

PLANNED GIVING DONOR PROFILES

It is important to define the characteristics of people who make planned gifts because this helps fundraisers to fully understand and appreciate prospects' motivation to make such gifts and the things likely to affect gift timing. These characteristics are listed in Exhibit 7.1.

Planned givers know the organization well, whether through having personal visits with its staff, administrators, or volunteers; attending its events; reading its newsletters, magazines, or direct appeals; or visiting its Web site. Planned givers are not the type of people who, without any education, cultivation, or involvement, wake up one day and say, "I think it's time I do a trust with Organization XYZ." They require much cultivation and education on the topic of planned gifts before the right planned gift option can be offered to them, and sometimes this preparation can take years. Their economic station in life, combined with uncertainty in the stock market and personal circumstances, can cause tremendous delays in their decision to make a planned gift. Planned givers are constant planners and predictors of how much money they need now and in the future for themselves and for their loved ones. They will give only if they know a group's mission, priorities, and direction and are drawn to supporting that group. Mission, priorities, and direction are usually defined and

EXHIBIT 7.1. *Characteristics of Planned Givers.*

1. They know about the organization and its mission, priorities, and direction.

2. They have confidence in the leadership.

3. They are satisfied with the organization's fiscal management.

4. They believe their gift will be perpetuated well into the future and that they will have a long and lasting legacy through the organization.

5. They give when the time is right for them economically.

6. They may have supported the organization in the past with smaller gifts, but a number of them will have no giving history with the organization.

7. They possess the assets to give without compromising their economic comfort level.

8. They want to ensure that their loved ones are taken care of in conjunction with the planned gift.

9. They tend to make several planned gifts over their lifetime.

10. They usually consult tax advisers, financial planners, attorneys, colleagues, and family members before making the gift.

driven by the leadership, namely, the organization's CEO or president and its board. Strong, visibly powerful, and effective leadership is required before people will unleash precious, hard-earned assets to make planned gifts to an organization.

Planned givers must also have confidence in the fiscal management of the organization. They want to see annual reports, they will ask questions on investment and spending policies, and they like to hear how other people's planned gifts are currently being invested and stewarded. Planned gifts are long-term legacy gifts, and when a person makes a planned gift, it is one of the biggest votes of confidence anyone can give to the organization. It signifies that the planned giver and the organization have a joint partnership in ensuring that the organization's mission will carry on for years to come.

For planned givers *it is all in the timing*. They will give when it is the optimal time for them to relinquish assets and property that they have worked long and hard to acquire. It takes an intense and soul-searching process to make a planned gift. Many people reflect on what they had, what they have, what they need now and later, and what they have over what they need. This becomes the basis for the planned giving opportunity. A mistake many fundraisers make is to use their own timing or the organization's fundraising goals or campaigns to drive the planned gift process and in some instances to try to force the gift. Again, although every fundraiser should keep steady and close contact with planned giving prospects, these prospects need some breathing room to think and reflect. They will make the gift when the time is right financially, emotionally, and philosophically for them and their families.

Although later in this chapter we will explore the planned giving prospect pool, it needs to be mentioned here as a characteristic of planned givers that even though many of them will have supported the organization in some capacity in the past, usually with small gifts, many will not have supported the organization previously at all. This may come as a surprise; however, many planned giving prospects do not view themselves as being able to make large outright gifts, so they wait until they have accumulated appreciated assets that they can give in ways that will not diminish their lifestyle. Many planned giving prospects are overlooked because of their past giving records, which as time has shown are not a reliable indicator of their potential and willingness to make a planned gift.

Planned giving prospects who have families and loved ones usually make sure that these important people in their lives are provided for via the planned gift. For instance, if a prospect wants to put a group in his will, family and loved ones are named first, and only after they have been provided for does the group receive the remainder of the estate. Families and loved ones are often the beneficiaries of charitable gift annuities and trusts, and it could well be a missed opportunity if the fundraiser did not make this a key selling point for these types of gifts.

Once prospects have made a planned gift and the organization shows it is managing and stewarding the gift properly—by giving the prospect timely financial reports, payments, and updates on how the gift is benefiting the organization and its constituency—many of them make repeat gifts. By now they are totally knowledgeable about how planned gifts work and the benefits these gifts bring, and they are comfortable and confident with these ways of giving. Many, many people make multiple gift annuities and then move on to trusts. Planned gifts become a way of life for them and a means to manage and control their finances while satisfying their ongoing dream to help the organization.

Even when the planned giving prospects have a financial background or are active businesspeople, it is always advisable for the fundraiser to suggest that the prospects consult legal or financial counsel. Many planned giving prospects do so and then also consult their family and other loved ones before the planned gift is made. This way everyone is aware of the prospect's plans to support the organization with a planned gift, and knows what assets will be used to fund the gift. There should be no surprises for either the prospect about what financial benefits the planned gift will bring or for the family and other loved ones. The last thing anyone wants is for the family or other loved ones to be unaware that assets or property that might have been given to them in the future are being used now to fund the planned gift. It does happen, but care should be taken to avoid it, because the family or other loved ones may not only be upset with the donor, they may also be very upset with the organization, causing bad feelings about the organization and possibly bad public relations. Request that your prospects seek as much advice as they feel comfortable with so that the organization will never be perceived as coercing or misinforming planned giving prospects.

The Planned Giver Prospect Pool

Compared to the prospect pool for annual givers and major gift donors, the prospect pool for planned giving has less definition and fewer guidelines. It contains the widest range of potential givers— young, old, female, male, single, married, divorced, wealthy, and those living on fixed incomes (Ashton, 2004, p. 51). Additionally, one cannot judge the potential for a planned gift by a person's prior giving history. As mentioned, many good planned giving prospects have made small gifts to the annual fund or *have made no gift* to the organization (Barrett and Ware, 2002, p. 86).

If gender, wealth, and prior giving history cannot be guideposts for determining the planned giving pool, perhaps the age of the donor would provide some structure. It might be assumed that donors sixty-five to seventy years old are the ideal planned giving prospects because these folks are probably retired and have appreciated and accumulated wealth. Although people in this age bracket do indeed make a significant number of planned gifts, recent studies suggest that younger people are also making a number of planned gifts. For instance, the National Committee on Planned Giving did a survey in 1992 of 170,000 households who had placed a charitable bequest in their wills or had signed a charitable gift annuity or remainder trust. The 1,579 households who completed a follow-up questionnaire to the survey yielded the following results. Forty-three percent of those naming a charity in their wills and 34 percent of those making charitable trusts *were under the age of fifty-five.* In fact, the average age of individuals making their first will was forty-four and the average age of people making their first charitable trust was forty-nine (Bigelow, 2001). Think of the number of charitable annuities and trusts an organization would miss out on if it did not market these gift opportunities to a younger audience or did not cultivate this age group for these types of planned gifts. In another study of bequests, sponsored by the Association of Fundraising Professionals and Mal Warwick & Associates, five U.S. nonprofit organizations soliciting legacy gifts compared the attitudes of those donors who pledged to make a legacy gift with the attitudes of those who were asked but had not committed. Although legacy pledgers were more likely to be female and older and less likely to have children, the balance of the charity's contributors *had no key differences or factors that would segment the donor base* (Association of Fundraising Professionals, 2004b). This again illustrates that there are no hard-and-fast rules governing the pool of planned giving prospects. Age, sex, and family history may be factors, but they do not dominate or determine with any great precision who will constitute the majority in the planned giving prospect pool.

The bottom line when managing any organization's planned giving prospect pool is that the net needs to be cast far enough and broadly enough so that good prospects are not missed. One cannot put on blinders and narrow the pool by demographics, particularly age, family status, and prior giving history. Planned giving prospects represent a fresh new group of prospects, and identifying them can and should be considered an opportunity for the organization to expand its existing donor base.

PLANNED GIVING PROGRAM PREREQUISITES

As with any comprehensive fundraising program, a number of systems must be in place before the organization successfully starts or enhances a planned giving program. The organization does not want to be in the position of asking for and accepting planned gifts when it lacks a means to produce planned giving forms and agreements, to invest these gifts, to send payments to donors, or to have legal counsel to review the complex situations that may arise. Exhibit 7.2 displays a checklist of considerations for any planned giving program.

If the organization is young, perhaps in existence for less than five years, launching a full-fledged planned giving program may not be a good idea. Although any organization should be able to accept bequests from individuals, young organizations may not be in a position to accept charitable gift annuities or trusts because they do not have all the elements listed in Exhibit 7.2 in place. It is best to take the time to put all the financial and legal systems in place before embarking on a comprehensive planned giving program.

In addition there must be approval and total buy-in for the planned giving program by the CEO or president, CFO, and the board. Many top administrators do not want planned gifts because many of these gifts, especially bequests, will not bring the organization money until well into the future. Many top leaders *discourage* planned gifts and would rather place all the emphasis on outright major gifts. Surely this is not a healthy approach, because gifts are determined by the donors, not top administrators and leaders. Donors will give the organization money when the time is right and with the gift vehicle that is best for each donor's financial situation, whether that vehicle is an outright gift or a type of planned gift. Leaders, fundraisers, top administrators, board members, and consultants need to understand that the group will lose huge gifts if it does not accept and embrace the donors' desire to give via planned gifts.

EXHIBIT 7.2. *Considerations Before Starting or Enhancing a Planned Giving Program.*

1. The number of years the organization has been in existence
2. Approval of the program by the CEO or president, the chief financial officer (CFO), and the board
3. Board-approved gift levels for each planned gift
4. Board-approved investment policies and spending rules for planned gifts
5. Incorporation of planned giving into the organization's strategic plan or capital campaign, or both
6. A budget to cover all program expenses
7. A financial organization that will oversee all aspects of planned gifts from agreements to payments
8. Legal expertise to answer the donor's and the organization's questions
9. Forms and agreements to give to planned giving prospects
10. Acknowledgment and stewardship programs for planned givers

Board approval is also needed for the gift level for each type of planned gift and for investment and spending policies. If the organization has an up-to-date gift acceptance policy, these issues should be covered in that policy. For instance, the group needs to set the minimum amount it will accept for a charitable gift annuity and for a trust. Many groups set a minimum of $5,000 for gift annuities and anywhere from $100,000 to $250,000 for a charitable trust. Additionally, the policy should state how the organization invests these types of gifts, and the amount of interest the gift will generate for the donors. Remember, you do not want to lack a policy when faced with a prospect who wants to give $50,000 for a charitable trust when your organization has had a pattern and practice of accepting not less than $100,000 for a charitable trust. Without a written policy to point to, your organization can find itself in an uncomfortable place with this prospect and may face bad press and ill will.

A key point to be made about any planned giving program is that it needs to be integrated into the organization's total picture. We will address this later in this chapter. For now it is important to note that if your group has a strategic plan or a capital campaign case statement, or both, the role and importance of planned gifts for the organization should be incorporated into these documents. If this does not occur, there is a risk that planned gifts will be deemphasized and that people will decide that acquiring these gifts does not need time and attention. Many people think that planned gifts take time to close because the prospects need this time to consider a myriad of financial consequences and, therefore, that if these gifts are going to happen they will happen on their own, without effort from the organization. Nothing could be further from the truth. This is why the planned gift program should be part of the strategic plan and campaign case statement, so that planned gifts are on a level playing field with major gifts.

The one factor that can make or break any planned giving program is its *budget*. The organization must consider whether it has the funds now and in the future to support

- Salaries for planned giving directors, officers, and support staff
- Trustee fees for administering charitable trusts
- Computer software for planned giving illustrations
- Attendance at seminars and conferences for planned giving staff
- Marketing materials to promote planned gifts to targeted constituencies
- Planned giving seminars the organization may wish to host
- Recognition societies and events
- Stewardship activities
- Travel to cultivate planned giving prospects
- Fees for legal counsel to address complex issues

The organization can begin slowly and work its way up to budgeting for all these factors, but at some point in time, especially if the group is progressing well with its planned giving program, all these needs will have to be funded.

A choice the organization has in managing the planned giving program is whether to keep it in-house or to have an outside financial organization handle investment, payment distribution, and tax reporting. I strongly suggest that whenever possible all this financial and technical activity be covered by an outside financial group. It can be laborious and time consuming to have a planned giving officer with one person in the finance department send quarterly annuity checks and annual tax forms. It would be better for the planned giving officer to use that time stewarding those gifts and cultivating prospects for new gifts. Small groups may want to keep these functions in-house at first, and then as the planned giving program progresses, move to outside help. The point is not to get so wrapped up with the bookkeeping end of planned gifts that it takes precious time away from planned giving donors and prospects.

Without a doubt, at some point in time the group will need outside counsel to answer a prospect's or a donor's questions. Planned gifts are complex vehicles, and even if the group has in-house legal counsel, that person may or may not have all the estate and tax expertise needed to answer important questions. If you do, terrific. If not, start having a series of discussions with the leaders of your group to retain good planned giving counsel so that that person will be on hand when a question arises that cannot be answered within the group. Fees for this legal expertise are money well spent, and you do not want to be in the position of not being able to address prospect or donor questions. Prospects and donors usually have more than one group they support, and you run the risk that they will make the planned gift with another group if you cannot answer their questions to their satisfaction. An additional reason for having good legal counsel is that every planned gift has a form or agreement for the prospect to fill out and sign. These forms and agreements need to be approved by legal counsel and ready to hand out before any planned gift is requested.

Lastly, there is a need for programs that steward and recognize planned givers. At Pace University, anyone who has made a planned gift to the university is enrolled in the Edward J. Mortola Heritage Society, named after a former Pace president. Each year the university has a luncheon for these members and their guests, and it does not charge them for this event because it is a recognition event. Each year the planned giving staff project the cost of this event, minus projected event sponsorship, and that figure goes into the planned giving budget. At any organization, costs for all recognition societies and stewardship events and activities must be projected on a yearly basis and incorporated into the planned giving budget.

COORDINATING THE PLANNED GIVING PROGRAM WITH ALL FUNDRAISING PROGRAMS

The success of the planned giving program rides on the degree to which it is integrated with all the other organizational fundraising programs. This leads us to a further guiding principle:

Guiding Principle 7

Any organization's planned giving program must be coordinated with all other fundraising programs.

The planned giving program cannot operate in a vacuum (Ashton, 2004, p. 55). As stated earlier, many planned giving prospects will be annual fund donors. This means that the annual fund director and the planned giving director must communicate regularly with each other, so that each prospect continues to make enhanced annual fund gifts while being cultivated by the planned giving director for a planned gift. The two go hand in hand. There is no room for prospect territorialism, and it is totally inaccurate to think that if the prospect makes a large annual fund gift she will not *at the same time* consider a planned gift. Use your prospect management meetings to form solid strategies for each prospect so that you will never face the serious problems that can arise when one department is working with a prospect at the same time another department is working with that same prospect and neither is aware of the other's activity.

In my experience the planned giving department will have its largest connections with the major gifts and capital campaign departments. Here's an example that illustrates this point. A prospect is approached for a $1 million gift to support a children's aid society. The prospect has made modest gifts to the group before, has served on its advisory board, and has the capacity and inclination to make this gift; however, she is in transition with her job and needs time before she can make a commitment this large. She is also a single mother with one daughter about to attend a private college.

Under these circumstances all three directors—planned giving, major gifts, and capital campaign—need to be communicating with each other on the right strategy for this prospect. Obviously, this is a major gift that will count toward the campaign, and given the size of the gift, the president and the campaign director make the ask. The prospect has said she needs time, so she is asked if the president and campaign director can visit with her again in a month. During that time the three directors design three different strategies, using a mix of outright gifts through the transfer of her stock and a variety of planned giving options that will give her the income she needs while her daughter is in college so that she will be able to make the $1 million gift.

This prospect did not start out as a planned giving prospect but she quickly turned into one because giving $1 million outright was simply not going to happen considering her circumstances. This demonstrates why everyone must be a good listener, sensitive to the prospect's needs, and willing to work with others on behalf of the organization to create the best gift opportunities for each prospect, financially, philosophically, and philanthropically.

Many organizations have one person performing both the major gift and planned giving roles. Under these circumstances the coordination effort is easier; however, it still must be plugged into the annual fund as well as any existing campaign or capital fund efforts. The bottom line is that fundraising can work only if each member is a team player and if prospect coordination is viewed as the key to success.

Building a Planned Giving Program

The best way to build a planned giving program is to start with the easiest planned giving vehicle to market, manage, and maintain, and then, when the organization is ready, to add the more complex vehicles. Remember, as I described in the Introduction, the emphasis in this book is on the ask. This section therefore is not going to cover all planned giving vehicles, just the most popular ones, which will also be the ones used at the end of this chapter in the examples of doing the asks for planned gifts.

Bequests

Bequests are the transfers of wealth that occur upon the donor's death and that include transfers by means of a will or a trust. Bequests can take several forms:

Specific bequest: a certain amount of cash, securities, or property—for example, "5,000 shares of IBM stock"

General bequest: property that is similar to all other items distributed—usually cash

Percentage bequest: a stated percentage of the donor's estate—for example, "35 percent of my gross estate"

Residual bequest: all or a portion of what remains of the estate after specific and general bequests are distributed

Many planned gift donors prefer to give an organization a sizeable gift at death. This allows them to maintain control and use of their earnings and assets during their lifetime. If an organization lacks a bequest program, this large, underutilized group of people will not be supporting the organization at all. When bequests come to an organization, they are like newfound money because the organization has no way of knowing when a donor will pass away or the size of his estate at death. More often than not, the organization will have had no idea the donor had assets of this value in his estate, and therefore bequests can be real windfalls for any group.

The hard part is to get your donors to state that they have placed your group in their wills. That is why many groups are so surprised when they receive notification that a donor has passed away and that the group was named in the will. The rule is to make it as effortless as possible for a donor to let your group know that it is in the donor's will. A simple *notification of bequest* form (Resource E) can be used when someone discovers through cultivation visits that a donor has placed the organization in his will. This form can also be used as a marketing tool to get donors to tell the fundraising office that they have placed the organization in their wills. Another simple method of getting this information is to place a tear-off form with lots of check-off boxes in all your publications. Then the donor can easily indicate that he has placed your group in his will, the amount of the bequest, whether it involves a life insurance policy, and whether it is a specific, general, percentage, or residual bequest. *Always* include a box the donor can check to receive additional information on other planned gifts and another box that gives you permission to list the donor as a member of your planned giving society.

Charitable Gift Annuities

One of the simplest and most popular forms of life income gifts is the charitable gift annuity. It involves a simple agreement whereby the charity accepts a gift of cash, securities, or property and agrees to pay a specified, fixed dollar amount to the *annuitant* (the donor or another beneficiary). The fixed amount is set by the American Council on Gift Annuities and is based on the annuitant's age at the time the annuity is established. Because the gift is irrevocable, the organization maintains control of the gift and is responsible for paying income for the lifetime of each annuitant.

For tax purposes it is a very attractive planned giving vehicle. The donor receives an immediate tax deduction for the remainder value, a portion of the annuity payment is tax-free income because it is regarded as return of principal, the remaining portion is taxed as ordinary income, and if the charitable annuity has been funded with an appreciated asset, the taxable income portion of the payment is split into ordinary income and capital gain income, and the latter is then spread out over the annuitant's expected lifetime. After that, it is taxed as ordinary income.

Charitable gift annuities are so popular because for a relatively low investment (most groups have an entry level of $5,000 for a charitable gift annuity), the donor receives a steady stream of guaranteed income. Especially in economic climates when interest rates are very low, charitable gift annuities can provide a very good rate of return and are a wise investment.

Deferred Charitable Gift Annuities

A deferred charitable gift annuity is funded with cash or stock that is exchanged for the organization's promise to pay the annuitant(s) income at a future date. At the death of the last annuitant, the remainder goes to the organization. Because the donor's assets are tied up for a number of years, the rate for the deferred annuity can be considerably higher than the rate for a charitable annuity that goes into effect immediately. Furthermore, because the income is not paid for a number of years, the principal remains untouched, making the eventual income rate higher, and the immediate income tax deduction is also larger than the deduction allowed for the charitable gift annuity that is not deferred.

Deferred gift annuities are an ideal way to plan for retirement and for uncertainties that may occur at a later time in the donor's life. For people who have reached the maximum amount on their individual retirement accounts or 401(k)s, the deferred gift annuity payments can supplement their retirement benefits. Additionally, there are no limits on the contributions to a deferred charitable annuity, so this is a further incentive for donors to add a deferred charitable gift annuity to their retirement portfolio.

Charitable Remainder Trusts

A charitable remainder trust is very attractive to donors with highly appreciated assets in the six-figure range and above. With this planned gift, the donor irrevocably transfers assets into a trust. The trust pays income to the donor or other beneficiaries during their lifetimes, and the remainder goes to a qualified nonprofit organization. The donor receives a charitable income tax deduction for the gift value, income for life, possible avoidance of capital gains tax, and possible reduction of gift and estate taxes. Charitable remainder trusts may be established during the donor's lifetime or at death. The payments the donor receives must not exceed 50 percent of the initial amount contributed, and the present value of the amount that will pass to the nonprofit must be at least 10 percent of the market value of the assets transferred to the trust. The donor usually names a bank or trust company to serve as trustee of the trust.

The two types of charitable remainder trusts are the annuity trust and the unitrust. With an annuity trust the donor receives a fixed income that is at least a 5 percent return on the trust amount, and the donor cannot make additional contributions to the trust. This type of trust is attractive to donors who desire a fixed income and is particularly attractive to older donors. A unitrust is much more flexible because the payments can vary and the donor can make additional contributions to the trust. The donor selects the payout rate, and the trust pays that percentage of the assets, revalued each year. Annual income will obviously increase or decrease with the market value of the trust assets. This type of trust appeals to donors who want income growth and the flexibility to make additional contributions and receive maximum tax benefits.

Marketing a Planned Giving Program

Planned gifts need to be sold. By that I mean you need to get the word to all your donors that you stand ready and willing to help them fulfill their philanthropic dreams of supporting your group, without depleting their savings for themselves and their loved ones. The underlying message of this whole chapter is to start out slowly and build. This also applies to the marketing efforts for your planned gifts. Start out by using your existing publications, direct appeals, Web site, and special events to advertise the types of planned gifts offered by your group. Make sure you list a single specific person as the planned giving contact person, with a telephone number, e-mail address, and mailing address. On your Web site, link giving opportunities listed on your home page to a planned giving section that presents the types of planned gifts your group accepts, the minimum level for each gift, and most important, the *benefits* for each gift. This seems obvious, but for medium-size to large organizations, the coordination of this effort with the marketing or communication department can be an arduous task that finds fundraisers fighting for space in organization newsletters and magazines. If you find yourself in this tug-of-war, rally the troops from your board and volunteers, and let them proclaim the benefits of advertising and marketing planned gifts. Let them know that *mailed solicitations and advertisements in the charity's literature and Web site* are the best way to solicit bequests and other planned gifts (Association of Fundraising Professionals, 2004b).

Once you have the budget, move on to newly created material. Create a planned giving newsletter that goes out to current planned givers as well as to those who have inquired about a planned gift and to any other audiences you can target for these gifts. If your group receives gifts primarily from older donors, then everyone in the donor pool should receive the newsletter. If your group has donors of all ages and if you have the funds, it should again go out to everyone. If you do not have the funds for a broad mailing, then start with people fifty years old and above. If that is too many, try sixty years old and above. Keep in mind that, as stated earlier, many people are planned giving prospects, *regardless of age,* so to the extent you can find the funds, mail a separate planned giving brochure or newsletter to as many people as possible in your donor base.

ASKING FOR PLANNED GIFTS

We are now ready to go through three scenarios with specific language to ask for a bequest, a charitable gift annuity, and a charitable remainder trust. There are three questions that must be answered during the ask. I have found that if I get the answers to these questions incorporated into the ask, a planned gift will surely follow.

1. What assets are the most logical to use to fund the gift?
2. What gift vehicle is best suited for the donor and any other beneficiaries?
3. When will the gift be made?

If you can get the answers to these questions during the ask, there is no doubt that you will close on the ask much more quickly than you will if you do not have these answers. Any asker needs to know up front the assets that can fund the gift because the nature of the assets will largely determine the best gift vehicle. If the prospect wants to give a limited cash gift or a few appreciated securities, she may lean toward a gift annuity, whereas if she is considering real estate or a large amount of appreciated securities, she would lean in favor of a charitable remainder trust. Next the asker needs to be sensitive to the donor's economic needs now and in the future. The asker needs to further explore the best planned gift vehicle for the donor. The donor may like a steady fixed income or may be attracted to the fluctuating investment. Lastly is the question of timing. When will the gift be made? One cannot assume that just because a prospect is discussing a planned gift now the gift will be made soon. Planned giving prospects generally take their time and mull many things over before they commit pen to paper. The world economic climate or their personal and business situations may change between the time of their first consideration and the time they make the planned gift. People asking for planned gifts need to be up to speed on how those personal circumstances can affect the original planned giving opportunity.

Asking for a Bequest

This first example of a planned gift ask is for an academy, a small organization that has one director of development, Ann, who is responsible for all aspects of fundraising, including building a bequest society. The donor, Trisha, forty-seven years old, has made steady gifts to the annual fund. Ann called Trisha to thank her for her most recent gift, and Trisha told Ann that she wished "she could do something more" but that she "needs to save" so she does not outlive her assets. Ann asked Trisha if she could stop by and chat with her about ways she could increase her support. Trisha agreed and the meeting was arranged. Here is what was said during that meeting:

Ann: Trisha, thank you for taking the time to meet with me today, and thank you for your wonderful and loyal gifts to the annual fund. Without loyal supporters like you we would not be able to give our students the best elementary school education they deserve.

Trisha: You're welcome, and I'm happy to help. I'm sure that the costs for books, good teachers, and outside activities only increases each year.

Ann: Absolutely, and thank you again. Trisha, you mentioned that you wanted some suggestions on how you could increase your support without decreasing your disposable assets.

Trisha: Yes, I wish I could do it. It's just that you can never know how much you will need in the future for health care, to cover living expenses, and everything that may come up.

Ann: That's perfectly understandable. Your needs come first, and predicting as best you can, with the help of an attorney or financial planner, how much you need in the future should put your mind at ease. There is a way however to take care of your needs while you are living and also support the academy in a significant way.

Trisha: How does that work?

Ann: You can leave a set amount or a percentage of your estate to the academy in your will.

Trisha: Too late; I've already done my will, and it is so costly to do another. I left some to my church, and the rest to my sister, niece, and nephew.

Ann: That's great that you have included your church in your will. That shows you believe in your church's mission, and your estate will reap tax benefits as well. You can still make this type of gift without creating another will. Simply ask your attorney to draft a codicil that will modify your will. I can provide the language for you to share with your attorney. How does that sound to you?

Trisha: I'll have to think about it, because I'm not very fond of these legal documents.

Ann: I can understand. When and if you are ready, this is just our suggestion of a way for you to do something really meaningful for the students of the academy without depleting your present-day income.

Trisha: Of course. When I return from a business trip, then the holidays with the family, I'll give it more thought.

Ann: Trisha, that would be great, and I'll make a note to call you after the holidays. In the meantime, thank you for all you do for the academy. We know how busy you are, but we would love to have you come back and, if you have the time, spend some time with the students. Give it some thought. In the meantime, we wish you and your family a wonderful holiday season.

Once a donor agrees to place your group in her will, it is very important that she indicate this in writing. Resource E is a sample bequest notification form you can use when prospects have agreed to make provisions in their wills for your group. I strongly suggest that you give this form to them in person and have it filled out in your presence and returned to you. Too often these forms are mailed to donors and never returned to the organization. Then the fundraiser has the task of calling the donors to get the forms returned. If at all possible hand deliver the form to the donor right after she has stated that your group is in her will, so that you have accurate records in your files on your bequest society members.

Asking for a Charitable Gift Annuity

The next example is an illustration of how to ask for a charitable gift annuity. Prospect Josh has just received a Jewish organization's charitable gift annuity mailing. The organization did a targeted mailing to all its donors who had made an annual gift within the last two years and who were sixty years old and above but who had not made a planned gift to date. Josh fits these categories. His interest was piqued by the possible rate of income he could receive from a charitable gift annuity, so he called the number on the brochure to find out more information. Planned giving officer Jerry received Josh's call, and Josh agreed to meet with Jerry at Josh's home to learn more about the benefits of a charitable gift annuity. This is the first time Josh has met with anyone from the organization.

Jerry: Josh, it's great to meet with you at your home. When we spoke you said that you just recently retired. Tell me, are you more busy now than you ever were?

Josh: You know I heard that from a lot of people and never believed them until now. You can't believe the number of things that I have going on.

Jerry: Well, good for you and congratulations on your retirement from all of us at our organization. We are very proud of you. You mentioned on the telephone that you received our brochure on charitable gift annuities and had some questions. I'm here to help.

Josh: Well, from the brochure it sounds like I could get a good rate of return, but I don't know how much that would be. A steady income now would surely help.

Jerry: OK, Josh, I brought my laptop with me to show you exactly how this will work. If you want me to show you now I can; if not, I can send it to you or e-mail it to you in no less than two days from now.

Josh: No, go right ahead.

Jerry: OK, let me pull up PG Calc. It's a software program that will calculate the exact annuity rate, payments, and tax deductions and exemptions that may apply. Ready. Josh, I'll need your full name and date of birth.

Josh: Josh Appleton, June 19, 1936.

Jerry: For you, the rate would be 6.3 percent. The organization would pay you in quarterly installments for as long as you live. Part of that payment is tax free, and part is taxed as ordinary income. After you pass away (you know, I just hate to say those words), the organization would use the proceeds for a variety of purposes that we can discuss. I'd be happy to print this out this illustration and send it to you so that you can think about it and review it with anyone you desire—family, attorney, financial adviser.

Josh: No, it will be just my decision. And I just want to give it to the Jewish organization. They can decide how best to use the money.

Jerry: That's terrific, Josh. Yes, you are absolutely right; the organization has a real need for unrestricted gifts so that we can maintain our programs while improving our outreach to serve our community.

Permit me to explain how gift annuities work. Josh, our annuities begin at the $5,000 level and can be funded with cash or appreciated securities. You mentioned on the phone that you were considering something in the $5,000 to $10,000 range. Remember, if you make a $10,000 gift now, that will give you $630 a year, and you can take an immediate tax deduction of $3,578. Those numbers would be smaller with a $5,000 gift. And the best part is that it is projected that your gift would ultimately give the organization $25,002, which would be a fantastic and meaningful gift for so many of our beneficiaries.

Josh: Well, I was prepared to write a check for $10,000, if I was convinced this was right for me.

Jerry: And, Josh, right now, how do you feel about this gift opportunity?

Josh: It all looks good, and I like the amount of money each year, plus I could use the tax deduction this year. What do we do next?

Jerry: I will send you this illustration so that you can see the amount of your quarterly payments, how they are taxed, and the charitable deduction you would be eligible to claim on your taxes. I'll also send a gift annuity contract. You should have it in no less than two days. I'll give you a call then and follow up on any questions you may have.

Josh: I need to do this before the end of the year, so please assure me this paperwork won't get in the way.

Jerry: You have my word. We have more than a month to process it, but let's say we will meet or speak next Monday, just so we keep this on track.

Josh: Mondays are not good but, hmm, Tuesday first thing in the morning would work.

Jerry: Done! Why don't I plan to drop by Tuesday, around 9:00 AM, and we'll complete everything for you.

Josh: Sounds good.

Jerry: Josh, please know that your prospective gift is so much appreciated. Your prospective gift, combined with others, will make it possible for the organization to continue its good work well into the future. Thank you so much.

Whenever possible use planned giving software, such as PG Calc, to illustrate how the planned gift can benefit the prospect. In the previous example Josh was shown how much he could prospectively take as a tax deduction, how much he would receive each year, and how much the organization would receive once Josh passes away. Resource F displays the materials sent to Josh to explain his $10,000 cash gift for a charitable gift annuity. Ideally, you will have enough information to bring materials like these with you on your visit to the prospect. You would then leave them with the prospect so that he has them as a reference that he can review and also can share with other decision makers who may have a say about the gift.

Asking for a Charitable Remainder Unitrust

The last example features a couple, Matilda and Clyde Tucker, both seventy-two years old, who are in the midst of some financial planning with an attorney. The attorney has advised them to consider a charitable trust to lift appreciated assets out of their estate in order to avoid potentially high tax liabilities. The Tuckers have supported an African American organization for the past three years, making consistent gifts of $2,500 each year, so if they were going to do a charitable trust, this organization would be their first choice. Bill, a major gifts and planned giving officer for the organization, has met with the Tuckers on several occasions, the last being a trip to their Florida home. Each time, Bill introduced the idea of a major or planned gift, but the Tuckers were not ready to increase their gift level and were always going to do some financial planning but "things got in the way." After the Tuckers' meeting with the attorney, Clyde called Bill to set up an appointment to learn more about charitable trusts. They agreed to meet at Bill's office.

> *Clyde:* Hi, Bill, you remember meeting my wife, Matilda, late last year.
>
> *Bill:* I sure do. Welcome back. Why don't we walk around the corner. I reserved us a conference room. I ordered coffee, water, and soda, but would either of you like something to eat?
>
> *Matilda:* Oh no, thank you, we just ate. What a great view of the river you have.
>
> *Bill:* Thanks. Yes, our offices do have good views. So, how long will you be in town?

Matilda: Oh, just two more days. We're going to visit with some friends, then we are flying back to Florida.

Bill: It's great that you are taking advantage of the city. Clyde, you said on the telephone that you and Matilda were considering a charitable trust.

Clyde: That's right. We met a few months ago with our attorney to review our wills and our estate since I am worried that we may be hit with big taxes under the new tax laws. I still don't understand the estate tax that may go away in 2010 and then may come back, but either way our attorney knows we are charitably inclined and suggested we explore a charitable trust to protect our assets.

Bill: Well, we are honored that you both are thinking of our African American organization. Tell me, what size trust are you considering, and what assets will you use to fund this trust?

Clyde: Well, we're not sure. We have an oceanside property in Virginia that we bought back in 1954 for what was then a large amount. We decided that we no longer wanted to make the trips from up north to Virginia, and then we moved a few years ago to Florida. We put feelers out to several realtors, and they tell us we can get about $1.2 million, can you imagine!

Bill: Haven't real estate prices just gone over the top? Clyde and Matilda, I'm assuming that just the two of you own it and that no one else, family member or other relative, is expecting that this will be given to them at some time?

Matilda: Oh, no. As you know, we don't have any children, and our family members, just my mother and Clyde's brother, are well taken care of in our wills.

Bill: OK, then, the timing could not be any better for you to consider making this gift of a highly appreciated and what sounds like a jewel of an oceanfront home work for you. I would suggest that you use this property to fund a charitable trust, and this is how it works. You transfer the property to the trust and designate both of you as beneficiaries of the trust. You will receive a fluctuating income for as long as either one of you is living. You will be able to deduct a portion of the value of your gift against income taxes, and since you are using an appreciated asset, you will escape a high amount of taxable capital gains. Let me stop here and ask you how you feel about making this type of gift.

Clyde: Well, it sounds all right, but can we see how this works?

Bill: Absolutely, now that I know the approximate size of the trust and the assets you would be using to fund the trust, I can draw up an illustration. The illustration will show you the exact amount of tax deduction you can take, the income you will receive for the first year, the amount of capital gains you will avoid, and the amount that is projected to come to the organization at the very end.

Clyde: Let's see the paperwork for the fluctuating trust.

Bill: I'd be pleased. Why don't we step back into my office, and I can do this right away. Then you can think it over, discuss it with your attorney, and I'll call in a week or so to answer additional questions.

In this example Bill could not prepare an illustration beforehand because he did not know the amount of the trust or the type of assets—cash or appreciated stock or real estate—that would be used to fund the trust. It is incumbent on Bill to do the due diligence and to send the illustration right away to the Tuckers. Resource G displays this illustration.

In each of the examples in this chapter, the asker answered the three key questions: What assets will fund the gift? What gift vehicle should be used? and, When will the gift be made? Notice that these questions and answers are woven throughout each dialogue and are a natural extension of the conversation that the fundraiser is having with the prospect. Lastly, each dialogue sets a definite time and date when the fundraiser will follow up with the prospect, ensuring that there will not be a gaping hole of time between this meeting and closing the gift. *Always* set a time and date for the next meeting in order to keep these planned giving opportunities alive.

Conclusion

Some of the largest gifts any nonprofit organization will receive will be planned gifts. People who make planned gifts want to leave a long and lasting legacy and impression with their chosen organization, and their planned gift assures them that they will be remembered throughout the group's lifetime. Generally, planned givers are extremely knowledgeable about the organization and have tremendous faith in its leadership and fiscal management. They will make planned gifts when the time is right for them personally and financially, that is, when they are ready.

As with any comprehensive fundraising program, a number of prerequisites must be in place before an organization begins a planned giving program. Because most planned gifts require legally binding contracts, an organization will want to have a board-adopted policy and levels for planned gifts, sound financial and legal counsel on hand to draft and review agreements, and a mechanism to ensure that each gift is properly invested and stewarded. When launching any planned giving program, the organization should start with bequests, the easiest planned gifts to manage, and work up to the more complex gifts of life insurance, charitable annuities and deferred annuities, charitable remainder trusts, and retirement plans.

When asking for any planned gift, make sure that the three key questions are answered during the ask: What assets are the most logical to use to fund the gift? What gift vehicle is best suited for the donor and beneficiaries? and, When will the gift be made? This can easily be done if the asker steers the conversation to the financial and personal needs of the donor. The end result should be that donors feel they are on a new and heightened level with the organization because they have tied their lives forever with the life of that group. It does not get much better than that.

Looking Ahead

The last type of ask to be discussed is the ask for the capital campaign gift. The next chapter explores the uniqueness and importance of campaign gifts, the phases of the campaign, the gifts that constitute campaign gifts, and the people who should be considered campaign prospects. Two specific campaign asks, along with a simple yet highly adaptable campaign marketing piece that can accompany and complement the ask, will illustrate how any group can effectively ask for capital campaign gifts.

Asking for Complex and Challenging Capital Campaign Gifts

I get asked constantly for money; I need to hear why I should support
your request.

—Herbert Henkel, Chairman, President, and CEO,
Ingersoll Rand Company, Woodcliff Lake, New Jersey

AT SOME POINT IN TIME, MOST ORGANIZATIONS will embark upon a capital campaign. A capital campaign is a concentrated organizational effort within a set time frame to raise a substantial amount of money for a specific and well-defined purpose. This chapter explores the importance and uniqueness of a capital campaign, the distinct phases of a capital campaign, the gifts that constitute campaign gifts, and the people who are campaign prospects. This will serve as background to the latter part of the chapter, which shows how a simple yet highly effective campaign piece can be used for a campaign ask by any organization of any size and which also discusses two specific examples of asking for campaign gifts.

DEFINING THE CAPITAL CAMPAIGN

I consider capital campaign gifts to be Cadillacs among gifts. In the hierarchy of fundraising, capital campaign gifts rank the highest because they usually have the highest monetary level of any gift any organization will receive. Capital campaigns are a cost-effective, intense fundraising effort. The purpose is to raise a substantial amount of money during a specific time period so that the organization can achieve new heights. It is a concentrated, major fundraising effort. Because they are time specific, whether five years, seven years, or ten years long, campaigns give people a reason to make the gift *now*. The campaign represents the donors' chance to boost the presence, stature, and success of the organization.

Capital campaigns can improve an organization's status and position within the community by providing the funds that result in more and better services to the organization's constituency. They can transform an organization when they serve as catalysts for the clarification and realization of long-term goals. For instance, an organization may have planned for years to expand or renovate its facilities, to add several new programs, or to undertake bold, entrepreneurial new projects. Without a substantial influx of *new money* none of these goals could be achieved.

Like most fundraising programs the capital campaign needs to be *all inclusive*. By that I mean that everyone and anyone associated with the group should be *invited* to give at some point during the lifetime of the campaign. Through the concentrated efforts of everyone associated with the organization, all internal and external constituencies, and an intensive volunteer effort, the capital campaign will be a success. Capital campaigns are not just a few lead gifts from board members or major corporate and foundation supporters. Campaigns have been conducted this way, but what a missed opportunity not to invite all associated with the group *to join in and be a part* of the transformation of the organization.

So why are capital campaigns unique? Exhibit 8.1 sets forth the distinctive features of a capital campaign.

Capital campaign goals need to be ambitious and yet realistic. That may sound contradictory but it is not. Before any organization can have any idea of what goal to set for the campaign, it should have

---

EXHIBIT 8.1. *Unique Elements of the Capital Campaign.*

1. Its fundraising goals are ambitious.

2. It asks people to make stretch gifts.

3. It drives the entire focus and direction of the organization until the campaign goals are met.

4. It coincides with and complements the organization's strategic plan.

5. It includes all types of existing fundraising programs, such as annual, major, and planned gifts programs.

6. It is well organized, with a beginning, middle, and end.

7. It causes the organization to expand its volunteer base.

8. It serves as a means to get prospects and donors to give now.

9. It is a highly cost-effective way to raise substantial money.

10. It can create a positive change in the culture of the organization.

---

a feasibility study done by an outside consulting group. During the feasibility study a select group of people—donors, nondonors, community leaders, board members, and administrators and other staff—are asked a series of questions about the organization. All the resulting data are compiled and analyzed to produce a monetary campaign goal that can be reached, the numbers and levels of gifts needed to reach that campaign goal, the individuals and corporate and foundation supporters who most likely will make gifts at each level, and the projects and programs that these campaign prospects will support. The organization is then in a position to know realistically what it can raise. It is then up to the leaders of the organization to decide whether to stay at the suggested goal level or to set the bar a bit higher, if they feel the organization is strong and solid enough to raise more than the feasibility study has suggested. For instance, a feasibility study may have revealed that the organization could raise $50 million, but the leaders have projected needs that amount to $75 million. The leaders, together with any campaign cabinet or committee that has been formed, are then in the position of having to decide whether $75 million is too ambitious or whether they are willing to set the goal at this level and, if need be, *extend the time of the campaign or count regular, noncampaign gifts, such as gifts to the annual fund, as contributing to the goal.* This is what makes capital campaigns ambitious and realistic at the same time.

During the life of the campaign, prospects will be asked to make stretch gifts. *Stretch gifts* are gift opportunities set at an amount much higher than the amount the prospect may have intended to give. They challenge the donor to consider not only a larger gift amount but also the organizational significance and the impact this larger gift will have (Dove, 2000, p. 128). For instance, you might have a prospect who you know could comfortably make a $100,000 gift to the campaign over five years. The organization's leaders might emphasize the importance of the campaign and the need for top supporters to stretch their thinking about their prospective gifts and, for this time only, to consider a much larger-than-usual gift of $250,000. That would be a stretch gift for this prospect. Capital campaigns give the organization this golden opportunity to encourage donors and prospects to think about their giving at a heightened level.

There is no such thing as a simple capital campaign. Any capital campaign is a complex, organized, and focused effort. If it is not, it will surely not succeed. It is fair to say that everyone in the organization should live and breathe and concentrate on the campaign every day throughout its duration. It should be the force that drives the choice of prospects to be seen, cultivated, and briefed, starting with the most likely prospects and working in stages until all the prospects have been asked for campaign gifts, including administrators and other staff. If the organization has a strategic plan, then logically the campaign should coexist with and complement that plan. Otherwise the organization is at risk of having either too many plans and goals to fund or divergent goals that are at odds with each other.

The beauty of capital campaigns is that they have something for everyone. People can make a campaign gift that supports the annual fund, or they can make a major or planned gift, or a combined major and planned gift, that will support the campaign. The giving options and combinations are endless and should be maximized and marketed in this manner. All you need is creativity and flexibility within the bounds of ethics and your board-adopted gift acceptance policy, and you will be well on your way to securing multiple campaign gifts.

Capital campaigns have a definite structure, a beginning, middle, and end that makes it very easy to judge at each phase whether the organization is on track to reach the campaign goal. Campaigns cannot be run loosely, otherwise the time allotted will need to be unnecessarily extended. Groups run the risk of *campaign burnout* if they do not stick with the defined parameters and time frames for their campaigns. This is why it is important that any organization have many volunteers for each of the different campaign stages. Although the leaders and the members of the campaign cabinet or committee may be expected and willing to see the campaign through to completion, many other volunteers will give the group and its campaign only a finite amount of time. So the more volunteers you enlist, the stronger and better the position of your group can be throughout the campaign.

Because capital campaign gifts are the largest gifts the organization will receive, they are extremely cost effective compared with other types of gifts (Kihlstedt, 2002, p. 1). Campaigns do take time in their planning and preparation, and most groups do employ outside fundraising counsel to assist with the campaign. However, because everyone is working in unison on the campaign, efforts are streamlined, and the return on the investment is quite high.

Lastly, capital campaigns should be an exciting, dynamic time, not only for the organization but also for the *people* working and volunteering for it. It is wonderful and uplifting to have everyone working together for a common goal. It is very energizing and can give fundraising staff and volunteers the confidence they need to say to any prospect, "We need you and we need you *now.*" I use the expression, "It gets people to move off the dime." When individuals are being asked for a gift ordinarily, they may make that gift now, later, or much later. Capital campaigns give them a reason to make the gift *now* rather than later. The organization has a set of accomplishments it wants to carry out now, and support is needed now to make this happen. This circumstance is very persuasive and empowering, and it keeps the campaign asks flowing.

Phases of the Campaign

It is worth briefly outlining the phases of a capital campaign for those of you who are new to campaigns. These phases apply regardless of the size of the organization or the goal of the campaign.

Preparation Phase

The first phase is the *preparation*. During this period the organization plans for the campaign by initially identifying organizational needs that should be part of the campaign, ensuring that the campaign goal is realistic, identifying campaign leaders who will make leadership gifts and who can also identify and solicit lead gifts, and drafting an initial list of campaign prospects. A feasibility study tests all these initial efforts and, through data analysis, should refine the goal; determine the projects, programs, endowment, and unrestricted funds that campaign prospects may wish to support; and identify prospects who can make gifts at various levels in order to achieve the goal.

Once this work is completed a case statement should be drafted and approved by the leaders and capital campaign cabinet or committee. Exhibit 8.2 lists the elements that should be part of any case statement.

The case statement is the blueprint for the campaign. It must be shared with all campaign prospects so that they have a clear idea of how the organization began, where it wants to go, why it is unique, what priorities it has among its funding needs, and how its leaders will ensure the campaign is a success.

Silent Phase

The second stage of the campaign is the *silent phase.* During this phase the campaign is kept in-house, and top prospects are asked for their gifts before the campaign is announced. This makes these prospects feel like *insiders,* the supporters closest to the organization because they have been asked before anyone else and before the campaign has gone public. It makes them feel elevated because they become the internal stakeholders for the group.

EXHIBIT 8.2. *Elements of a Case Statement.*

1. The history of the organization, including the year of its formation and its mission, its leaders, and its accomplishments over the years

2. A few unique and distinguishing characteristics of the organization

3. The organization's future plans and the reasons why they are important

4. The campaign goal, detailing areas to be supported—such as the endowment, capital projects, and unrestricted funds for special needs—and giving the breakdown of the amount that needs to be raised for each area

5. The campaign time frame

6. The composition of the campaign committee, and the campaign positions locally, nationally, and internationally that make up the committee

The silent phase has two components. First, anyone who is a prospect for a leadership gift is asked to support the campaign. Leadership gifts are considered the biggest ones the campaign will receive and come from the organization's top prospects. Each lead gift is unique and achieving it requires a minicampaign within the campaign (Dove, 2000, p. 129). For instance in a $100 million campaign, all gifts of $1 million and up are considered leadership gifts, as are all gifts from the board and top administrators. The second part of the silent phase is that additional major prospects are asked until the organization has raised 50 to 60 percent of its goal. The group needs to ask all its top prospects first so that there is a solid commitment from the best prospects. This will set the example for others to make campaign gifts. Many prospects want to know what the top leadership and top prospects have done before they commit to the campaign. The time needed to acquire 50 to 60 percent of the campaign goal varies with each organization because it depends on how many top prospects the organization has and how many will commit to the campaign. This is why it is crucial for the organization to have layers of prospects to go to and not to rely just on top prospects. The campaign will need to take in a series of midsize and small gifts, whether those gifts are for $10,000, $25,000, or $250,000, depending on the organization, in order to be a success. As we will see later in this chapter in an illustrative gift chart, only a rich and deep prospect pool can make this happen.

Public Phase

The next phase is the *public phase,* or general phase, during which everyone is invited to participate. Generally, this is the time when direct-mail campaigns kick in, employees are asked to participate, and phone-a-thons occur. The most important feature of this phase is that now the campaign has gone public. Now the organization can announce internally and externally everything about the campaign—its goal, the amount raised to date, and with each donor's permission, the names of the people who have already made gifts, the levels at which they made these gifts, and what they selected to support. This is a great time to showcase how the campaign will be transformational for the beneficiaries, highlighting them in internal and external media. This is the home stretch for the campaign, and by going public now, it can and should gather new momentum for that final push to meet the goal.

Closing Phase

The last phase of the campaign is the *close.* In this phase all asks are followed up and solidified; all pledges are firmed up and tracked; prior gifts to the campaign are stewarded; publicity continues for all new gifts; leadership, volunteers, and staff are thanked and recognized; and a thorough report is done on all gifts and the amounts funded for each area of the campaign. Whether you are raising $10 million or $100 million, if you stick with and accomplish each phase, within your time frame, your campaign will be a success.

DEFINING CAMPAIGN GIFTS AND PROSPECTS

A campaign gift may be a large gift to the annual fund, a major gift, a planned gift, a gift in kind, or any combination of these gifts. Campaigns can and should be *fun and creative*. This is where the leaders, campaign cabinets or committees, volunteers, and fundraisers come together to brainstorm on the best and most attractive campaign gift opportunities, selecting for each prospect the opportunity that will not only meet her economic needs but, more important, will also recognize her passion and desire to be a part of the present and future success of the organization.

Even if you are working at a two-person operation, coordination of identifying and prioritizing campaign prospects for gifts is a must. I strongly suggest that in the planning stage of the campaign, all top individual, corporate, and foundation prospects be identified and that the best contact for each be listed, whether that be the president or CEO, a board member, the director of leadership gifts, the corporate and foundation officer, or the director of development. It is likely that the best person will be the one who has the closest personal relationship with the prospect. For instance, for individual prospects the list might include all board members and anyone who has supported your group over the last ten years at a major gift level or who has the capacity and interest to do so but has not given to date. For corporate and foundation support, it may be that these funders have given to your organization at a major level or that they have not given to date but the campaign goals and case statement fit squarely within their giving guidelines. Once you have this list then the prospects must be prioritized. Top prospects who can make lead gifts must be asked first, followed by the next tier of prospects. The best prospects to ask for campaign gifts first are those people who have the capacity to give the largest gifts and who have demonstrated a willingness and desire to support the campaign. The two must exist together. The next tier of prospects are people who could make gifts at the next level and who also have demonstrated a willingness to support the campaign.

The sizes of the lead gifts and the sizes of the remaining gift levels should be clearly defined in a gift chart. A gift chart details the number of gifts needed at each level in order to achieve the goal. Table 8.1

displays an example for a $100 million campaign. For this campaign the organization has determined that all gifts of $1 million or more will be considered lead gifts, followed by a middle tier of gifts ranging from $100,000 to $500,000, followed by numerous gifts of any amount up to $100,000. A gift chart can be drafted for any size campaign. For instance, if a group is raising $10 million during a capital campaign, it might determine that it needs one gift of $1 million, four gifts of $500,000, eight gifts of $250,000, and many gifts below this level to reach its goal.

A gift chart is a great tool to use when asking any prospect, and particularly top prospects, for a campaign gift because it illustrates that a collection of devoted, passionate investors can make the goal happen. It shows that there is a road map and that if one special person commits to the campaign followed by another dedicated person and then another, the campaign will be a success and each participant will have made it happen.

TABLE 8.1. *Table of Gifts Necessary to Raise $100 Million.*

Gift Level	Number of Gifts Needed	Providing	Cumulative Total
$10,000,000	1	$10,000,000	$10,000,000
$5,000,000	3	$15,000,000	$25,000,000
$2,500,000	5	$12,500,000	$37,500,000
$1,000,000	15	$15,000,000	$52,500,000
$500,000	25	$12,500,000	$65,000,000
$250,000	40	$10,000,000	$75,000,000
$100,000	60	$6,000,000	$81,000,000
$50,000	100	$5,000,000	$86,000,000
$25,000	200	$5,000,000	$91,000,000
$10,000	400	$4,000,000	$95,000,000
$5,000	800	$4,000,000	$99,000,000
Below $5,000	Many	$1,000,000	$100,000,000
Total gifts	1,649+		$100,000,000

PREPARING CAMPAIGN MATERIALS TO USE
DURING THE ASK

Every prospect who is asked for a campaign gift should have some written matter that explains the core objectives of the campaign. Put simply, the case statement should include the areas—projects, programs, endowment—that need to be funded; the amount that needs to be raised in each of those core areas; why there is a need for this funding; and the ask amount. This leads to another guiding principle:

Guiding Principle 8

Every campaign prospect must be asked for a specific amount, with guidelines on how to fund the gift and with a proposed time frame.

It is not enough to spell out all the organizational needs and ambitious goals that need to be met; in addition, the asker needs to give each and every prospect a specific ask amount. The leaders, campaign cabinet or committee, fundraising staff, and counsel also need to make logical, well thought out suggestions for how the gift should be made. Does the prospect have the liquid assets to make the gift or will it probably be a gift that is part outright and part planned? Many groups do a specific ask without carrying out the two steps of suggesting how and when the gift can be funded. Naturally, if the campaign is a seven-year campaign and everyone feels the prospect can make the gift now, then a shorter time frame, such as one to three years, should be suggested. Conversely, if this is a real stretch gift for the prospect but is doable as long as he has enough time to fulfill all the pledges, then logically a five- to seven-year time frame would be best for the prospect. Remember, each prospect should receive his own mini campaign, and each ask must be tailored to meet the unique needs of each prospect.

Although I highly suggest that each campaign ask be accompanied by materials in writing, this decision can vary depending on the size of the organization as well as the funds devoted to marketing the campaign. If you have the funds set aside for new brochures or folders into which you can insert a variety of campaign pieces, terrific. However, groups with small budgets or who are in the silent phase and will use their resources at a later time for campaign material have the option of using desktop publishing for simple yet effective presentations. Resource H is an example of materials used by many institutions, including Pace University, early in a capital campaign. These materials are prepared in the form of a laminated, flip-chart-style piece to be shared with each person who is asked for a lead gift early in the campaign. This piece can be produced entirely in-house and costs barely anything to make, and any group could use these materials as a model for a similar piece. They include the core campaign objectives, the funding needed for each objective, why the funding is needed, the campaign plan, a gift table, the progress to date, the *ask* (with suggested areas of funding), how and when the gift can be made, and the benefits of making a leadership gift. Prospects could take this campaign piece home, review it with family members or advisers, and refer to it when they had questions or comments. Any group can put something in writing to share with each prospect during the campaign ask or to leave with the prospect after the ask. If this is truly a very special time for your group, then highlight its significance by creating a campaign piece that will accompany the ask.

ASKING FOR CAMPAIGN GIFTS

The best way to see how this all comes together is to illustrate two sample campaign ask dialogues. Remember, add or subtract the zeros in the ask as necessary. The ask amount is not what is important. It is the way the ask is made, and how it is tailored for each prospect.

The first ask is for a $2 million lead gift for a hospital, made by the CEO and the vice president for development. The couple being asked have been long-time volunteers for the hospital and have been generous donors to the hospital's signature gala event.

> *CEO Carol:* Bill and Maria, please come in, and why don't we sit here at the conference table. I hope you didn't have too much trouble coming to see us. I heard there was a bad accident on the freeway.

Bill: Oh, not too bad. We gave ourselves extra time.

VP Charles: Good to see both of you. I'll sit over here. So tell me, do the two of you have any vacation plans this year?

Maria: Well, as soon as our eldest gets back from college, we plan to spend some time fishing and hiking upstate.

CEO Carol: Yes, you mentioned your place the last time we met. We are glad you could meet with us today. Our purpose is twofold—first, to thank you both for your outstanding leadership and voluntary activities with the hospital. Maria, we cannot tell you how invaluable you have been to our finance committee, and Bill, we certainly have appreciated your volunteering to be cochair of our gala.

Bill: Carol, we're glad to help the hospital. We wish we had more time to give, but we do what we can. And every time we come to the hospital we are reminded that our daughter had the best doctors and nurses caring for her.

CEO Carol: We never get tired of hearing that, thank you. Our other purpose is to bring you up to date on our capital campaign and to discuss your involvement with the campaign. Now I know you have heard at board meetings and from me personally that our goal is to raise $50 million to build a whole new state-of-the-art patient waiting area and to upgrade our department of surgery. This will be a transforming experience for the hospital. But in order for the campaign to be a success we need a few families to help us. Charles will share with you our progress to date.

VP Charles: Well, Carol and I have made four campaign asks totaling $10 million. We are working very hard to secure these commitments, and we are extremely optimistic that this will happen. Over the next few months we will be meeting with terrific supporters and enthusiasts for the hospital, like both of you, asking for significant gifts. As you can see, Carol and I and others will be very busy, but what an exciting time for the hospital.

CEO Carol: Bill and Maria, we turn to you now, two of our most trusted and treasured family members, and ask you to consider a transformational $2 million gift for the campaign. We are asking our top supporters like you to consider this stretch gift. We have a handout we prepared that you can look at later describing a variety of areas to which you can target your gift, the timing of your gift, and suggestions on how you can fund the gift. Of course we would be so pleased to provide you with a number of naming opportunities if you so desire. Your pledge would also have the exponential effect of raising the sights of other families and hospital supporters because it would give them an incentive to join with you to support the hospital in this significant way. Will you consider making this gift at this level for the hospital?

This ask has *flow* to it. Notice also that it takes the form of a natural dialogue that includes everyone; it is not, for example, a one-sided conversation between the CEO and just one of the donor couple, either Bill or Maria. This ask covers a lot of ground. First, it thanks both Bill and Maria for the time and expertise they have shared with the hospital, and then it turns to the point of the meeting. Bill and Maria knew in advance that the meeting would be about the campaign, but now the CEO tells them what specifically will be covered in this meeting. It is very important to get this out early in the meeting, otherwise too much time can be spent on small talk or current issues at hand, such as problems within the finance committee that Maria is serving on or with the gala that Bill is chairing. When the ask is being made of a couple or other family group, it is always a good idea to include the words *family members* in the ask. This brings the ask straight to the heart of the prospects' core values and their shared views on the importance of supporting the hospital. Lastly, this ask sets forth the progress to date on the campaign and asks Bill and Maria for a specific amount, followed by giving them information about the areas they could support, how the gift can be funded, the number of years over which the gift can be funded, and the recognition options they have. They are also told, best of all, that their gift will inspire other families and people to help the hospital, *now.*

The next example features the president and development officer of a public radio station who are asking a supporter for a $10,000 campaign gift. The supporter is in her forties, is very active with the radio station's membership committee, and has given yearly gifts over the past four years of $500, which were matched by her employer.

> *President Paul:* Monique, so good to see you again.

> *Director Jessica:* Yes, Monique, how are you? I hear we are keeping you quite busy on our membership committee.

> *Monique:* Yes, we have lots of new ideas to expand the membership. It's been fun. Sometimes my travel schedule gets in the way of attending all the meetings, but we have a good core group. Since I have been on the committee for a few years, I may step down soon to make room for others.

> *President Paul:* We thank you for your generous support. We are so glad that you take advantage of our matching gifts program. Also, thank you for all you have done to help us increase our base of supporters. Perhaps to the extent your schedule permits, we can keep you active and engaged with other activities for the radio station.

> *Monique:* You're quite welcome on both counts.

> *Director Jessica:* Will you be attending our annual singer/songwriter event next month?

> *Monique:* We'll see. I'm scheduled to be in Dallas that week but plans may change.

> *President Paul:* Monique, we certainly hope that you can attend should your plans change. Thank you for your time today. Our purpose is to once again thank you for all your hard work on the membership committee, to thank you for your past loyal support, and to update you on our capital campaign. You have been an inspirational leader for energizing new members to join the station. Thank you from all of us. Additionally, your steady gifts matched by your company for our membership drive has set such an example for others like you to give in this meaningful way.

> *Monique:* Any way I can help the station I will.

> *President Paul:* Monique, I would like to spend the rest of our time together bringing you up to date on our capital campaign and your prospective involvement. As you know from

my meeting with you and the committee, we are trying to raise $30 million, in part to increase our endowment and also to expand our format to include educational programs for children during school hours and to recruit new on-air talent for our political spotlight series. We have made good progress so far, and I'll let Jessica fill you in.

Director Jessica: Well, the president and I have been meeting with all our board members asking them for their leadership for the campaign. I'm happy to report that so far we have about 80 percent of them pledged for a total of $18 million for the campaign. In addition, we have other people we have met with and will be meeting with over the next six months who have expressed a desire and willingness to support the campaign in a significant way.

Monique: Wow, that's pretty good.

President Paul: Yes, we are very pleased with our progress to date. We wanted to speak with you personally because of your dedication to the station. Please know how important this campaign is for our future. We have such a positive momentum now and with the campaign we have the opportunity to strengthen our endowment and to expand our services to reach many more listeners. But in order for the campaign to be a success—and all indications are we are well on our way to reaching that success—we need our strong leaders like you to help us. Monique, Jessica mentioned that we would be meeting with other supporters over the next few months and many of them are leaders like you. We turn to you now and ask you to consider a $10,000 pledge for the campaign. This may be more than what you were thinking of, but we have some ideas on how to make this happen. Here is a handout I'd like to go over with you.

First, your gift can go to support the general endowment fund, or you can target your gift to support the educational program for our young listeners or the political spotlight series. Second, your gift can be pledged over five to seven years, and we will work with you and your company to get matching gifts to complete the pledge. Third, your pledge will help us to obtain similar gifts from other supporters. Your gift would be the wind beneath the wings of the campaign at this moment in time. Monique, will you consider making a $10,000 gift to the radio station?

As in the first ask, there is a nice balance in dialogue as well as a strong emphasis on thanking Monique for her gifts in prior years and for her years of service on the membership committee. I used this example for several reasons. First, I wanted to illustrate an ask of this size because, again, the zeros do not matter; it is the effectiveness of the ask that is important. Second, do not use age as a factor in prioritizing the tiers of asks. In this example, Monique's age may not seem to make her a good campaign prospect, but her dedication to the radio station makes her an excellent prospect. Third, always maximize and leverage matching gifts. In this example, Monique's prior gifts were matched by her employer, so it is highly likely that her campaign pledges will be matched as well. Her out-of-pocket costs may well be only half of the $10,000. If she pledged the gift for five years and her company made this match, then she would have to give only $1,000 a year. That is far more attractive and probably more doable than $2,000 a year. The bottom line is to be creative and flexible and to maximize the variety of ways people can give to the campaign.

CONCLUSION

Capital campaigns are a concentrated effort by everyone involved with the organization to raise a significant amount of money within a finite period of time. This concentrated focus can transform the future direction and stability of the organization. It gives all prospects and donors a reason to give *now*. Campaigns are *all inclusive* in that they can accept all forms of giving and combinations of these forms; they should co-exist with and complement the organization's strategic plan; they should be coordinated with existing annual, major, and planned gift fundraising programs in order to maximize gifts to the campaign; and at some time during each campaign, *all* prospects, administrators, and staff should be asked to support the campaign.

Well-structured campaigns include a feasibility study to set the parameters of the amount that can be raised, the areas to be funded, and the prospects that can or should make significant gifts to ensure the success of the campaign. A case statement needs to be drafted and adopted by the leaders and the campaign cabinet or committee. Perhaps the most essential step is to identify all top prospects—those with the *ability and willingness* to make leadership gifts—followed by a second and a third tier of prospects so that the organization has a rich prospect pool to draw on throughout the entire campaign. A gift chart detailing the number of gifts needed at each level and the number of prospects needed to make gifts at each level is an important and effective tool for benchmarking the progress of the campaign.

Every campaign prospect must be asked for a specific amount, with guidelines on how to fund the gift and with a proposed time frame. The ask should be accompanied with some written material that states the background and purpose of the campaign and the reason why each prospect's gift is important to the campaign. Even if the organization does not have a huge budget for large brochures, a simple desktop publishing packet, with pictures of the organization and a specific ask, including information about how the suggested gift can be funded within a suggested time frame, is a must. This packet has to be tailored to each prospect so that it emphasizes the importance and prominence of each person's participation in the campaign. Lastly, the person or team doing the ask must let the prospect know that each person's and each family's gift combined will have a powerful and transforming effect on the organization. It is the power of collective giving and the leveraging of present gifts to obtain future gifts that will keep the campaign on track and will make it a success.

LOOKING AHEAD

Now that we have addressed how to ask for each type of gift, the next step is to learn how to anticipate and to properly address the wide range of responses prospects will have when asked for each type of gift. Through numerous sample dialogues, the next chapter will prepare the reader to respond to any reaction or lack of reaction the prospect may have to each ask. Tips and suggestions on how to be the best listener possible, how to turn potential stumbling blocks into building blocks, and how to read the prospect's body language will be covered.

Addressing the Prospect's Response to the Ask

In my business the art of listening is crucial. Without it, my clients and I aren't effectively communicating. Likewise, when someone asks me to support a group that is near and dear to my heart, the art of listening takes the same precedence. If you're not listening to what I'm saying, how will you know why I would want to support you, or the best way to approach me?

—David Schellenberg, President, LinguiSearch, Inc., Philadelphia, Pennsylvania

EACH AND EVERY ASK WILL RESULT IN A UNIQUE response to the ask. How one handles that response is crucial to keeping the gift opportunity alive and viable. Only through preparation and anticipation of the prospect's response can any asker feel fully confident about answering the response. This chapter illustrates numerous responses to the ask, followed by suggested ways to address the prospect's concerns. These responses and suggestions apply to any ask, whether it be for a special event or community project, an enhanced annual fund gift, a major or planned gift, or an extraordinary capital campaign gift. This chapter also suggests ways to best prepare for the prospect's response, so that the conversation remains upbeat, the dialogue flows smoothly, and there are few surprises or unanticipated responses.

Preparing for the Prospect's Response

Askers should take a series of preparation steps before and during the ask to ensure that the ask and the response remain conversational. Exhibit 9.1 outlines these steps.

By now the asker or the asking team should know the prospect inside and out and therefore should be able to anticipate the prospect's response. For instance, if you are the asker and during cultivation the prospect has shared with you information about recent family illnesses or that his company may be moving to a new location or that his children are considering very expensive private universities, you should be alerted that this issue will come up when you ask for money. This is anticipating the prospect's response. It should not prevent or postpone the ask you were planning, but it should guide you in the overall preparation that needs to be done. *Sit down and make a list of what you (and anyone who is participating in the ask with you) think the prospect will say to the ask.* This is not to suggest that you will correctly guess the specific response all the time, but it is a powerful exercise for not getting caught completely off guard by the prospect's response.

Every asker must listen to the prospect's concerns and pay strict attention to the prospect's tone of voice and body language. *If you do not hear what the prospect's concerns are, how will you know what to say next?* The asker should let the prospect talk as long as she wants to, because then the asker will have the total picture of what is going on in the prospect's mind. As the asker is listening, he or she should be

---

EXHIBIT 9.1. *Steps for Keeping the Ask on Track.*

1. Anticipate the prospect's response.
2. Listen to every word the prospect is saying.
3. Pay close attention to the prospect's tone of voice and body language.
4. Avoid being overly aggressive in responding to the concerns.
5. Know that confidence, passion, and patience will lead to the gift.

---

careful not to interrupt the prospect or to show any negative reaction through body language. The goal is to keep the prospect focused on the ask and in the moment and to keep the atmosphere as conversational, inviting, and accepting as possible. The prospect's tone of voice and body language will also provide clues on her level of comfort. If the prospect is clearing her throat, looking down or out the window, tapping her foot, or turning red in the face, then the asker needs to address the prospect's concerns in a calm and soothing voice that exudes confidence and compassion.

Being overly aggressive will not win over any prospect. All too often people doing the ask are so wrapped up in the mechanics and script of the ask that they oversell the gift. When the prospect is finished speaking, then the asker or asking team needs to address all aspects of her concerns with confidence, passion, and patience. Closing gifts takes time, and it is highly unlikely that the prospect's first words after the ask will be, "All right," "OK," or, "Where do I sign?" Remember, these are people who love the organization and have demonstrated loyalty and commitment. They deserve to have the asker or asking team be 100 percent focused on their needs in a professional, polished, and passionate manner.

RESPONDING TO THE PROSPECT'S CONCERNS

Because there are so many responses one could receive when asking for money, the best way to illustrate the most examples is to categorize them. This way the asker can anticipate the prospect's concern, find the applicable category, and select the suggested responses that best address the prospect's needs and concerns.

The Ask Is Too High

1. "That's a lot of money."
   - "We understand perfectly, and believe us, we do not ask for this every day."
   - "You are but one of a handful of people we can turn to to ask for this very important gift."
   - "Is it the amount or the timing that seems troubling to you now?"

2. "That's too much money."

- "As a top supporter for the group, you are one of the few people we can turn to for this extraordinary gift opportunity."

- "We hope you take this as a compliment. Our intent was to make sure that you were among the first families to be offered this exciting and transformational opportunity."

- "We realize that our campaign goal is very ambitious, but we are asking our closest family members to consider a 'stretch gift' at this time. We would be happy to talk about the ways you can fund your gift as well as the timing for your pledge payments."

3. "What makes you people think that I have this kind of money?"

- "We can assure you that no one is going to determine what you will give but you and your family. We respect your honesty."

- "No one can know with certainty how much a person will give. Based on everything we have discussed over the past few months, your ideas and past support for *our* group, we wanted to ask you for this amount so that we could fulfill your desire to bring *our* group to new heights for our beneficiaries."

- "We would like you to consider this gift at this amount because you have expressed interest in this particular project [or program] in the past. We have no idea if you are willing to make this type of leadership gift, but as you are one of our top visionary leaders and long-standing volunteers, it was important that we come to you first."

Fear That Assets Are Insufficient to Make the Gift

1. "We don't think we can do this. Our daughter wants to go to a private school, and there is a chance that we may have to take care of my father's medical bills for quite some time."

- "Selecting the right school is an important decision. You must be very proud of your daughter right now."

- "We realize that taking care of the family comes first and thank you for sharing your concern over your dad's health. Just for the moment, putting those two things aside, how do you feel about the gift opportunity?"

- "Perhaps making this type of gift could actually help you instead of interfering with future family plans. Can we share with you some planned giving ways that could provide additional income to support your daughter and your father?"

2. "As you know, I'm nearing retirement so this may not be a good time."

   - "We know how hard you have worked, and we are most certain that you will be even busier during retirement! We cannot thank you enough for all you have done and continue to do for *our* group. We will be here with you to celebrate your retirement and to continue to keep you active with us."

   - "There are ways, through unique and individualized gift plans, that may actually increase your retirement income. May we share them with you?"

   - "We are sure that you have a lot to consider now and for the future. Let's plan to keep the discussion open, and we will touch base with you in a month or two. We are confident that we can help you during this transition to prospectively make a significant and meaningful gift to *our* organization."

3. "I'm a single person and may have to work for forty more years."

   - "Absolutely, and statistics show that we all will be living longer and working longer than our parents did. You have been an exemplary donor and tried-and-true volunteer. Please know that we had to ask you to join with others on this special occasion to make an important gift."

   - "You may be interested in gift plans that can give you income now or at a later time in life so that you will be taken care of for many years to come. Can we discuss them with you?"

- "What is important for all of us today is that you are interested in the gift opportunity we suggested, and we will work together for as long as it takes until you are comfortable with making this type of gift to *our* group."

Poor Timing

1. "You could not have asked at a worse time. My business is down, and I may not get the big contract I was hoping to get by the end of the month."

   - "Thank you for being honest. We are sure this was not an easy thing to share with us."

   - "We understand perfectly, and obviously this is not a good time for this discussion. Please know how we value you and your family. You have done so much for us, and now that we have so many great projects and programs going that are fulfilling our mission and strategic plan, we needed to include you in this very special time for *your* organization."

   - "Right now, if your business picked up and you were in the position to make a gift at this level, how do you feel about making this type of investment with *our* group?"

2. "As you know, the companies merged, and while I thought I could hang on to my job, that didn't happen."

   - "We are so sorry, and please know that if there is anything we can do to help we are here for you."

   - "When things come back on an upswing we can revisit this great gift opportunity. For now, we promise to stay in good contact with you as we have in the past. If there are any services we have that you feel may help you in your job search, please let us know."

   - "We are extremely grateful that under these circumstances you gave us the time to include you as one of our most treasured supporters. Our campaign [or fund drive] will continue for several years, and for now what is important is that at some point in time you would like to make this type of gift to *our* organization."

Wrong Ask

1. "I'm really not interested in supporting that project."

   - "Thank you for being so candid and honest with us today. Please know that we did think long and hard about the right gift opportunity for you. From our previous conversations we thought this gift opportunity would match your key interests."

   - "Can you tell us where your key interest lies within the organization? We want to hear more from you."

   - "Now that we know that you would rather make an unrestricted gift for the overall good work of *our* organization, we would be happy to share with you how unrestricted gifts benefit the entire organization."

2. "We are more interested in supporting a project and having a naming opportunity than in supporting the endowment."

   - "We understand that our donors choose to support things that interest them the most, and we are here to honor your philanthropic wishes and desires. Please know that many donors do like to support our endowment because it allows *our* organization to continue its good work well into the future and provides the financial backing for us to provide the very best services for our beneficiaries."

   - "Would you consider, with the gift level we suggested, splitting your gift and having a portion of your gift go toward the endowment to secure the future of *our* organization?"

Disagreement with the Organization

1. "Didn't you recently have a change in leadership? Now may not be the time to give. Let's wait and see what your new leader does."

   - "Yes, we do have a new president who will continue the important work of *our* organization. We ask you to think about the thousands of people we serve. We think you share our vision that they deserve continuous support from our loyal supporters like you."

- "We think you will be most pleased with the new director. Already she has had a tremendous impact with our beneficiaries and in our community. Here is some information on her, and we would love to have you meet with her sometime very soon."

2. "You recently received some pretty bad press. I don't think I want to make a major investment in your group now. There could be further fallout."

  - "We are here to listen to your views and to share with you the facts about the organization you have so generously supported over the years."

  - "We take your views very seriously and we would like to have our president [or CEO] personally contact you."

  - "A few donors shared your views, and in a short span of time we regained their trust. We are here to regain your trust and respect. We know that may take some time, but you are very important to us."

Give to Numerous Organizations

1. "We support a number of worthy causes, and making a larger gift to your group would give them less money."

  - "We understand perfectly. Many of our top supporters give to more than one organization."

  - "There are so many great groups to support. I have felt the way you do now, but after giving it much consideration, I simply had to make giving this larger gift a priority. We hope that you will think about this a bit and make it your priority as well."

  - "Our purpose here today is to introduce you to this exciting opportunity and to hear your thoughts about it. Obviously, you have interests with other groups, but right now, how do you feel about the gift opportunity we just described?"

2. "We are really overcommitted this year, so let me just give you our usual annual gift."

  - "First, let me thank you for your continued generous support for your group. Your gift to the annual fund makes it possible for us to provide programs and services to so many deserving people. However, the need we just described is urgent and is a top priority for the organization."

- "This request is really for our future needs and for the community. We welcome your annual support, but let's keep talking about the campaign. Gifts at this level will ensure the success of our organization for years to come."

- "We are asking everyone to consider what their combined extraordinary support can do for your organization. Right now, if what we have described for you is exciting and you want to join with others to make this happen, then we can apply your very special annual fund gift toward your commitment for this fantastic opportunity."

Need More Time

1. "This is really a serious request, and I'm going to need a lot of time before I can decide."

   - "Important decisions take time, and we are very happy to hear that you will give this gift opportunity serious consideration."

   - "How can we help you while you make this important decision? Do you need any additional information from us?"

   - "Right now, tell us how you feel about the gift opportunity we just described?"

   - "We would like to contact you in two weeks. If you need more time that is perfectly understandable, but we would like to listen to your thoughts and answer your questions as you reflect on this important and exciting gift opportunity."

2. "You are asking for a large amount of money, more than I have thought about giving. It will take us a long time to think this one over."

   - "We understand perfectly, and we are sure there are many factors you will want to consider. But right now, how do you feel about the gift opportunity we just described?"

   - "We are not surprised at all that you need some time, because this may be a larger gift than you might have anticipated at this time. As you know, this is an extraordinary time for our organization, and we need to rely on a handful of treasured families, like yours, to make this happen now."

- "We are asking our closest friends like you to stretch their giving a bit because we feel you share the dream that together we can accomplish great things for our beneficiaries."

Need to Discuss This with Family or Spouse or Attorney or Accountant

1. "I really should discuss this with my husband [or wife]."

   - "Absolutely, we want you to discuss this with important people in your life. We would be delighted to help you and your spouse make this important decision. Would our meeting with you two together be beneficial to reaching a joint decision?"

   - "Before I made my gift I felt exactly like you and that I needed to discuss this with my partner. Please take some time, and I would be delighted to be present or to answer any questions that you have in person or by telephone or e-mail."

2. "I have a meeting in a few weeks with my accountant, so let me discuss this with her and get back to you."

   - "That's terrific. I guess our timing is good to ask you for this special gift when you have a scheduled meeting with your accountant. We would welcome the opportunity to be a part of that meeting if you wish, or to answer any questions."

   - "You sound excited about this gift opportunity. We have found that if you share that excitement with others, such as your accountant, that she too will feel the magic of giving and will do everything to help you make it happen."

Stock Market or Economy Dictates the Gift

1. "I have been waiting for the past two quarters for the market to bounce back and it hasn't. I'm not in a position to make this type of financial commitment now."

- "I know how you feel. I have been watching the market also. But what we are hoping to accomplish today is that you are excited about the gift opportunity. Putting the stock market and the economy aside, we hope that this is something you would very much like to do."

- "What is important for now is that you intend to make the gift in the very near future. We can work with you so that you can fulfill your pledge payments when the timing is right for you. We are hoping to get our strong supporters like you on board so that we can go to others and seek their support."

2. "My portfolio is looking worse and worse each month. I want to wait until my stocks get stronger before I even think about making a gift this size."

   - "We absolutely understand, and hopefully the economy will be on an upswing very soon. And some people might question why we are asking our good supporters like you for a gift now. That's easy—because the needs of our beneficiaries don't go away, regardless of the economy. We think you share our vision that this is a special time for our organization, and we have but a handful of strong leaders like you to help us make this happen."

   - "Thank you for sharing that with us today. Please know that you and you alone control the timing of your prospective gift. We would never dream of asking you to make the gift while your stocks are not where you want them to be. We are asking you to seriously consider making a pledge to make the gift, and we can discuss at a later time when and how you can fund the gift."

More Comfortable Giving Lesser Amount

1. "You're off by a couple zeros. I really intended giving something in the ballpark of a smaller amount."

   - "That is wonderful that you were thinking of making a great gift to our organization. The reason why we asked you for this amount is because the program we just described requires funding at this level. We know from previous conversations that this program matches your key interest in the organization. Let's talk a bit more on how together we can make this happen."

- "Let's talk more about a variety of ways that you could make a gift this size. We have some ideas that you may or may not have considered."

- "We have heard this from a few donors, and once we spoke further about the funding needs of the project that would triple the benefits to our constituency and the community, they gave it great consideration and eventually pledged to make the gift over several years."

2. "That's really much more than I intended to give."

- "Thank you for your honesty. From what you said it sounds like you have given your next gift some thought. We really appreciate that. Let's explore how you could make this special gift over several years and in ways that are most beneficial for you."

- "You know, when I was asked to make a gift at this level I had the same reaction. But the president convinced me that this fundraising effort had such momentum and enthusiasm that it was attracting many good leadership gifts. My gift, combined with others, would serve to attract similar high-level gifts needed for the campaign."

ANALYZING THE RESPONSES TO THE PROSPECT'S CONCERNS

It is important to go over a few key concepts that are contained in these responses to the prospect's concerns. These concepts are listed in Exhibit 9.2.

First and foremost, your prospects should be thanked before, during, and after the ask. Even if you think prospects are really leaning in the direction of not making the gift because of the response, thank them. Thank them for their time, their past support, and their volunteerism and leadership, but most of all for their honesty. After all they did not have to tell you any personal details about themselves

---

EXHIBIT 9.2. *Key Concepts for Responses to Any Ask.*

1. At every opportunity thank the donor for his or her past support, leadership, and honesty.

2. Always use inclusive words—for example, our organization; shared vision.

3. Do not argue or try to be overly persuasive.

4. Share your insights about your own giving and the giving of donors who may have had the same reaction to the ask.

5. Tell the prospect why you are suggesting this gift, at this level, for this purpose.

6. Stay committed to the ask amount at this moment.

7. Have alternative ways the prospect can make the gift.

8. Do not be afraid to emphasize the priorities of the organization and the need for many gifts to fund these priorities.

9. If the timing is not right for the prospect to consider a gift or the prospect needs more time, suggest a definite time to meet or speak again to keep the ask alive.

10. Encourage all prospects to share the joy of giving by consulting with family members and legal or financial counsel.

---

or their situations. They are volunteering this very private and personal information, so the asker needs to be compassionate, sympathetic, and grateful that the organization has such a prospect who exemplifies integrity and honesty.

Just as it is important during the ask to use *we* instead of *I* so that the asker is truly representing the strength of the organization, the response to the prospect's concern should also use all-inclusive words such as *our,* as in *our organization.* Addressing the prospect's response should not be a *we* versus *you* conversation. It should be all inclusive. The asker and prospect should use words that speak to the good of the organization as well as the needs and priorities of the organization. This also serves to keep the prospect focused on the larger picture of what the group needs in order to be fiscally sound well into the future.

If the asker tries to argue with the prospect, even with the best intentions, the prospect is going to be turned off by this behavior. The same can be said for being overly persuasive or aggressive. This is not the time to come off as the only person in authority who knows what is good for the organization. It is the time to listen to the prospect and to discuss calmly and thoughtfully the issues the prospect has presented. The asker is not going to win the case of getting the gift if the prospect feels put upon or is uncomfortable. Being dedicated to the mission of the group, the beneficiaries it serves, and the need for substantial support is fine; however, this dedication should be conveyed in a compassionate and convincing manner.

Because the asker has made her or his own gift and probably has a fair amount of experience asking for these types of gifts, it is a good idea to share both experiences. When the asker was asked to support the group, no doubt there were issues the asker needed to address before the gift was made. So this is the time for the asker to share those experiences by saying, "Yes, I know how you feel. I had similar thoughts and this is how I reached my conclusion." Prospects are very receptive to those stories because now their problems or concerns are common and not so difficult to overcome. Likewise, if the asker has heard similar responses from other prospects, he or she might share, without using names, the stories of how those donors worked through similar concerns to the point of making the gift.

There will be times, no matter how well the asker knows the prospect, when the suggested gift is not a high funding priority or interest for the prospect. When this happens, the asker must let the prospect know why the gift opportunity was suggested. This shows that the asker thought long and hard about the right gift opportunity, the match, reflecting on past conversations during cultivation. In some instances the prospect may have suggested, inferred, or made outright statements that this was a project or program to support. Prospects are entitled to change their minds. A new and different project or program may have more appeal at this point in time. Of key importance is that the asker bring the conversation back to the gift opportunity by asking the prospect about the particular funding area the prospect would like to support. By asking the prospect questions about the key interest in the organization the asker will rejuvenate the prospect's enthusiasm for making a gift that is right for the prospect.

The next point is so important in responding to the prospect's concerns that it is a guiding principle.

Guiding Principle 9

At the initial ask, stay committed to the ask amount.

Let us place this in context. The asker or asking team has come up with a solid ask based on all previous contact and prospect research. The prospect's initial reaction is, "No, that is too high," or maybe even, "You folks are dreaming!" As tempting as it may be to lower the "price," do not. It is very natural to want to ask the prospect, "What gift level did you have in mind?" That is like nails on a chalkboard to me. Instead, the asker needs to set forth the following. First, the asker needs to acknowledge that, yes indeed, this is a high-end ask, and we do not ask this every day. That sets aside the idea that the organization brings in another prospect each day and asks for what feels like an exorbitant amount of money. Second, if the project or program to be funded needs a specific amount to start and to run for several years, then accepting a lesser amount will not accomplish a thing because there would then be insufficient funds for this type of gift. It is highly unlikely that the prospect would want to make a gift to a project or program that would come to a close shortly owing to insufficient funds. Third, do not be afraid that if the asker continues to stress the reasons why this amount is asked of this prospect and the need for gifts of this size, the prospect will make no gift at all. The same principle can be applied when the prospect hands the asker a check before the ask. Although the asker must thank the donor, the asker needs to get the ask that was intended for this prospect back on track. This could well include suggesting that the initial check the prospect is offering be a partial payment or the first pledge payment of the suggested gift. The bottom line is that during the first meeting of the initial ask, the asker should *stick to the ask amount and ask the prospect to think about it before giving a definitive answer.* Then the asker should set a time immediately to meet to answer questions.

While sticking to the ask amount, showing creativity and flexibility in the ways the gift can be funded and the years over which it can be funded goes a long way to closing the gift. Show the prospect, with the aid of a small chart, how gifts can be made outright, through a planned gift, or through a combination of both methods, and also display a time frame of one year, three years, or five years. This has enormous impact and practicality for the prospect. It makes the gift more doable and removes hesitation surrounding the ask amount.

Many prospects welcome the opportunity to hear about the organization's priorities because it gives them a clear idea of where the organization is headed and focuses their attention on helping the group reach those goals. Especially when your group is in campaign mode, you must share these priorities by putting them in your case statement. Offer your prospects the chance to divide their gift so that it will fund one or more of the organization's priorities and also support an area that is near and dear to their hearts.

The higher the ask amount, the more time prospects will need to consider the offer. This is why it is so important (as discussed in detail in Chapter Ten) that at the close of the initial ask meeting a specific time be established to meet again or to call. The length of time chosen must serve both the needs of the prospect to reflect and the needs of the organization to gather support within a specified period. This is the only way the gift opportunity can stay in the forefront of the prospect's mind. Otherwise months and sometimes a year or years will pass with no resolution to the ask.

Lastly, *do not lose sight of the joy of the moment.* When prospects say they need to share the idea with loved ones, this is truly a special moment. It means that prospects want to bring the people they are closest to in on this very important decision. The same is true when prospects wish to consult legal counsel and accountants. Many, many fundraisers feel that once the gift opportunity is in the hands of these experts they will convince the prospect not to make the gift. This does happen sometimes, but what good would it do for the asker to say, "We really suggest you make this decision on your own"? That is why it is so important for the asker to suggest that she or he come with the prospect to the meeting with these experts or at the very least be available for questions or to send backup materials. It is also recommended that each asker in this situation tell the prospect that it is important to convey to these experts the prospect's desire to make the gift and the prospect's passion and commitment to the organization. This way there is no doubt that that expert's role is to lend advice and to assist the prospect in making the gift that best suits the prospect's financial situation and philanthropic dreams.

CONCLUSION

The most effective ways to prepare for the prospect's response before and during the ask are to anticipate the response, listen carefully to what the prospect is saying, pay close attention to the prospect's tone of voice and body language, avoid being overly aggressive, and know that all good gifts come if the ask is delivered with confidence, passion, and patience. It is all about focusing carefully on the prospect with undivided attention. These people have demonstrated loyalty and commitment to the organization and deserve to have the unwavering attention of the asker or asking team.

Regardless of what the prospect has said in response to the ask, it is critically important that he be thanked for his time, and where applicable, his past support, leadership, and honesty. Whenever possible use inclusive words during and after the ask, such as *we* and *our.* Inclusive words place the prospect in the position of being a significant person to the organization. Avoid at all costs a *we* versus *you* conversation.

The asker or asking team needs to be open and honest with the prospect. Let the prospect know about similar donors who had the same hesitations or concerns about making a large gift and how these issues were resolved. The asker must be forthright but not belligerent or overly aggressive in asking for a stated amount. It is vitally important that the asker or asking team does not back off the ask amount, especially when the prospect responds that the amount is too large or that he had a smaller gift in mind. The asker or asking team needs to stay committed to the ask amount and be creative and flexible on how and when the prospect can make the gift. Two simple steps, *listen* and *make suggestions,* will keep the dialogue open and the prospect more willing to explore alternative ways to make the gift happen.

LOOKING AHEAD

The last chapter focuses on how to follow through with each and every ask. It closes the process that moves from the actual ask through responding to the prospect's concerns to all the follow-up steps that need to be covered in order to secure the gift. An ask without the follow-up will result in no gift. The final chapter also recaps the importance of the ten guiding principles for any ask, so that the reader will have the total picture of the wonderful world of asking for money.

CHAPTER

Following Through with Each Ask

There is a natural bond between individuals and their college and university. They are positive and energized about their educational experience and the impact it has made on their lives. My task is to match those interests with the needs of the institution so that a gift, regardless of amount or purpose, is a win-win for both the institution and the individual. If the donor feels positive about the impact of their gift, they are more likely to stay involved and to also consider additional gifts. Cultivation is the key to a successful ask and relationship.

—David A. Caputo, President, Pace University, New York, New York

IMPORTANT STEPS NEED TO BE TAKEN AFTER each ask to keep the ask in the forefront of the prospect's mind and ensure that questions are answered and additional material or expertise is provided. Because each person being asked will respond in a unique way, a check-off list of what to do after each ask is essential. This chapter describes these steps. It also explores how to juggle and balance your time so that you can make several asks while following up on each and every ask. The reality is always that after one ask is made, many more asks and many important follow-ups to previous asks have to be made. Without an organized system to manage the asker's time, things can slip through the cracks, resulting in too much time elapsing between the ask and the follow-through. The more time that tran-spires between the ask and the follow-through, the harder it will be to refocus the prospect on the gift opportunity.

Lastly, this chapter will recapitulate the ten guiding principles. The full list of the principles makes up a total picture of the ask and reinforces the essential elements of any ask.

THE NEXT STEPS AFTER EACH ASK

A check-off list of tasks must be completed after each and every ask. What good would an ask be if no one followed up? This is not the time when you want to leave the ball in the prospect's court. *Out of sight is out of mind and that is not where the asker wants to be.* Even though prospects may well need time to consider a variety of things and to reflect on the relationships they have had with people in the organization, the asker who follows the steps listed in Exhibit 10.1 will ensure that the ask remains a high priority for each prospect.

Immediately at the close of the meeting in which the prospect has been asked for a gift, the asker or asking team needs to look the prospect directly in the eyes, and with all the warmth and sincerity possible, thank her for her time, for her past support and volun-teerism, and most important, for giving the gift opportunity serious consideration. This thank-you needs to be followed up with a formal letter or personal note *no less than twenty-four hours after the prospect has been asked.* The letter or note should include more than a thank-you for time; it should trickle in something important or even hu-morous that was discussed at the meeting. For instance, if the prospect just returned from a fabulous vacation, then start the letter or note with, "It was so good to see you yesterday and to hear about your very adventurous vacation. I will have to keep that in mind for future vacation destinations." If the prospect revealed some personal discussion about family or business, then start the letter or note with, "It was great to see you yesterday, and congratulations on your new grandson," or, "Please keep us apprised of your company's prospec-tive acquisition of a new line of semiconductors." It keeps the ask per-sonal and important, and it shows that the asker or asking team really listened and focused on the prospect throughout the entire course of the meeting.

EXHIBIT 10.1. *Checklist for the Next Steps After the Ask.*

1. Thank the prospect in person and in writing.

2. Convey to the prospect the importance of this gift to the organization and the urgency of the gift.

3. Set a specific date, time, and place to further discuss the gift.

4. Send additional information where appropriate, within the shortest time possible.

5. Provide additional expertise, or speak with the prospect's family or advisers where appropriate.

6. Fine-tune or clarify the gift proposal if the prospect has requested this.

7. Continue to meet with the prospect, to telephone him, and to send him relevant materials, articles, and brochures if he has told you that he will need much time to reach a decision or if he has said he simply cannot give any more to the organization.

8. Convey to the prospect that her gift will be joined with others, so that the organization is portrayed as fiscally sound.

9. Neutralize any misgivings the prospect may have expressed about the organization or previous gifts to the organization so that focus and energy remain on the present gift opportunity.

10. Maintain a positive attitude throughout the follow-through and treat each prospect as if he has already said yes to the ask.

At the end of the meeting and in the follow-up letter or note, the asker or asking team needs to convey the importance and the impact this prospective gift will have for the organization and its beneficiaries. The prospect should not feel that if the gift is not made it's no big deal because there are plenty of other potential supporters who can make a gift of this size. Similarly, convey a sense of *urgency* about the gift. If the ask is for a fundraising event such as a community block event or for a campaign gift, then urgency is easy to convey because the organization needs to raise a precise amount within a tightly de-fined time. It is harder to convey urgency, and one must be creative when the ask is for an enhanced annual fund gift or a planned or major gift without a specific campaign or fund drive. Put yourself in the prospect's shoes. He could be thinking, "It's not a big deal whether I make the gift now, in a few months, or a few years; the or-ganization will receive it eventually." This is why it is very important with any ask that a sense of urgency for the gift be clearly spelled out for the prospect. For instance, tell the prospect why your group needs a particular number of gifts at this particular level *now* or why it has a need to increase the number of heritage society members and life in-come gifts *now*. Tell him how these gifts are needed now so that the organization can fulfill its mission, expand its services and commu-nity outreach, or achieve the important goals in its strategic plan.

At the conclusion of the meeting in which the prospect is asked for a gift, *make sure that a date, time, and place are set for the asker or asking team to speak or meet again with the prospect.* Ideally, the next meeting or conversation will be within a week or two. Some prospects will share their own preference for the time of the meeting, which is usually further away than the asker or asking team wants to hear. If this happens, then ask the prospect if you can mail, e-mail, or fax in-formation, so that communication can occur while the prospect thinks things over. Remember, it will be much harder to get the ask back on track once a month or more goes by from the date of the ask. Use whatever communication methods are best for the prospect, but make sure some form of communication occurs if the prospect resists a follow-up meeting within a week or two.

If the prospect has specifically requested that you send additional material, speak or meet with family or advisers, or change the pro-posal to add or delete certain parts, then make sure this happens within one week. Providing additional material and tweaking the proposal are all things that are within the control of the asker or ask-ing team, so there is no reason why this cannot occur within one week. The harder part is scheduling meetings with the prospect's fam-ily or advisers, because in most instances the prospect is more com-fortable if she makes these arrangements. Now the ball is in the prospect's court. Do not let it sit there too long. *Be gentle yet persistent by calling or e-mailing the prospect to schedule those meetings.* Granted, there will be times when scheduling a meeting or conversation with the family or advisers will take some time. The point here is that the asker can provide gentle reminders for the prospect that as soon as this meeting is scheduled the happier the prospect will be because her closest circle of family members or advisers will be helping her to make a very important decision.

Sometimes the prospect just needs a whole lot of time before deciding on the gift, or perhaps he simply has said that right now he cannot give any more to your organization. The key in both instances is to keep communication in a variety of ways at an all-time high and to continue strong cultivation. Closing a gift or getting a prospect to the point of reconsidering a gift when the initial answer to the ask was no can take months and even years. You must schedule periodic contact with the prospect. This is a time when the gift opportunity can really lose momentum and steam and when you can let a good donor drift. Use a tickler file, donor database system, or your personal calendar notation system to remind yourself that these prospects need some type of communication from you or others in the organization at least once a month. Ideally, try to meet or speak with these prospects and donors once a month. If their schedules do not permit a personal visit or telephone call, then set a date once a month when you send them newsletters, brochures, or annual reports with personal notes; send newspaper or magazine articles on their hobbies; pass along press releases or any media coverage on your organization; send e-mails, where appropriate, about recent gifts and events; and encourage them to visit the organization's Web site for the latest updates on the organization.

Many prospects need encouragement in the form of a reminder that their gift will not be the one and only gift of this size for the organization. No one likes to be a lone wolf in supporting an organization. Prospects may feel like lone wolves because they are alone or accompanied by just a family member when they meet with the asker or asking team. It is a private and special moment, and they cannot sense how many others have given or will give. This concern should be addressed in the following manner. Share with these prospects news of each and every gift your group receives that is similar in size to the gift the prospect is considering. If you do not have the other donors' permission to use their names, then talk just about the size of the gift and what that will do for your group. Preferably, call each prospect and share this good news. Let the prospects hear the excitement and enthusiasm in your voice. People want to give to forward-moving trains, to winning and successful organizations. This sends the clear message to prospects that now is the time they should invest with the organization because their gift, combined with others, will attract other meaningful and significant gifts.

Inevitably, at some point you will be dealing with prospects who really want to make the gift but who have some prior misgiving about the organization. It could be a disagreement about what exactly was paid or not paid on their past pledge, for example. In an ideal world the prospect's bookkeeping would mirror the organization's database, but that does not happen all the time. Some prospects may feel that their prior gifts were not stewarded with the amount of attention they deserved. Some prospects have very strong political views, and they may not like a board member or two, a lecturer who was invited to speak at the organization, or a project or program that they feel strays from the mission of the organization. Under these circumstances the best steps to follow are to *listen to the prospect, address the concerns honestly and openly, and invite the prospect to meet with others in the organization or other prospects who felt the same way but who now feel different and support the organization.* Do not, however, promise anything that violates the organization's mission or policies. I add this caveat because all too often the asker is so eager to get a positive response to the ask that he or she may be tempted to stretch the bounds of what askers can do on behalf of the organization. For instance, one should not tell the prospect that he will receive notification prior to any speaker selection when that selection may be under the exclusive provenance of a committee, or that he can have a special event recognizing his prior gift when gifts at that level do not receive that level of attention. Do your best to listen and to neutralize the situation without coming across as patronizing the prospect or just paying lip service to his prior issue with the organization.

Lastly, maintain a positive disposition throughout the entire follow-through process. This takes discipline and attention but it is worth it. In all of your follow-up communications with prospects, treat them every day as if they have said or are about to say yes to the ask. Even if they sound less optimistic or constantly tell you that their financial or personal situation is not getting any better, remain upbeat.

The last thing you want is to have your tone of voice or energy sink to the prospect's level when that level is less enthusiastic than yours. This will surely lead to a long postponement of the gift and maybe even a no to the gift opportunity. Do whatever it takes to prepare yourself before you see, call, e-mail, or write to the prospect. What works for me is that when I call prospects I stand up. I have much more energy standing up than I do when confined to the chair behind my desk, and I can project more positive energy this way. When I am ready to e-mail or write to a prospect, I either revisit the prospect record in my organization's database or take something out of the person's file that places me in the moment with him or her. This is all about customer service and personalized attention.

This brings us to the last guiding principle.

Guiding Principle 10

The ask without the follow-through will result in no gift.

Use the steps detailed in Exhibit 10.1. Make a check-off list for each prospect to ensure that no step is missed and that you and others are on track with steady communication with each prospect so that all asks will result in yes.

HOW TO JUGGLE AND BALANCE TIME AFTER EACH ASK

One of the hardest things for anyone who wants to raise money is learning how to strike the right balance between organizing time to ask for gifts and then staying on track with all the steps after the ask. We have just explored the checklist of the next steps that need to done after each ask to ensure that too much time does not elapse between the ask and the resolution to the ask. *Time and balance are essential components of the ask.* For instance, you do not want to be in the position of spending 75 percent of your time asking for gifts and only 25 percent doing the follow-through. If that happens, chances are you will carry out the follow-up with only a handful of the people you asked for gifts.

There is no formula that applies uniformly to all fundraisers for determining the appropriate number of asks per month or year in relation to the number of outstanding asks that need follow-ups. However, throughout this book I have given you guidelines for gauging how many asks the asker or asking team can or should do for each type of ask, considering many factors such as the size of the organization, number of askers to do each ask, time available, budget, and administrative help. Now it is time to add some structure to the amount of *time available for the asker or asking team to do the follow-through*. Take the "Chart to Track the Time Available for Asks" that appears in Chapter Three, Exhibit 3.3, and add one more column to it: "Time Available for Follow-Through After the Ask." When askers have completed this column, you may find that the people you need to make the initial ask do not have the same quantity of time to do the follow-through or that follow-up is something they do not like to do or want to do. Many board members, committee members, or donors who want to be "in on the ask" feel their job is done once the ask is made and now it is up to the fundraising staff and the president or CEO to do the follow-up. They want to hand off to the fundraiser the responsibility of doing whatever it takes to close the gift.

Whenever possible, encourage all those involved with cultivating the prospect and with making the ask to *stay active* with the prospect. Prospects are likely to feel they have been dropped if those whom they talked to during the cultivation stages and the ask are not part of the follow-through. Convince your leaders that you are inches away from getting the gift but you need just a "tad more of their time" to make it happen. Of course, if you do find yourself in a situation where it is up to you as the fundraiser to pick up the process and to coordinate and carry out the follow-through, then you need to factor in a significant amount of time to coordinate all the necessary follow-up steps.

These are suggestions and guidelines on how to juggle and organize time during and after the ask. Again, it is one of the hardest tasks to get right on a consistent basis because even though the asker or asking team may be able to control the course of the ask meeting and the setting and tone of the ask, from that moment on *it is the prospect who can require anything from a little of your time to all of your time.* Some prospects are *low maintenance* but others are *very high maintenance*. Plot your time as best you can, and stay flexible. If you find that you are overwhelmed and things are getting way out of control, then you need to cut back on the number of asks and concentrate on the follow-through, and when you see a clearing, get back to asking for gifts. Stay positive, learn from your mistakes, communicate constantly with everyone involved with the ask and the follow-through, and you will have learned the fine art, the dance, of how to juggle it all.

THE TEN GUIDING PRINCIPLES FOR ANY ASK

I can think of no better way to conclude than to ask you to review the ten guiding principles presented in this book. They provide a full and complete picture for any ask. I *really* hope that you walk away with many things from this book, but most of all, these ten guiding principles should be your road map for all your asks.

The Ten Guiding Principles for Any Ask

1. The more personal and sincere you are with the people you are cultivating, the quicker you will be able to make the ask.

2. Every prospect must be treated separately and distinctly.

3. Anyone asking for a gift must make his or her own gift first.

4. Ask for a specific amount for a specific purpose.

5. Consistent givers can and will make larger gifts.

6. Always use *we* instead of *I* in any ask. *We* connotes that the ask is being done with all the strength and backing of the organization.

7. Any organization's planned giving program must be coordinated with all other fundraising programs.

8. Every *campaign prospect must be asked for a specific amount*, with guidelines on how to fund the gift and with a proposed time frame.

9. At the initial ask, stay committed to the ask amount.

10. The ask without the follow-through will result in no gift.

Well, there you have it! Follow and practice these ten guiding principles, go over the exercises and numerous dialogues and examples in this book, and you will be ready, focused, and energized to ask for gifts in your own winning style.

Please feel free to e-mail me your success stories at lfredricks@ pace.edu. Believe me, I learn as much from you as you learn from me. In this wonderful world of philanthropy, we all need to share our experiences so that together we can feel proud that in some small but significant way we did make a difference!

RESOURCE A
Sources for Fundraising Software

Access International
423 Columbia St.
Cambridge, MA 02141
(617) 494-0066

Advance Solutions International Inc.
901 North Pitt St., Ste. 200
Alexandria, VA 22314
(800) 727-8682

Portfolio, from Amergent, Inc.
9 Centennial Dr.
Peabody, MA 01960
(800) 370-7500

Best Software
313 East Anderson Ln., Ste. 120
Austin, TX 78752
(800) 647-3863

Blackbaud Inc.
2000 Daniel Island Dr.
Charleston, SC 29492
(800) 443-9441

Campaign Associates
195 McGregor St., Ste. 410
Manchester, NH 03102
(800) 582-3489

Convio
11921 North Mopac Expwy., Ste. 200
Austin, TX 78759
(512) 652-2600

Donor 2
8848-B Red Oak Blvd.
Charlotte, NC 28217
(800) 548-6708

eTapestry.com
9201 Harrison Park St.
Indianapolis, IN 46216
(888) 739-3827

Helix Ltd.
7300 Warden Ave., Ste. 503
Markham, ON L3R 9Z6
(877) 479-3780

PledgeMaker, by Softrek
30 Bryant Woods North
Amherst, NY 14228
(800) 442-9211

RESOURCE **B**

Prospect Research Providers
and Web Sites

Amergent
9 Centennial Dr.
Peabody, MA 01960
(978) 531-1800

Bentz Whaley Flessner
7251 Ohms Ln.
Minneapolis, MN 55439
(952) 921-0111

Claritas
1525 Wilson Blvd., Ste. 1000
Arlington, VA 22209
(800) 234-5973

FocusWise, Inc.
4112 Roenker Ln., Ste. 100
Virginia Beach, VA 23455
(888) 704-5700

iWave Information Systems
PO Box 143
Charlottetown, PE C1A 1K8
Canada
(800) 655-7729

Magic Inc.
133 Carnegie Way, Ste. 1200
Atlanta, GA 30303
(877) 54MAGIC

www.edgaronline.com

www.stockmaster.com

www.finance.yahoo.com

www.realestate.yahoo.com

www.10kwizard.com

www.wealthengine.com

www.hoovers.com

www.internet-prospector.org

www.wealthid.com

www.foundationcenter.org

RESOURCE C

AFP Code of Ethical Principles and Standards of Professional Practice

STATEMENT OF ETHICAL PRINCIPLES

Adopted 1964; amended October 2004

The Association of Fundraising Professionals (AFP) exists to foster the development and growth of fundraising professionals and the profession, to promote high ethical standards in the fundraising profession and to preserve and enhance philanthropy and volunteerism.

Members of AFP are motivated by an inner drive to improve the quality of life through the causes they serve. They serve the ideal of philanthropy; are committed to the preservation and enhancement of volunteerism; and hold stewardship of these concepts as the overriding principle of their professional life. They recognize their responsibility to ensure that needed resources are vigorously and ethically sought and that the intent of the donor is honestly fulfilled. To these ends, AFP members embrace certain values that they strive to uphold in performing their responsibilities for generating philanthropic support.

AFP members aspire to:

- practice their profession with integrity, honesty, truthfulness and adherence to the absolute obligation to safeguard the public trust;
- act according to the highest standards and visions of their organization, profession and conscience;
- put philanthropic mission above personal gain;
- inspire others through their own sense of dedication and high purpose;
- improve their professional knowledge and skills, so that their performance will better serve others;
- demonstrate concern for the interests and well-being of individuals affected by their actions;
- value the privacy, freedom of choice and interests of all those affected by their actions;
- foster cultural diversity and pluralistic values, and treat all people with dignity and respect;
- affirm, through personal giving, a commitment to philanthropy and its role in society;
- adhere to the spirit as well as the letter of all applicable laws and regulations;
- advocate within their organizations, adherence to all applicable laws and regulations;
- avoid even the appearance of any criminal offense or professional misconduct;
- bring credit to the fundraising profession by their public demeanor;
- encourage colleagues to embrace and practice these ethical principles and standards of professional practice; and
- be aware of the codes of ethics promulgated by other professional organizations that serve philanthropy.

STANDARDS OF PROFESSIONAL PRACTICE

Furthermore, while striving to act according to the above values, AFP members agree to abide by the AFP Standards of Professional Practice, which are adopted and incorporated into the AFP Code of Ethical Principles. Violation of the Standards may subject the member to disciplinary sanctions, including expulsion, as provided in the AFP Ethics Enforcement Procedures.

Professional Obligations

1. Members shall not engage in activities that harm the members' organization, clients, or profession.

2. Members shall not engage in activities that conflict with their fiduciary, ethical, and legal obligations to their organizations and their clients.

3. Members shall effectively disclose all potential and actual conflicts of interest; such disclosure does not preclude or imply ethical impropriety.

4. Members shall not exploit any relationship with a donor, prospect, volunteer, or employee for the benefit of the members or the members' organizations.

5. Members shall comply with all applicable local, state, provincial, and federal civil and criminal laws.

6. Members recognize their individual boundaries of competence and are forthcoming and truthful about their professional experience and qualifications.

Solicitation and Use of Philanthropic Funds

7. Members shall take care to ensure that all solicitation materials are accurate and correctly reflect their organization's mission and use of solicited funds.

8. Members shall take care to ensure that donors receive informed, accurate, and ethical advice about the value and tax implications of contributions.

9. Members shall take care to ensure that contributions are used in accordance with donors' intentions.

10. Members shall take care to ensure proper stewardship of philanthropic contributions, including timely reports on the use and management of such funds.

11. Members shall obtain explicit consent by donors before altering the conditions of contributions.

Presentation of Information

12. Members shall not disclose privileged or confidential information to unauthorized parties.

13. Members shall adhere to the principle that all donor and prospect information created by, or on behalf of, an organization is the property of that organization and shall not be transferred or utilized except on behalf of that organization.

14. Members shall give donors the opportunity to have their names removed from lists that are sold to, rented to, or exchanged with other organizations.

15. Members shall, when stating fundraising results, use accurate and consistent accounting methods that conform to the appropriate guidelines adopted by the American Institute of Certified Public Accountants (AICPA)* for the type of organization involved. (* In countries outside of the United States, comparable authority should be utilized.)

Compensation

16. Members shall not accept compensation that is based on a percentage of contributions; nor shall they accept finder's fees.

17. Members may accept performance-based compensation, such as bonuses, provided such bonuses are in accord with prevailing practices within the members' own organizations, and are not based on a percentage of contributions.

18. Members shall not pay finder's fees, or commissions or percentage compensation based on contributions, and shall take care to discourage their organizations from making such payments.

Thank-You Letter After the Ask

Dear David:

It was an absolute delight spending time with you yesterday and we are so appreciative of the time you so generously gave us. We particularly enjoyed hearing about the details of your recent trip to Vancouver and the success you and the family had catching salmon. The next time, do not hesitate to bring us back a sample!

David, as we discussed, the time could not be better for our organization to reach out to many of our top supporters like you, and ask you to consider making a significant gift of $250,000 to support our endowment. As a successful and esteemed business community leader, you know how important it is for an institution to be fiscally sound now and for years to come. That does not happen overnight, but it does happen when people like you, who are dedicated and devoted to our mission, know and appreciate the need for a sound endowment. It can and will position our organization, the one you helped build and shape, to have a greater and more meaningful outreach to our beneficiaries, as we discussed in our gift proposal.

Yesterday, we could not set another date to meet because you needed some time to consult your travel calendar. I will call your assistant in a few days to set the most convenient time for you to meet with us again, preferably within this month.

David, on behalf of all the people who have benefited from your generosity, thank you for being part of our family.

Sincerely,
[*Name and Title*]

RESOURCE E
Notification of Bequest

NOTIFICATION OF BEQUEST

Today's date _____

Name _____

Home address _____

Work address _____

Home phone _____ Work phone _____

Date of birth _____ Social Security number _____

Bequest is in _____ Will _____ Revocable trust _____ Other

Please check appropriate box:

[ ] Outright bequest

[ ] Contingent bequest

Approximate value of gift: $ _____

Purpose of gift if not for the general purposes of the charity:

_____

_____

Execution date of will/trust _____

Attorney of record _____   Phone _____

Address _____

Executor of estate _____   Phone _____

Address _____   Phone _____

Relation to you _____

[ ] I have attached a photocopy of the relevant portion of my will or revocable trust.

Please return to: [*Title*]
                     [*Charity name*]
                     [*Address*]
                     [*Phone number*]
                     [*E-mail*]

Sample Prospect Materials
for a Charitable Gift Annuity

Prepared for:
Josh Appleton
November 5, 2004

Deduction Calculations

Taxation of Gift Annuity Payments	**Cash**

6.3% Charitable Gift Annuity

ASSUMPTIONS

Annuitant	[6/19/1936] 68
Date of gift	11/5/2004
Principal donated	$10,000.00
Cost basis	$10,000.00
Annuity rate	6.3%
Payment schedule	quarterly
	at end

CALCULATIONS

Charitable Deduction	$3,578.20

Number of full payments in first year	0
Days in payment period (10/1/2004 to 12/31/2004)	92
Days in credit period (11/5/2004 to 12/31/2004)	57

Annuity	$630.00
Quarterly payment	$157.50
First partial payment	$97.58

BREAKDOWN OF ANNUITY

	Tax-Free Portion	Ordinary Income	Total Annuity
2004 to 2004	56.79	40.79	97.58
2005 to 2021	366.66	263.34	630.00
2022 to 2022	131.79	498.21	630.00
2023 onward	0.00	630.00	630.00

After 17.5 years, the entire annuity becomes ordinary income.

IRS discount rate is 4.6%

These calculations are for illustration purposes only and should not be considered legal, accounting, or other professional advice. Your actual benefits may vary depending on the timing of the gift.

WHAT IS A CHARITABLE GIFT ANNUITY?

A charitable gift annuity is a simple contract between you and the charity.

In exchange for your irrevocable gift of cash, securities, or other assets, the charity agrees to pay one or two annuitants you name a fixed sum each year for life. The older your designated annuitants are at the time of the gift, the greater the fixed income the charity can agree to pay. In most cases, part of each payment is tax-free, increasing each payment's after-tax value.

Payments may be made annually, semiannually, or quarterly.

EXAMPLE

If you irrevocably transfer $10,000 in cash to the charity in exchange for a $630 annuity for an annuitant, age 68,

BENEFITS INCLUDE

1. You will qualify for a federal income tax deduction of approximately $3,578. Your deduction may vary modestly depending on the timing of your gift. Note that deductions for this and other gifts of cash and nonappreciated property will be limited to 50% of your adjusted gross income. You may, if necessary, take unused deductions of this kind over the next five years, subject to the same 50% limitation.

2. Your designated annuitant will receive fixed payments in quarterly installments totaling $630 each year for life. In addition, $366.66 of each year's payments will be tax-free for the first 17.5 years.

3. Your estate may enjoy reduced probate costs and estate taxes.

4. You will provide generous support of the charity.

Prepared for Josh Appleton   November 5, 2004

These calculations are for illustration purposes only and should not be considered legal, accounting, or other professional advice. Your actual benefits may vary depending on the timing of the gift.

Sample Prospect Materials for a Charitable Remainder Unitrust

Prepared for:
Clyde & Matilda Tucker
November 5, 2004

Deduction Calculations

Summary of Benefits	**Real property**

5% Charitable Unitrust

ASSUMPTIONS

Beneficiary ages	72
	72
Principal donated	$1,200,000.00
Cost basis of property	$120,000.00
Payout rate	5%
Payment schedule	quarterly
	3 months to 1st payment

BENEFITS

Charitable deduction $543,264.00

First year's income $60,000.00
(future income will vary with trust value)

IRS discount rate is 4.6%

These calculations are for illustration purposes only and should not be considered legal, accounting, or other professional advice. Your actual benefits may vary depending on the timing of the gift.

WHAT IS A CHARITABLE REMAINDER UNITRUST?

A charitable remainder unitrust ("unitrust") is a gift plan defined by federal tax law that allows you to provide income to yourself or others for life or a term of years while making a generous gift to the charity.

As a unitrust donor, you irrevocably transfer assets, usually cash, securities, or real estate, to a trustee of your choice (for example, [name of charity] or a bank trust department). During the unitrust's term, the trustee invests the unitrust's assets. Each year, the trustee pays a fixed percentage of the unitrust's value, as revalued annually, to one or more income beneficiaries named by you. Payments must be at least 5% of the trust's annual value and are made out of trust income, or trust principal if income is not adequate. Payments may be made annually, semiannually, or quarterly.

When the unitrust term ends, the unitrust's principal passes to the charity, to be used for the purpose you designate.

EXAMPLE

If you irrevocably transfer $1,200,000 in property, with a cost basis of $120,000, to a unitrust that pays 5% of its value each year for the lifetime benefit of individuals, age 72 and 72,

BENEFITS INCLUDE

1. You will qualify for a federal income tax deduction of approximately $543,264. Your deduction may vary modestly depending on the timing of your gift. Note that deductions for this and other gifts of long-term appreciated property will be limited to 30% of your adjusted gross income. You may, if necessary, take unused deductions of this kind over the next five years, subject to the same 30% limitation.

2. Your designated income beneficiaries will receive payments in quarterly installments for life. In the first year, these payments will be approximately $60,000. Payments in future years will vary with the value of the unitrust.

3. Your entire gift property will be available for reinvestment, free of capital gains tax. If you were to sell and reinvest this property yourself, you would owe tax on $1,080,000 of capital gain.

4. Your estate may enjoy reduced probate costs and estate taxes.

5. You will provide generous support of the charity.

6. Your gift will benefit from expert asset management, provided by the same professionals who manage the charity's endowment.

Prepared for Clyde & Matilda Tucker   November 5, 2004

These calculations are for illustration purposes only and should not be considered legal, accounting, or other professional advice. Your actual benefits may vary depending on the timing of the gift.

Sample Capital Campaign
Marketing Materials

THE CENTENNIAL CAMPAIGN FOR PACE UNIVERSITY

Presentation for

THE FUTURE—
FIVE-YEAR
STRATEGIC PLAN
2003–2008

Three Core Objectives

1. Strengthen Pace's Academic Excellence and Reputation

2. Reinforce Our Commitment to be a Student-Centered University

3. Strengthen Pace's Financial Situation

CENTENNIAL
CAPITAL
CAMPAIGN

OBJECTIVES

1. Building the University's Endowment	$45 million
a. *Endowment for Faculty Excellence*	
b. *Endowment for Student Excellence*	
c. *Endowment for Strategic Initiatives*	
2. Creating Tomorrow's Campus	$30 million
3. Strengthening Annual Giving	$25 million
TOTAL	**$100 million**

ENDOWMENT

In the highly competitive world of higher education, the ability of an institution to grow in quality and reputation can be directly related to its financial resources—specifically its endowment.

Pace University's current endowment of $92.8 million is relatively modest, given our size and age. Pace's endowment per full-time student is also lower than our peers, putting us at a disadvantage.

ENDOWMENT

A successful campaign will strengthen our endowment. A strong endowment will help to ensure financial success by providing important benefits:

- Financial stability

- Resources not tied to fluctuations in enrollment

- A steady stream of funds for faculty and student excellence and to attract top faculty and students

- A regular influx of unrestricted funds to respond to pressing needs and opportunities

ENDOWMENT

Endowment for Faculty Excellence

- Attract and support best faculty available

- Faculty chairs and professorships

- Recognize outstanding teaching and scholarship

- Support classroom innovation, curriculum development, professional travel, part-time research, technology, and library support

- Support faculty sabbaticals and professional development

ENDOWMENT

Endowment for Student Excellence

- Scholarships

- International education

- Civic engagement

- Internships and externships

ENDOWMENT

Endowment for Strategic Initiatives

- Rapid investments as needs arise

- New technologies

- Support for programs that bring national distinction

- New academic programs

- Match or attract sponsored research funding

- Graduate student assistantships

- Student recreational activities

METHODS OF GIVING

Campaign supporters can contribute to Pace University in many ways, each offering tax advantages.

Gifts of Cash: An outright gift of cash by a donor, for which the donors receives an income tax reduction as prescribed by current law. Pledging a gift over five or more years may allow a donor to make a more substantial gift, while affording the opportunity to adjust the timing and amount of each payment to achieve the most beneficial tax benefit and/or needs of the donor.

Gifts of Securities: A gift of stocks or bonds that are readily marketable. A donor who assigns appreciated securities held for at least one year to Pace University may deduct the fair market value of the gift from declared adjusted gross income *and* avoid any capital gains taxes.

Gifts of Real Estate: Property may be donated outright once approved by the University President and Executive VP for Finance and Administration. An immediate tax deduction is available and capital gains taxes may be avoided.

All gifts are tax deductible to the extent provided by law. This publication provides general information only. For legal and tax advice please contact your attorney, accountant, or financial adviser.

References

Ashton, D. *The Complete Guide to Planned Giving.* (3rd ed.) Quincy, Mass.: Ashton Associates, 2004.

Association of Fundraising Professionals. *Code of Ethical Principles and Standards of Professional Practice.* Alexandria, Va.: Association of Fundraising Professionals, Oct. 2004a.

Association of Fundraising Professionals. "New Strategies for Bequest Solicitations." [http://www.nsfre.org/tier3_print.cfm?folder_id=2345&content_item_id=17348]. July 20, 2004b.

Barrett, R. D., and Ware, M. E. *Planned Giving Essentials: A Step-by-Step Guide to Success.* (2nd ed.) Gaithersburg, Md.: Aspen, 2002.

Bigelow, B. "Planned Giving in the United States: A Survey of Donors." *Journal of Gift Planning,* 5(1), 2001.

Canada Revenue Agency. "Charities Directorate." [www.ccra.gc.ca/charities]. 2003.

Dove, K. *Conducting a Successful Capital Campaign.* (2nd ed.) San Francisco: Jossey-Bass, 2000.

Dove, K., Lindauer, J., and Madvig, C. *Conducting a Successful Annual Giving Program.* San Francisco: Jossey-Bass, 2001.

Giving USA Foundation. *Giving USA 2004.* Glenview, Ill.: AAFRC Trust for Philanthropy, 2004.

Greenfield, J. *Fundraising Fundamentals: A Guide to Annual Giving for Professionals and Volunteers.* (2nd ed.) New York: Wiley, 2002.

GuideStar. Home page. [www.guidestar.org]. 2004.

Hartsook, B. *Getting Your Ducks in a Row.* Wichita, Kan.: ASR Philanthropic, 2001.

Irwin-Wells, S. *Planning and Implementing Your Major Gifts Campaign.* San Francisco: Jossey-Bass, 2002.

Kihlstedt, A. *Capital Campaigns: Strategies That Work.* (2nd ed.) Gaithersburg, Md.: Aspen, 2002.

Lysakowski, L. "Getting Grassroots Boards to 'Move and Shake.'" [CharityChannel .com]. 2004.

Matheny, R. *Major Gifts Solicitation Strategies.* (2nd ed.) Washington, D.C.: CASE Books, 1999.

Nichols, J. *Pinpointing Affluence in the 21st Century.* Chicago: Bonus Books, 2001.

"Non-Cash Gifts: Generational Transfer Won't Be All Cash." *NonProfit Times,* Apr. 20, 2004.

Panas, J. *Asking: A 59-Minute Guide to Everything Board Members, Volunteers, and Staff Must Know to Secure the Gift.* Medfield, Mass.: Emerson & Church, 2004.

PNN Online. "87% of Donors Motivated to Give When Asked by Someone They Know." [http://www.pnnonline.org/article.php?sid=5362]. Jul. 30, 2004.

Wagner, L. *Careers in Fundraising.* New York: Wiley, 2002.

Warwick, M. *The Five Strategies for Fundraising Success.* San Francisco: Jossey-Bass, 2000.

The Author

Laura Fredricks is vice president for philanthropy at Pace University in New York City. She oversees all aspects of fundraising and alumni relations for a staff of forty on five campuses and is helping the university to raise $100,000,000+ for its capital campaign and to engage all alumni and donors in Pace's centennial celebration in 2006. She is the author of the book *Developing Major Gifts: Turning Small Donors into Big Contributors* (published by Jones and Bartlett, 2001).

For the past twelve years Fredricks has been teaching nonprofit business management; leadership; and annual, major, planned, and capital campaign courses on the certification and master's degree levels for the University of Pennsylvania, Columbia University, Duke University, and the Smithsonian Institution. She is an international presenter and motivational speaker. Her speaking engagements include numerous presentations at the International Conference of the Association of Fundraising Professionals (AFP), four international audio conferences for AFP, numerous AFP chapter conferences, several district conferences for the Council for Advancement and Support for Education, and a master class on the ask at the International Fundraising Congress in The Netherlands.

Previously, she was associate vice president for development at Temple University, Philadelphia, where she managed and coordinated the major and planned giving programs, corporate and foundation funding, and alumni relations for fifteen schools and colleges, two hospitals, and the athletic program. Additionally, she has served as major gifts manager for the Deborah Hospital Foundation, assistant director of development for the Temple University School of Medicine, and director of the Philadelphia Bar Foundation.

She is a journalism graduate of Rutgers College, and she holds a JD degree from Western New England College School of Law. Prior to her fundraising career she practiced law for over six years as a deputy attorney general IV for the Attorney General's Office of the Commonwealth of Pennsylvania, specializing in civil litigation.

She has been active with the AFP as an executive board member for the Greater Philadelphia Chapter for six years and as a committee member on the national level. She has been involved for many years as a volunteer for the Bedford, Barrow, Commerce Block Association; Community Cares; Philadelphia YMCA; and Big Brothers/Big Sisters of Philadelphia, and she serves as an advisory board member for the University of Pennsylvania Special Programs and the Columbia University master of science in fundraising program.